C000081157

COLT'S

SINGLE ACTION ARMY REVOLVER

"Doc" O'Meara

© 1999 by
Robert H. "Doc" O' Meara

All rights reserved.
No portion of this publication may be reproduced or transmitted in any form or by any means,
electronic or mechanical, including photocopy, recording, or any information storage and retrieval
system, without permission in writing from the publisher, except by a reviewer who may quote brief
passages in a critical article or review to be printed in a magazine or newspaper,
or electronically transmitted on radio or television.

Published by

krause
publications

700 E. State Street • Iola, WI 54990-0001
Telephone: 715/445-2214

Please call or write for our free catalog.
Our toll-free number to place an order or obtain a free catalog is 800-258-0929
or please use our regular business telephone 715-445-2214
for editorial comment and further information.

ISBN: 0-87341-7941

Printed in the United States of America

DEDICATION

To my beautiful wife, Betty - for love, patience and impatience.
And, to Russi, for a lifetime of love, faith and squabbles.

ACKNOWLEDGEMENTS

To Howard Dove - He made them beautiful; to Pete Stebbins and Tom Eiben - we played together and learned together for most of a lifetime; to Bill Dascher - for the variety and the contacts; to Al DeJohn, Marty Huber, Kathy Hoyt and Beverly Rhodes - who opened doors and opened books; to Ken Hurst, Paul Mobley and Marty Rabeno - whose art inspires.

And, a special thank you to John Downing, Editor Extraordinaire, who has the heart of an Australian patriot, but whose soul is pure American Cowboy. I'll ride the river with you any time, Amigo.

SPECIAL THANKS

We are indebted to the following persons, for their kindness in allowing items from their personal collections to be photographed and shared with others: William A. Dascher; Jim Dick; George Eastes; Tom Eiben; Jeff Faintich; Roy Jinks; Robert Mason; Raj Singh; Peter J. Stebbins and Steve White. Without their generosity this book would not have been possible.

These corporations, museums and their personnel were especially helpful in providing test specimens of their products and the opportunity to photograph their wares and collections: Anthony F. Imperato, of Colt Blackpowder Arms Co.; Mike Harvey, of Cimarron Firearms Co.; Boyd A. Davis, of EMF Co., Inc.; Richard C. Rattenbury, of the National Cowboy Hall of Fame; The Oklahoma Historical Society and Tom Mix Museum; Syl Wiley and Margaret Sheldon, of Sturm, Ruger & Co., Inc. and Maria Uberti, of Uberti USA.

TABLE OF CONTENTS

CHAPTER 1

THE MYSTIQUE OF THE COLT SINGLE ACTION ARMY REVOLVER

From the most cosmopolitan urban centers to the most remote outposts of civilization, the Colt Single Action Army revolver is the most recognizable handgun ever made.

As an example I offer a brief event: One afternoon in the spring of 1982. While I was serving in the U.S. Navy, my ship was making a port call at Tangier, Morocco. I was walking on the outskirts of the town, still trying to regain my land legs, when I passed a movie theater just as the film's matinee showing was over. The billboard advertised an old Western film of the mid-1950s, featuring "B" movie actor, John Payne. I couldn't decipher the title, because it was written in bold Arabic script. There was Payne in Western costume with a low-slung holster and a drawn and cocked SAA Colt in his hand.

The nature of the film was obvious; especially when about 100 little boys came running out of the place yelling at each other and pointing index fingers with raised thumbs that fell suddenly when they mimicked the sound of gunfire. The words were foreign, but the meanings were obviously the same as those of my own childhood. The Colt Single Action Army was and is the gun of the cowboy. As uniquely American as the cowboy may be, his image is known around the world.

During World War II it was fairly common for American G.I.s to take personal handguns with them into combat zones. Those who carried the old SAA were sometimes held in awe by the locals in more isolated areas. I've been told that it was the most feared firearm in the Far East. Even in the most remote villages in China and Burma, people had seen those old "B" Westerns from the Lone Star, Monogram and Republic studios, and "knew" that in the hands of a "good guy" the Colt's accuracy was unfailing and it never ran out of ammunition. Modern audiences certainly know better, but there is still something magical about the look and feel of this most graceful of cartridge revolvers. It hasn't been state-of-the-art for more than 100 years, yet it continues to be one of the most popular handguns in the world.

In the 1830s the concept of a firearm capable of shooting multiple rounds without reloading was in its infancy. Numerous attempts were made to increase firepower, but most used rotating barrels. This made such firearms very heavy, relatively inconvenient to carry and difficult to shoot. The fundamental idea upon which all revolving-cylinder handguns are based began when Sam Colt was a youngster of 16, on a voyage aboard the ship, Corvo. While he watched the helmsman at the ship's wheel, the notion for a separate revolving cylinder with a fixed barrel was conceived.

Colt's ultimate successes outweighed his early failures and turned his products into a synonym for the word "revolver." When those upstarts at Smith & Wesson came out with their fixed-cartridge revolvers with bored-through cylinders based upon the Rollin White patent, Sam Colt wasn't concerned. They couldn't compete in terms of power with his handguns, so

Long barrel and gutta percha (black hard rubber) grips peg this as a gun to be used by "bad guys." Never mind that a number of real western lawmen thought highly of SAA's in this configuration.

There was a transition period in the late 1860's and early '70s, during which percussion revolvers were converted to use self contained metallic cartridges. This 1862 Pocket Navy revolver was altered to use .38 rimfire ammunition.

the market for serious military use, personal protection and law enforcement on the expanding frontier remained almost entirely his.

However, as the end of the life of the patent's exclusivity approached, experimentation with self-contained cartridges of greater size and power began to take place. It became obvious throughout the arms manufacturing community that there would be big money to be made with handguns using fixed cartridges large enough and powerful enough to interest the Army.

Colt's success with the Models of 1851 and 1860 made those the natural basis upon which to develop fixed cartridge revolvers. In the beginning these percussion designs were converted for use with rimfire ammunition. Soon the Conversion step was eliminated and they were built from scratch to take the fixed cartridges. Then, came the Model of 1872. Like nearly all of its percussion predecessors, this revolver had no top strap. The greater power and the attendant pressures of large fixed cartridges would require the addition of such a strap for strength and safety. Thus, was born the Colt Single Action Army revolver.

Adoption of this revolver by U.S. Military forces brought it to the immediate attention of the public. The resulting demand for these handguns over the next 20 years saw a remarkable production level. In that time, nearly 150,000 of them in many calibers and configurations were sold.

The SAA is most often associated with the Old West, but over the course of its initial 67 years of production (during which time more than 357,000 revolvers were made) it was used by shopkeepers, hunters, explorers, householders, lawmen, soldiers, outlaws, farmers and ranchers throughout the world.

By today's standards its lockwork would be considered fragile, but in its heyday it was considered exceptionally rugged. Its internal working parts are subject to a phenomenon known as metal fatigue. Each of them, particularly the springs, is more or less subject to this form of stress. In order of frequency of breakage they are: the cylinder bolt spring, the cylinder bolt, the trigger sear, hammer notches, hand (or pawl) spring, and the mainspring. Yet, the mechanism that causes the revolver to discharge a cartridge is so simple that in an emergency it can be made to function with any one or all of these parts malfunctioning, as long as the firing pin remains in place on the hammer. Still, the wise owner of one of these revolvers who uses it on a regular basis will at the very least keep a spare bolt spring, bolt and trigger in his kit for emergency repairs.

There are some simple home gunsmithing tricks that can lessen the frequency of breakage of various parts. But that subject deserves a chapter all its own, because it's too complex to go into in sufficient detail here. Suffice it to say that if the revolver is properly tuned and is not subjected to such harsh abuse as the practice of fast-draw or fanning, it can serve for many years and thousands of rounds of shooting between repairs.

As the American frontier gave way to civilization and the real West became the Old West of story, song and legend, the Colt Single Action Army came to be a symbol of that age. Between 1900 and 1907 more than 100,000 of these guns were made. That's an average of 55 a day, every work day, at a time when there was no such thing as automated machinery as we understand the term today. That doesn't even begin to consider how busy the plant might have been with the production of other products.

Much of the SAA's appeal during that period was certainly due to the popularity of the Wild

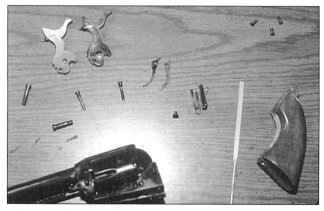

Single-action revolver mechanisms are simple, and easily repaired, but one must have a knowledge of proper fit and relationship of the parts to do it correctly. It pays to keep spare parts handy.

West Shows of Buffalo Bill Cody, The Miller Brothers 101 Ranch Show, Pawnee Bill's extravaganzas and the Western features of the burgeoning motion picture industry.

For the first 70 years of this century the great morality plays of the silver screen were often based on the theme of "Manifest Destiny," the term used to justify the expansion of the United States from the Atlantic to the Pacific coasts. The faces changed over the years. From the live performances of Cody, Frank Butler and Annie Oakley, we turned to celluloid. By the 1920s we began seeing the stone face of William S. Hart. Then came Bronco Billy Anderson, Hoot Gibson, Tom Mix and Jack Hoxie. In the 1930s and '40s John Wayne, Gene Autry, Roy Rogers and William Boyd, as Hopalong Cassidy began to dominate the genre.

Along the way, let's not forget the likes of Lash LaRue, Sunset Carson, Gordon "Wild Bill" Elliott as Red Ryder, Crash Corrigan and Rex Allen.

All of these, and more, kept legions of kids around the world entertained at the Saturday matinees. Their parents were more likely to take in a feature starring Randolph Scott, Gary Cooper or Joel McCrea. The thrill was much the same for them. The only significant difference was that the hero kissed the girl rather than his horse at the end of the picture.

Palominos, white horses and white hats predominated. Never mind that no self-respecting frontiersman would want a horse or hat that stood out so boldly in hostile territory. These were symbols of good. In the 1950s we began to see a transition of the popular screen cowboys to television. As the decade wore on, the era of the "Adult Western" began. Such television series as *Gunsmoke* and *The Life and Legend of Wyatt Earp* appealed to young and old alike.

Throughout the entire period, one thing remained constant. No matter by whom the lead character was portrayed, the Colt Single Action Army was a featured player. Often, in the hands of the hero it would be nickel plated and/or engraved, usually with 4-5/8-inch barrel; making it easier to be fast on the draw. The "bad guys" carried blued and color case-hardened SAAs, mostly with 5-1/2-inch barrels, or Remingtons and an assortment of double-action Colts or Smith & Wessons that could be of nearly any vintage. It was as easy to tell which character was which by their guns as by the hats or the black-maned bay horses the villains rode.

When it came to comic relief, the "sidekick" was also easily recognized. He usually rode a pinto horse, smaller than that of the hero, but sometimes he would be mounted on a mule or burro. His hat might be of any color, but the brim was always misshapen and often had holes or tears in it. The handgun he carried in a slovenly fashion in worn-looking leather was most often a Colt SAA, but usually had a well worn finish and a long barrel.

Many of the Westerns done during the war years of the 1940s had a contemporary theme. If the script dealt with Axis spies, for example, the hero's SAAs were pitted against that great symbol of Hitlerian evil, the P-08 pistol; better known as the Luger. Never mind that by then it was being phased out in favor of the P-38; we're at the movies, here. Gene Autry even went up against science fiction ray-guns in the 1935 motion picture serial *The Phantom Empire*.

It may strike some as strange that in many of the "B" movies of the 1930s, '40s and '50s the hero still rode a horse, while the film's villains drove a car or truck. That's a valid observation until one realizes that it's all but impossible for a cowboy hero to have a personal relationship with an automobile (although Roy Rogers' TV sidekick of the early '50s, Pat Brady, did it nicely with his jeep, NellieBelle), but he could certainly do so with such valiant steeds as Gene Autry's sorrel, Champion and Roy Rogers' palomino, Trigger. These animals were fine performers in their own right. Audiences, especially in rural areas, understood perfectly well that in many parts of the west hayburning horsepower remained a common mode of personal transportation.

I recall as a child, living in El Paso, Texas, seeing cowboys coming into town on horseback. That was in the mid-1940s. In the early '50s, when my family first moved to Las Vegas, Nevada it was still a small town, little more than a wayside stop on the highway between Salt Lake City and

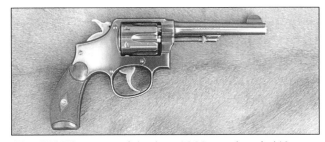

The "B" Westerns of the late 1930s and early '40s often had a contemporary setting and the film's villain would be armed with a revolver better suited to a cops and robbers "film noir" presentation, like this vintage Smith & Wesson M&P.

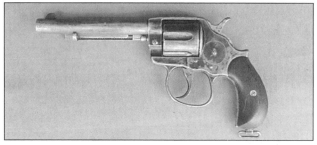

The villain in a Western set in the 19th century would very likely be armed with a Model 1878 Double Action Army revolver similar to this one. However, this is actually a US military issue revolver, Model of 1902; the so called, Philippine or Alaskan Model.

On rare occasions the hero might carry a double action revolver such as the New Service. Some movie cowboy heroes used them, because they lacked the manual dexterity to thumb cock an SAA rapidly enough to suit the camera.

Los Angeles. Even then, there were still hitching rails in front of some of the saloons and gambling establishments on Fremont Street.

At that time, it remained common in places throughout the West to see men carrying guns, often Colts, on their hips. There were no show-downs at high noon or challenges to get out of town before sundown. One almost never heard a cross word spoken. These were simply working men who wore their guns as part of the regular equipment of a rough outdoor trade. It was sometimes necessary to shoot a snake, dispatch injured stock or defend oneself against an aggressive steer. A well-placed shot from his handgun might also provide for the addition of some animal protein to supplement an otherwise dull meal of canned beans. A working cowboy, even in this day and age, sometimes has to do without the comfort of a bunkhouse and a home-cooked meal; camping overnight on the range.

By the 1970s the Western had fallen out of favor, replaced by other formats for the Hollywood morality play. Still, the Western continues to surface on occasion. And, the SAA continues to play its role. However, in the past few decades

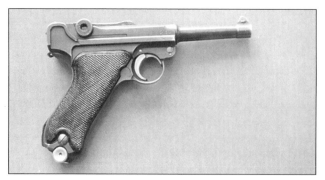

During the war years the plot often formed about Axis spies and the SAA was called upon to face that classic symbol of Hitlerian evil, the P-O8. Naturally, it was no match for the Peacemaker.

the original Colts that were kept in the studio armories have become valuable antiques and have been sold off to collectors and replaced by the excellent copies now made in Italy by such masters of the replica firearm as Aldo Uberti, and Armi San Marco, among others.

Decoration of the Single Action Army revolver started long before the motion picture and television industries were thought of, but the entertainment industry certainly contributed to the fact that the Colt SAA is the most commonly decorated firearm in history.

In the 19th century, engraved firearms were usually either presentation pieces given to prominent citizens for services appreciated by the community or status symbols ordered by their wealthy owners. In either case these firearms were generally regarded as tools to be used and were nearly always carried like any other firearm.

Today, the owner of an engraved SAA usually regards shooting it, especially if it's a recently done special order piece, as tantamount to sacrilege. My old friend, the late Howard Dove, who was regarded by many as the premier practitioner of the engraver's art of the modern era, told me that, with rare exceptions, an engraved firearm should be used. He believed that its owner will usually be a better marksman, because he wants to demonstrate that the gun's worth goes beyond its beauty. I've found this to be a sound assessment. The nickel plated 2nd Generation SAA that I've had since 1969 has a fine set of staghorn grips and some simple engraving on its backstrap and butt. I've used it to shoot the National Match course, just to prove that it could be done with such a piece, and scored in the expert class (barely) with it.

This is not to indicate that the SAA is a match-grade revolver. Most specimens in good condition can be regarded as adequate if they produce 2- or 3-inch groups. However, some well-tuned pieces are capable of surprisingly precise shot placement. For example, I had the opportunity to shoot a 5-1/2-inch barreled .357 Magnum that had belonged to Ed McGivern. Ed's speed and accuracy with a revolver was so great that some of his records still stand more than half a century after they were set. That old Colt is a precision paper puncher of the highest order and I'll have more to tell about it later.

Though many of the sixguns used by our favorite movie cowboys were highly decorated, many others were recognized by the audience as belonging to the hero simply by the addition of custom grips made of some distinctive material. The most commonly seen were staghorn, ivory and mother-of-pearl. This carries forward to the modern period. In most of the movies John Wayne made during in the last couple of decades of his life he carried a worn old Peacemaker that had actually been made in the 1890s. On it was a set of darkly yellowed ivory two-piece grips. It was worn in a simple holster, high behind his right hip. Although it may not have been a fancy outfit, it was certainly distinctive. It became as familiar to movie audiences as Bob Hope's nose and Cary Grant's smile.

Few of us have the wherewithal to afford quality engraving, but the addition of stocks made of some exotic material can make an otherwise ordinary Single Action Army appear very special, indeed. One of the best sources for such stock materials that I know of is Eagle Grips. They can supply fine examples made of exotic woods, such as ebony, rosewood and teak, as well as East Indian and western Pacific buffalo horn in addition to the more traditional ivory, staghorn and mother-of-pearl.

The Colt SAA is so beloved by gun enthusiasts, even recently manufactured revolvers have lately come to be regarded as collectors' items. They've also become very expensive and, for that reason, I rarely add one to my collection. Like many of us, I just can't afford to do so any more. But once in a while temptation rears its head and I fall prey to its lure. Not long ago, I was overcome by the urge, because the caliber and barrel length offered were exactly what I'd been seeking for quite some time. I waited 20 long months for the 4-5/8-inch barreled .38-40 to arrive.

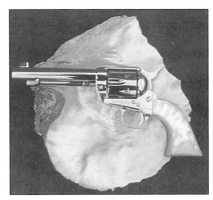

Mother-of-pearl is rare and expensive these days, but Eagle Grips manages to keep a limited supply on hand. For some, it's just the ticket to make a sixgun look as though it came from the holster of a Western movie hero.

A special edition, made exclusively for the membership of the Colt Collectors Association, it has a Royal Blue finish. The case-hardened colors of its frame, done in the fashion of the 19th century, have the same visual appeal as they've always had. It wore walnut grips when it arrived, but they were quickly replaced by staghorn from Eagle Grips.

Most of those who ordered them regarded them as commemoratives, to be kept in factory new condition and used only for display. I got mine to shoot, and shoot it does; quite well, thank you very much.

The Colt Single Action Army is no longer a valid option for military or law enforcement use, but it still has a place in the holster of the outdoorsman. It has been a part of our history and has entertained us. It has worked for us and protected us. Now, thousands of aficionados, world-wide, have taken up the sport of Cowboy Action Shooting, providing yet another reason for interest in the old "Thumb-buster." Moreover, many of these guns are works of art with great aesthetic appeal just as surely as are the Mona Lisa and the ceiling of the Sistine Chapel. No firearm ever made has such appeal. It is a timeless beauty that everyone who loves guns will appreciate.

Colt produced SAA revolvers chambered for the old .38-40 cartridge during the early 1990s. That's when the author added this one to his collection. It started out with factory walnut stocks, but these staghorns, from Eagle Grips, quickly replaced them.

CHAPTER 2

THE GUNS OF THE FORTY-NINERS

James W. Marshall was an ambitious and determined man. He intended to become a man of wealth and power in the Territory of California, newly independent from Mexico and, briefly, a nation in its own right.

In January, 1848, the sawmill he had constructed on the American River with his partner, John Sutter, was found to be faulty. The tailrace was not deep enough. The water backed up, preventing the flutter wheel from turning. Correcting the problem would require that the dam gate be closed, to divert the river, in the hope that the faster running water would wash away some of the sand and gravel.

The plan succeeded and later, after the water had done its work, among the debris left behind Marshall spied a glittering substance lodged in the crevice of a large chunk of granite. His first thought was that it might be copper, but it proved to be soft, not brittle, as is characteristic of copper in its unrefined form. Collecting several more specimens, he returned a few days later to Sutter's Fort and shared his discovery with his partner.

Tests, using boiling lye, proved it to be what Marshall had suspected. He and Sutter decided to keep the discovery secret, but little by little word got out that there were untold riches to be found in the vicinity of Sutter's Mill.

Gold! The word engenders visions of wealth and power. It's the stuff of which dreams are made. Unfortunately, it's axiomatic that those who usually gain the greatest wealth from such discoveries are the ones who provide goods and services to those who come to seek their fortunes in the mines. Ironically, neither Marshall nor Sutter profited in any way from the discovery of gold on their property.

Where there is gold, one will usually find guns. It was a wild time and people felt a real need for personal protection. Handguns were common tools and there was money to be made for those who could provide miners with the best tools at the best price. This era of economic expansion provided some of the push that eventually helped create the Colt Single Action Army revolver. The history of the gold rush is as much a part of the development of the Single Action Army as is the development of new industrial technology.

By 1849, the discovery of gold in California was common knowledge throughout the world. People of all sorts and from many nations made their way there by wagon train across the North American continent. Some brave souls crossed the Isthmus of Panama, risking the swamps and prevalent tropical diseases, to get to the Pacific Coast. Others risked the legendary horrors of the winds, storms and currents of the Strait of Magellan around Cape Horn, at the tip of South America. The transcontinental journey averaged about six months. The voyage by sea was for the prudent; it took about three months and was relatively safe. With luck, if malaria or yellow fever didn't intervene, those in a hurry who survived the route through Panama might do it in two.

The monumental hardships involved are difficult to comprehend in an age when

Many authorities believe Colt's 1851 Navy Model revolver to be the finest revolver of the percussion age. It was favored in the California gold fields by miners, lawmen and outlaws alike. Its popularity continues among modern black powder shooters.

the same coast-to-coast journey can be made in four days by automobile or as many hours by airplane. But the lure of gold and the wealth it could bring made the trip worthwhile in the minds of many thousands.

The tiny harbor village of Yerba Buena, so named by its Spanish founders for the wild mint that grew in abundance in the area, had recently been renamed San Francisco. By 1850, its population had grown from 9,000 to about 25,000, but something on the order of 80,000 passed through and were frequent return visitors. In that year, half the buildings in the city were saloons, hotels and restaurants catering to the crowds of miners spending the proceeds of their labors on the creature comforts of that wild and corrupt city.

America was a young land; its interests in California only just begun. But that great population influx allowed it to be rushed to admission as a state in 1850. The gold rush lasted less than 10 years, but the changes wrought were to affect the world forever. Newcomers from all parts of the globe had come to a raw wilderness, far from the civilizing influence of well-regulated government, organized society and establishments of law and order. This made it necessary for people to be responsible for their own security. In short, people routinely carried knives and guns, both for personal protection and for food gathering.

It was a period of transition in many aspects of the arms industry. Flintlocks remained commonplace, but caplock firearms dominated the scene. The pinfire breach-loaders of LeFaucheux had their following. Military muskets and handguns, many from the recent war with Mexico, were favorites of the veterans of

Simple pocket pistols like this, which bears no maker's name, were common among the Forty-Niners. The barrel screws on and off easily for cleaning.

that conflict. European immigrants brought representative pieces from the arsenals of their homelands. The revolvers of Colonel Sam Colt's fledgling arms factory in Hartford, Conn. and his earlier enterprise in Paterson, New Jersey, were among the most highly prized. But virtually anything that could be made to shoot might be found in the hands, pockets or on the hips of the gold seekers.

In a time and place where vice is more common than virtue and armed robbery and government corruption a fact of daily life, one must be prepared for the worst. The Forty-Niners faced just such circumstances. Their choice of weaponry was based upon economic means and general availability as much as personal preference, but one thing was certain, virtually everyone was armed.

Among the most popular firearms of the period was the pepperbox revolver. At least 20 different makers produced handguns of that type, but by far the best known were those of Ethan Allen. They were manufactured in Norwich and Grafton, Connecticut, under the label Allen & Thurber and later in Worcester, Massachusetts, with the name Allen & Wheelock. Allen and his partners made their (usually) six-shot multi-barreled revolvers in a variety of small calibers. Most common are those of .25, .28, .34 and .36 calibers. Characteristically, the entire barrel assembly rotates with a double action pull of the trigger, at the same time as a hammer, either hidden or top-mounted on the Allen products, was raised, tripped and dropped under spring pressure to ignite the cap on the nipple beneath. A few, such as those of Stocking & Co., of Worcester, Massachusetts, differed in that their barrels had to be rotated by hand. Pepperboxes are heavy revolvers but, in the baggy clothing of the period, were easily

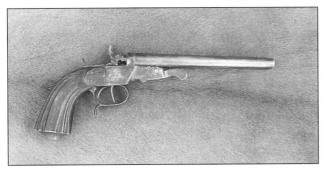
First made by the Parisian gunsmith, M. LeFaucheux, around 1835, this pinfire design was the first successful breechloading cartridge pistol. The self-contained cartridges it used provided a big advantage in speed when loading.

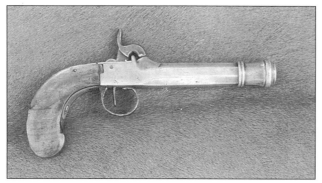

This Belgian pistol, with plain wood and brass barrel is typical of the inexpensive European pistols that were to be found in the gold fields of California. It shows the wear of long, hard use, a few minor repairs and wood shrinkage, but it was well-made and is still serviceable.

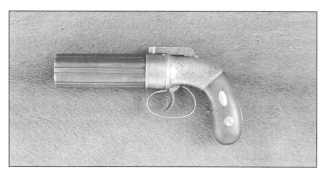

Pepperbox pistols were tough and reliable firearms. Many Forty-Niners confidently depended upon them to help protect their mining claims.

concealed and much favored for their multiple shot capability.

Most of the pistols then available were single-shots and the ability to fire multiple rounds without having to reload gave the shooter a major advantage. Allen also made a small number of rifles and shotguns, both single- and

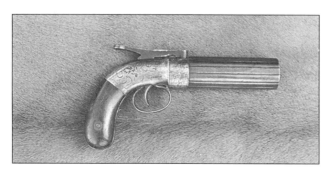

More than 20 different manufacturers made pepperbox pistols. Most were made so that their barrels rotated with a double-action pull of the trigger. A few, such as this .31 caliber by Stocking and Co., of Worcester, Massachusetts, required the user to rotate the barrel assembly manually for the next shot.

Military firearms of many nations, such as this German naval pistol were brought to California by immigrant gold-seekers. This one has a unique swinging block safety device.

double-shot types. His revolving rifles were made in such small quantity that it's doubtful many made their way to the Pacific Coast.

Military handguns likely to have seen service in the gold fields include those of government contractors North, Ames, Evans, Waters and Aston. All these were New England makers, from the Connecticut River Valley, which produced primary martial arms for the U.S. Army and Navy. As the naval presence in California was greater than that of the Army, those with naval marks were more likely to have been used there.

To illustrate the diversity of arms that came to California's shores, one that may have seen use there is a German naval pistol, the photo of which appears among the illustrations for this chapter. It's similar in most respects to those of other military pistols of the period, but with typically Teutonic innovation and consideration for firearms safety. It's equipped with a block upon which the hammer rests. The block swings up and out of the way when the pistol is

Double-barreled and other multi-shot rifles, such as this by Bown & Tetley, of Pittsburgh, Pennsylvania, were highly prized by the Forty-Niners. In an age when single-shot firearms were the norm, having immediate access to another round gave the shooter an advantage that could mean the difference between survival and death on the lawless frontier.

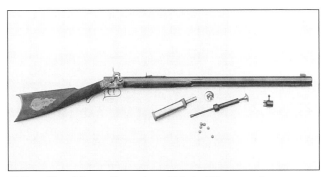

Rifles like this replica of an Edwin Wesson, have many of the characteristics of the Plains Rifles, such as a shorter barrel and larger caliber than the rifles that were popular in the East.

cocked and ready to fire.

As the gold rush of 1849 was beginning, the period of the Mountain Man was ending. These intrepid adventurers traveled vast distances by horseback, canoe, riverboat, and on foot to find the best trapping grounds, the swiftest routes and the natural wonders that lay beyond the Great Plains. Most of the early guns making the trip west were rifles.

Early on, they found that the full-stocked Pennsylvania "Long Rifles" that had been so popular in the East were too long, heavy and ungainly to use effectively from horseback. These guns were downright useless in a canoe and much too heavy to carry conveniently afoot. To answer the requirements of this immense new land, gunsmiths such as S. O'Dell, of Natchez, Mississippi, and Jacob and Samuel Hawken, of St. Louis designed an entirely new style of rifle.

Both these cities were on the primary river routes to the West and became centers of the trade in furs and other goods. It was, therefore, natural for them to become gunmaking centers, as well. The arms made for use in the West came to be known as "Plains Rifles" and, as the movement over the Rocky Mountains continued across the desert to the Sierras, and on to the shores of the Pacific Ocean, those rifles went along. They were lighter, shorter and of larger caliber than those favored in the East. A typical Hawken had a barrel of 36 or 38 inches and was bored .50 or .60 caliber. The majority were flintlocks, preferred for the ease with which replacement flints could be acquired on the trail. Percussion caps provided more reliable ignition, but it was a long way between gun shops and, if one ran out of caps, a rifle made to use them became a less-than-efficient club, nothing more.

These new rifles were better suited to take such large species as elk, buffalo and mule deer. The smaller caliber rifles had been adequate for white-tailed deer and the occasional black bear found in the East. The new rifles were also important as long-range man-stoppers. Hostile Indians, outlaws and renegades quickly learned to respect the performance of the Plains Rifle in capable hands. Less than capable hands didn't last long, anyway. Many of these guns found their way over the Sierras to the gold mines.

Still, no firearms on the California frontier were more highly prized than those of Colt's. The first of his production revolvers, the Paterson Models, were already long out of production by the time gold was found, but some saw service in the mines and surrounding areas.

Considering the brief period of their production before the New Jersey-based enterprise went bankrupt, a remarkable number of variations were manufactured. Total numbers of all varieties are in the neighborhood of 4,700 pieces, about 2,850 of which were handguns. Five models, from the Pocket or Baby Paterson through the Belt Models to the Holster Model, better known as the Texas Paterson, gave the customer as many options as his potential needs might require.

The handguns were made in .28, .31 and .36 calibers, corresponding to the three basic frame sizes of the gun's design. It was long supposed that there were guns produced in .34 caliber, as well, but the research of arms historians, Philip R. Phillips and R.L. Wilson, has failed to turn up any evidence of them actually having been made in that bore size.

The Patersons are single-action five-shot revolvers that differ in one major respect from the revolvers that evolved from them. They have no trigger guards and the trigger itself folds up and out of the way against the bottom of the revolver's frame. When the hammer is cocked for use, the trigger drops down, ready for action. These were by no means the first revolvers, but they were the first production models made with a cylinder that revolved independently of the barrel. This made them lighter and easier to aim accurately than other handguns of their time.

The rifles made at the Paterson factory were quite different from the handguns in appearance. The 1st and 2nd Models were operated by

Colt's Walker revolver remains one of the most powerful handguns ever produced. At more than 5 pounds, it's the heaviest military handgun ever produced, but its size and weight make it easy to control.

means of a ring lever. The 1st is found in calibers .34, .36, .38, .40 and .44. The 2nd was made only in .44 caliber. Both models had the capability of firing eight shots, an enormous number for the time. A small number of both models were also made with ten-shot cylinders.

The Model 1839 Carbine was the most popular of the Paterson long guns and was unusual in that it had a .525 caliber smooth bore. A 16-gauge shotgun of like bore dimensions was also produced using that design. The two are almost identical in outward appearance, but can be told apart by the length of their cylinders. The carbine's measures 2.5-inches, while the shotgun's is 3.5-inches.

It was management problems that led to Colt's failure in New Jersey. The guns made there were well received by the public and attracted military contracts, as well. A few years passed before Colt was back on his feet.

In 1847, Sam Colt was back in his home state of Connecticut, trying to find a way to revive his enterprise, when he was sought out by a young soldier named Samuel Walker, who was newly arrived from Texas. The U.S. was on the verge of war with Mexico. The experience the Texas Rangers had with the Paterson revolvers impressed Walker. He was a thoughtful man with an appreciation for fine firearms and a level of military experience such that he conceived a number of improvements that would make Colt's revolver even better in the field.

The two Sams hit it off well and began a collaboration. The result was the manufacture of the Walker Model, which was accepted for government purchase almost immediately. This led to the revival of Colt's gun-making operation. Only 100 of the Walkers were made for the civilian trade. There is no way to know how many of them might actually have found their

way to California, but some of them and a few of the military-issue pieces certainly must have made it to the gold country.

It's interesting to note that the Walker revolver's ballistic performance using recommended powder and ball specifications was so impressive that, loaded to its full potential, it remained the world's most powerful revolver well into the 20th century. Only the creation of the .357 Magnum knocked the Walker off the top spot.

In the course of the next five years the Walker evolved rapidly into the 1st, 2nd and 3rd Model Dragoon revolvers. Each new change made them simpler to use and more efficient to manufacture. They and the Walkers were designed for use by mounted troops and were generally carried in pairs of holsters slung over the pommel of the trooper's saddle. Carried in a hip holster, they were too large and heavy for comfort and would interfere with movement on the march or in combat. It's no mystery why they were referred to as "Horse Pistols."

Colt's Model 1851 Navy revolver is arguably the most attractive handgun of the period. Its handling qualities are such that its influence carried on through the next two decades and can be seen in the designs of the 1860 Army Model and the Single Action Army Revolver of 1873. The .36 caliber revolver was light enough for comfortable carry on the hip and powerful enough by the standards of the period, to be regarded as an excellent defensive handgun. In the decades to come it would become a favorite of gunfighters like James Butler "Wild Bill" Hickok. It arrived in the marketplace early enough in the gold rush period to become one of the best respected arms on the scene.

Of all the firearms used by the Forty-Niners, the Colt revolver of 1849 was by far the most sought after among the miners. Small and relatively light, its size was appreciated. In most cases all that a man needed in the fields had to be carried there on his person. Like the modern backpacker, every item in his possession was carefully selected for its utility and portability. The Model 1849 Pocket Revolvers were the Detective Specials of their day. Easily carried and more potent than their size would imply, the little handguns could send bullets off at 960 fps with only 14 grains of FFFG black powder. This gave the tiny .31 caliber, 49-grain ball about 100 foot pounds of energy, roughly equivalent to

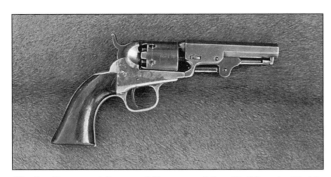

By far the most favored firearm of the California Gold Rush was Colt's Model 1849 revolver. This one is nearly 150 years old and has seen hard use, but remains shootable.

a .32 S&W Long cartridge, using a bullet of about twice that weight. By modern standards that's pretty anemic for personal defense use, but anyone who has ever taken small game with that round will appreciate that it's no toy.

During its 24-year production history the Model 1849 revolvers and their variants were made in enormous numbers. By the end of production, in 1873, more than 340,000 had been sold. Nearly half that number were made in the first decade; a large percentage of which were destined for the gold fields. Of all the handguns available at the time, none was more suited to that purpose.

Without individual documentation it's impossible to say with certainty that any given firearm did or did not see service during the wild and turbulent period of the California Gold Rush. Failing a verifiable documented history of an individual piece, the best one can do is relate the probabilities. Without question, many arms makers served the needs of the fortune seekers and their associates. Some, like Colt, owed much of their success to that segment of the market. By the same token, the lessons learned there greatly influenced the development of firearms for the rest of the 19th century and beyond and set the stage for the development of Colt's firearms and others.

CHAPTER 3

CASE-HARDENED CLASSICS BY COLT

Six years and a number of false starts after he came up with the idea for a firearm with a revolving cylinder, Sam Colt got his first factory rolling in New Jersey. A number of prototypes had been made up to that point, but it was the revolver made in the Paterson factory that first brought his invention to the attention of the public.

Between 1836 and 1873, more than a dozen basic models with over 60 recognized variations of the cap-and-ball revolvers, with quantities numbering in the millions had been manufactured. All this had made Col. Colt America's first

multimillionaire and the firm he founded one of the most important in the nation. Then, Colt began making guns for those new-fangled fixed cartridges that their chief competitor, Smith & Wesson, had for the previous 17 years monopolized by virtue of the Rollin White patent.

The general availability of fixed-cartridge revolvers caused the rapid demise of cap-and-ball weaponry. By the 1880s few remained in use and their manufacture had ceased throughout most of the world. The technological changes in the last three decades of the 19th century were so rapid and extensive that the guns that had made Colt so wealthy in his lifetime were all but useless for any practical purpose and rapidly became curiosities and collectibles. No one would ever have expected to see them returned to production. But the guns were classics and classics never seem to die.

In the early 1960s with the Civil War Centennial at hand and the increasing popularity of Western movies and television, there developed a renewed interest in the guns of that period. Gunmakers in Belgium, Italy and Spain cashed in on this phenomenon, selling their wares in the U.S. and elsewhere around the world.

As useful as most of these reproductions were, many shooters, particularly those involved in re-enactment groups, wanted as much authenticity as possible in their activities. Worn, but serviceable original Colts were highly prized. Most who used them recognized that

More than 200,000 1860 Army Colts saw service in the Civil War and beyond. Even by today's standards it was a powerful handgun. It was one of the most popular revolvers in the reissue series.

the remaining specimens in good mechanical condition with original parts and finish were too rare and valuable to shoot. Firms such as Dixie Gun Works provided parts to repair and service both junkers that held little collector interest and good pieces with altered or missing parts. However, there just weren't enough of those beat up old pieces to go around.

The black powder renaissance continued well after the Civil War anniversary and, smelling a good thing, Val Forgett of Navy Arms, one of the country's largest suppliers of reproduction firearms, talked to Colt about reissuing the 1851 Navy revolvers, by far the most popular model among collectors and shooters, under the original maker's name.

Tooling and setting up for the manufacture of a new firearm is an extremely expensive and time consuming process. Needless to say, the machinery for the manufacture of the '51 Navy no longer existed at Hartford. Colt was properly reluctant to invest the kind of money it would take to bring the old warhorse back into the stable, so an arrangement was made that became one of the most closely guarded secrets in the industry. Navy Arms would quietly team up with a foreign manufacturer. The secret was kept, in spite of rumors and suspicions, for more than a decade before it became common knowledge.

No manufacturer of replica firearms in the world commands greater respect for authenticity and the quality workmanship of its products than the firm of Aldo Uberti, of Brescia, Italy. They were already tooled up to make the '51 Navy and had been doing so for many years. In fact, that model was only one of several close copies of the originals they had in production. On the other hand, Italian law requires all firearms, including the black powder types, to be proof tested and so marked before being offered for sale. This would cause marketing problems, because a lot of Americans would be reluctant to look upon such guns as authentic with foreign proof marks on them.

The solution was simple. There is no requirement in Italian law for the proofing of parts, only fully assembled guns. The 1851 Navys were shipped in pieces, then assembled, finished, and packaged in the United States. Subsequently, they were shipped from the Hartford plant and carried Colt's warranty of reliability and service. Spare parts were kept on hand so that factory repairs could be made without the delays of international shipment and the risk of running afoul of Italian law.

The result in the marketplace was astounding. Initial demand for the new guns was such that more replicas were sold in their first six years of production than were Pythons sold during the first six years of that model's production. I attended the gun show at the 5th Regiment Armory in Baltimore in 1973, shortly after the '51 hit the market. Walking around the show I noticed one dealer who had four stacks of 25 boxes containing the new Colts on the floor next to his table at the end of one of the rows. He sold all 100 revolvers before the end of the first day. Similar sales successes were seen throughout the country.

Another factor that had to be considered before such a project could be undertaken was the need to protect collectors from those unscrupulous enough to try to pass a reissued Colt off as a 19th century original. This was done by starting the serial numbers of this new run where they had left off when the original

production had ceased. In addition, the rifling of the barrels was different and, of course, the screws had metric threads (a dead giveaway as to their origin, but few people noticed).

The popularity of the 2nd Generation 1851 Navy was so great, with more than 35,000 made, including all variations, that additional models were added to the line. The 3rd Model Dragoon came along in 1974, followed by the 1860 Army in 1977. Ultimately, there were 10 basic models, with at least 47 variations offered. Some of these variations are very scarce. The total of the entire black powder series production is at least 88,736. There is certainly enough variety among them to challenge and interest any collector.

Unfortunately, by the early 1980s the secret of the Colt-Uberti deal was fairly common knowledge. Buyer interest began to wane and the project fizzled. Colt continued to maintain that the guns were a home-grown project right up until the mid '80s. As late as 1985 I personally queried a Colt executive, who shall remain nameless, and was told the truth but admonished to say nothing in print, as the firm would not admit to it publicly. By that time, however, a few guns had managed to slip through with parts that had inadvertently carried Italian proof marks and the game was up. At this point just about everybody with an interest in the subject knows the truth and not many care.

However, there remain those that have been offended by the Italian connection. Others, including myself, recognize the fact that subcontractors have always been used throughout the arms industry. Sam Colt himself, used them in his early years and he was certainly not alone. It continues to be common practice in many firms. The fit, finish and function of the black powder revolvers Colt sold was up to their standards of quality and backed by their own warranty and service facilities. They were and are as fine as any of the guns Colt has sold in any period in its history.

A few special editions have been issued since 1982, but regular production ended that year. There was some speculation that a new Paterson revolver would be offered in the sesquicentennial year of 1986, but that never came to pass. I always thought it remarkable that the Paterson had been neglected. I've been told that the reason it wasn't made had to do with safety concerns. Others have done it, so I personally don't see the validity of that reasoning, but in our present litigious climate, I'm not surprised that any suggestion of possi-

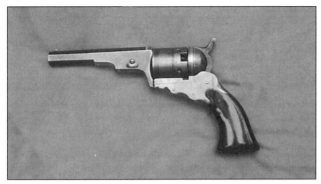

Sam Colt's first production revolver, the Paterson, was a success with the public, but management problems caused him to fall back and regroup. Nevertheless, it was the beginning of a manufacturing empire that greatly influenced world history. The Paterson was never a part of Colt's reissue series, but the author thinks it should have been.

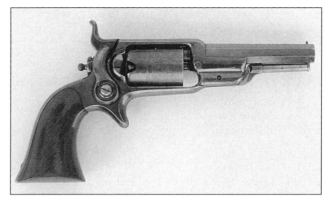

The Root revolvers are distinctive, because of their external sidehammer. They were also the first handguns with a topstrap made at the Colt factory.

ble legal problems would deter production.

The 1855 Sidehammer model, known to many as the Root revolver, after Elisha Root, who was Sam Colt's hand-picked successor as president of the firm, is another I'd like to have seen made. That particular piece was the first Colt revolver to add a solid topstrap to its frame.

For a time after the secret was out there was a bear market in the black powder reissue series, but little by little they are regaining popularity and collector interest is increasing. With that increased interest it has become necessary to develop and categorize the available records regarding serial number ranges and production figures so that goals may be set and values established, based upon rarity and desirability. With the help of friend and fellow collector, Alex

Schlitten, I've prepared the table that appears in Appendix I as a guide. The records of these guns are not precise on all accounts, so it's possible that minor variations from the figures listed may be found. For example, factory records seem to indicate that the last stainless steel 1860 Army Model shipped was number 212540S. Yet, Mr. Schlitten reports hearing of one (unconfirmed) with a number three digits higher. The data presented is as complete as I can provide at this time. If any reader can offer additional information I would be pleased to know about it.

Another area of collector interest not to be taken lightly is that of the accouterments and memorabilia associated with Colt's black powder series. They are myriad, including such things as cap tins, powder flasks of various types, casings of both the original style and French-fit, oilers, molds, promotional hat pins, advertisements, etc. There have even been miniatures. This can be seen as an area of collector specialization all its own.

As for the guns themselves, most I've seen remain mint, if not new in the box. Most collec-

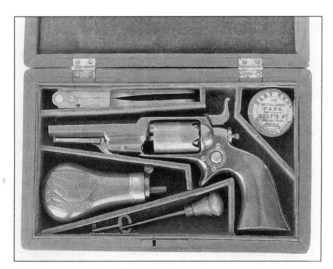

This is an original Colt Root revolver, cased, with accessories. The author would like to have seen this model among those reissued in the 1970s and '80s.

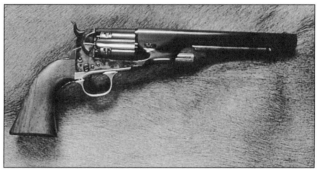

The author's personal favorite among the black powder Colts, the fluted cylinder 1860 Army, was very rare among the originals. It's one of the more scarce 20th century reissue revolvers, as well.

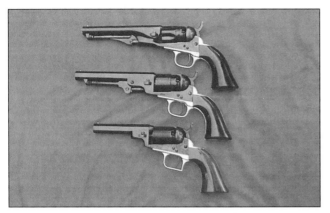

Colt's 1862 Pocket Police revolver (top) was numbered in the same series as the Pocket Navy Model (center). Both these .36 caliber variations were built on frames the same size as that of the .31 caliber Baby Dragoon (bottom).

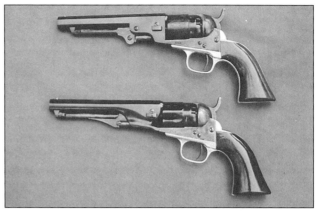

The 1851 Navy Model (top) is regarded by many to be the best of the Colt percussion revolvers in terms of accuracy and handling qualities. Wild Bill Hickok thought highly of them. He carried an ivory-stocked pair tucked in a sash, butt forward for a crossdraw. It's been the odds-on favorite of modern black powder shooters, as well. But, for its beauty and grace, the 1862 Pocket Police Model is the author's preference.

tors seem to treat the entire series, not just those marketed as such, as they would the commemoratives. Few pieces seem to see any shooting. As is the case with any collectible, shooting lowers the value of these guns compared to those that remain unfired.

There is a special grace to their look and a feeling of living history to these revolvers. They remain as natural a choice for engraving and commemoration of historical events and special presentations today as they were when Sam Colt was handing them out in high places more than 140 years ago. Colt's Custom Shop continues to use them on occasion.

If your desire is to have a good shooter, they'll serve that purpose admirably. If, on the other hand, you are interested in collectibles, the reissue revolvers and accessories made between 1972 and 1984 offer an extremely interesting specialty that can provide lots of fun, many challenges and the promise of investment security. What's more, they certainly look good in a wall display.

But we're not done with the modern Colt black powder saga. In 1994, Colt reissue firearms became available once again as the Signature Series, from Colt Blackpowder Arms. Made under a licensing agreement with Colt, the Signature Series muskets and revolvers bear a likeness of Sam Colt's autograph. Among these firearms are some of the standard issue pieces, such as the 1851 Navy and 1860 Army revolvers, but several variations that were not made available during the 1970s and '80s, such as the 1849 Pocket Model and the Whitneyville Walker, among others, are now in production. These handguns and muskets are true to the form of

the originals in fit, finish and function. In addition, many authentic accessories that were not made available with the earlier reissue revolvers are now readily available, including holsters, shoulder stocks for some revolvers, bayonets for the muskets and other items.

As the 20th century comes slowly to a close, firearms technology has advanced far beyond anything Sam Colt could have envisioned. Yet there remains a link with the past that many shooters continue to maintain. Black powder firearms bearing the Colt name will always have a place in the scheme of things as long as the elegant lines of the front-loading case-hardened classics continue to be appreciated for their historical and intrinsic worth.

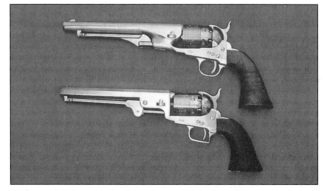

The stainless steel 1860 Army and 1851 Navy revolvers were intended for shooters interested in avoiding the corrosion that often goes with shooting black powder firearms. However, production was low and shooting would seriously reduce the value of these rare variations.

CHAPTER 4

MORE ABOUT THE SIGNATURE SERIES REVOLVERS

One of the first purchases I made as a serious firearms collector was a pair of 1849 Pocket Model Colts. They came from an antiques dealer in Hackensack, New Jersey, who had obtained them from an estate sale. That was in the early 1960s and I still remember them well. The pair had consecutive serial numbers and retained about 85% of their original blue, with case hardened colors just starting to turn grey and nearly all of the silver plating on their backstraps and trigger guards. Their 4-inch barrels had bores that remained bright and clean, with crisp rifling and no pits.

Being young and inexperienced, with no concept of their scarcity in such nice condition, I shot them without hesitation. In fact, they provided my introduction to the world of black powder shooting. The mold I purchased for use with them all those years ago is still among my inventory of handloading tools.

Over the years many guns have come and gone, but I've regretted selling only a few. These two guns are among them. Not the least of reasons is that I'd paid about $100 for the pair, but

in today's market would not be surprised to see them for sale with a mid-four figure price tag. As they say, "Hindsight is 20/20."

When, in 1984, the 2nd Generation Colt black powder series production was ended many felt

The .36 caliber Model 1851 Navy revolvers continue to be the most popular of the cap-and-ball Colts among collectors of originals, reissue Colts and the new Signature Series.

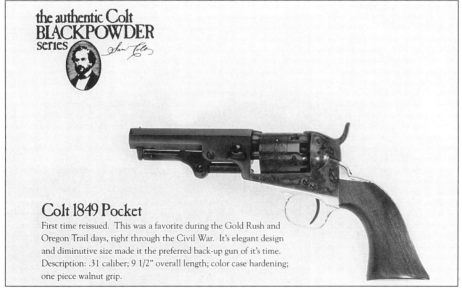

The Signature Series 1849 Pocket Model from Colt Blackpowder Arms is one of several variations that was unavailable from Colt during the time that they marketed their 2nd Generation reissue revolvers.

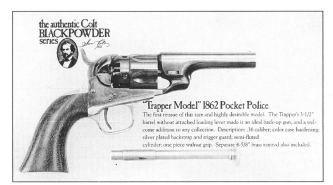

the authentic Colt
BLACKPOWDER
series

"Trapper Model" 1862 Pocket Police
The first reissue of this rare and highly desirable model. The Trapper's 3-1/2" barrel without attached loading lever made it an ideal back-up gun, and a welcome addition to any collection. Description: .36 caliber; color case hardening; silver plated backstrap and trigger guard; semi-fluted cylinder; one piece walnut grip. Separate 4-5/8" brass ramrod also included.

Very rare, an original Trapper's Model version of the 1862 Pocket Police revolver would be much too valuable to shoot. The owner of a Signature Series version of it can have all the fun of doing so for a small fraction of the cost. Many other rarities are now being reissued.

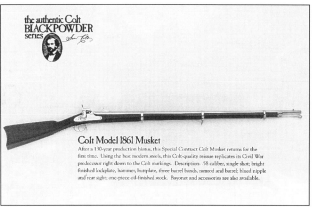

the authentic Colt
BLACKPOWDER
series

Colt Model 1861 Musket
After a 130-year production hiatus, this Special Contract Colt Musket returns for the first time. Using the best modern steels, this Colt-quality reissue replicates its Civil War predecessor right down to the Colt markings. Description: .58 caliber; single shot; bright finished lockplate, hammer, buttplate, three barrel bands, ramrod and barrel; blued nipple and rear sight; one-piece oil-finished stock. Bayonet and accessories are also available.

Civil War re-enactors can now match their authentic reproduction revolvers with the .58 caliber Colt Signature Series Model 1861 Musket.

the move was premature. A few years ago a new outfit stepped in to bridge the gap in the market that can only be filled by Colt. Known as Colt Black Powder Arms Company and working under license to use the Colt name, and the prestige that goes with it, a new series of cap-and-ball revolvers has been developed. Most of the original pieces, like the 1851 Navy, the Walker, the Dragoon series and the 1860 Army are again available. They've also added several variations that were absent from the 2nd Generation series.

Originals of the .36 caliber 1862 Police revolver in the so-called Trapper's variation (lacking the attached loading lever) and the Whitneyville Hartford Dragoon, are very rare and highly desirable collectibles, far too valuable to shoot. Yet, anyone who wishes to fire such guns may now obtain them from

among the Signature Series. Re-enactors of historical events, such as the members of the North/South Skirmish association will find the .58 caliber Model 1861 Artillery Musket a delight.

Except for the distinctive signature of Sam Colt on the backstrap of the revolvers and on the trigger guard of the musket, they are, externally, almost identical to the ones that were being shipped from the Hartford plant that Col. Colt built, ran and developed into one of the great manufacturing enterprises of the 19th century.

Although Colt vocally denied industry rumors that their percussion revolvers were made with imported Italian parts provided by Uberti, the truth was finally admitted near the end of their production. The current production's sources aren't being kept secret. Parts are being provided by Uberti, Armi San Marco and others. But meticulous care is

the authentic Colt
BLACKPOWDER
series

Colt 1860 Officers Model
An exclusively featured, deluxe version of the standard sidearm issued to U.S. troops during the Civil War. This includes an extremely rare, elegantly handcrafted brilliant blue finish used only on a handful of revolvers Sam Colt reserved as presentation Colts. In addition, the traditional "crossed sabres" emblem is executed in 24 karat gold above the wedge. The 4-screw frame is cut for optional shoulder stock. Sam Colt's signature is roll engraved on the backstrap. Description: 8" barrel; 6-shot rebated cylinder; one piece walnut grip.

A few commemorative variations have also been issued among the Signature Series from Colt Blackpowder Arms. This one is the 1860 Officers Model.

being taken to maintain the quality of appearance and function that Old Sam would demand of any product that bears his name. The color

By modern standards, the Signature Series 1860 Army revolver is the smallest of the .44 caliber percussion Colts, it's also the easiest of the big bore revolvers to carry and shoot, so it is very popular among re-enactors.

case hardening is correct, the blue is deep and rich, although not of the same charcoal type as the originals. However, it is just as attractive and far more durable. Backstraps and trigger guards are made of brass, or blued steel, whichever is appropriate to the originals represented and, in those instances where it is historically correct, those parts are silver plated. Of significant importance to many is that the proof marks required under Italian law to be stamped on any firearm made there do not compromise the originality of these pieces. Because, like the 2nd Generation revolvers from Colt, they are exported as unassembled parts and exempt from such regulation.

Of more than passing concern is the matter of such realistic reproductions being artificially aged and passed off as originals. The first deterrent to that is the serial numbering of the current production. The revolvers are numbered above those in use at the time the originals were discontinued in 1873. The character of the rifling is different, as well. Such subtle differences don't affect the authenticity of their outward appearance, but make fakery much more difficult to accomplish successfully.

Grips on these pistols are made of good Italian walnut, some of it nicely figured, but the precision of the fit of wood to metal varies. Most is quite good, but we have seen a few examples that have been slightly over or under size.

There are those who will look upon these handguns as some sort of commemoratives and keep them pristine, unfired, with the cylinders unturned. What a waste. These revolvers are made of high quality steels that the metallurgists of Sam Colt's era couldn't even imagine. They are made to be shot, and should be. Every one of the Signature Series black powder firearms is worthy of that purpose.

Choosing from among them will depend upon the activities in which the shooter wishes to engage. Mexican War buffs will be most interested in the Walker and Dragoon models. Most Civil War and frontier history aficionados will be inclined to pick up the 1851 Navy and 1860 Army revolvers. These will also suit a large percentage of Cowboy Action Shooters, but many of them will want to use something a bit more handy. The 1849 Pocket Model, 1862 Pocket Navy and Pocket Police variations, as well as the aforementioned Trapper's Model are well suited to the sort of fast handling required for such shooting.

Getting started is simply a matter of obtaining the gun that suits your fancy, adding some black powder or some modern substitute for black powder, balls of appropriate size, percussion caps and either over-powder wads or an appropriate grease to seal the mouths of the chambers. The latter component provides lubrication for the projectiles and prevents cross ignition, sometimes termed chainfire or flashover, from one chamber to another during firing.

Novice black powder shooters should be aware that the guns in question launch their projectiles with relatively low velocities and rainbow-like trajectories. The rear sight of the revolver is a notch in the hammer, visible only when it is cocked. Most of these handguns are made to shoot roughly to point of aim at a distance of 25 yards, using full-power loads. Any significant decrease in the distance will place the shot high. At 10 or 15 yards this can mean several inches, depending upon the individual revolver model and the powder charge being used. The crudeness of the rudimentary sights on these revolvers is such that changing them by deepening the notch on the hammer or raising or lowering the front sight simply isn't sensible. It's far better to determine where the revolver shoots at any given distance and adjust one's point of aim to compensate for any deviation. Alternatively, the powder charge may be adjusted to change the point of impact.

It is well to remember that, while today's black powder revolver shooters use their guns for fun and for the novelty of the experience, our forebears used guns just like them for fighting wars, for protection and food gathering on the expanding frontiers of several continents. The power level of the .31 caliber revolver is the rough equivalent of our modern .32 S&W Long cartridge. That of the .36 caliber 1851 Navy Model closely approximates the .38 S&W round or a mid-range wadcutter .38 Special, while the .44 caliber Dragoons and the 1860 Army Model are more potent than the .44 Special cartridge in its standard loadings. Actually, the energy delivered by a Walker loaded to full-power was greater than that of any revolver ever made until the .357 Magnum came along in 1935. We are not dealing with toy guns here. The rules of safe firearms handling apply, and a few more, specific to their type, must be added.

We must also consider the nature of black powder. Unlike smokeless powder, which is classified as a propellant because it burns progressively, black powder is an explosive. When ignited, the smokeless propellant in a modern cartridge seems to go off all at once, but it actually burns at a specific fixed rate, depending upon the manner in which its chemical components have been compounded. When ignited, the gases that are generated will build to a peak level of pressure, then drop off. In so doing, the brass cartridge case expands against the walls of the chamber, sealing it to accommodate the initial pressure and prevent gas blowback, then contracts to allow for easy extraction from the chamber of the firearm.

The black powder in a muzzle-loading firearm's chamber goes off all at once, literally exploding within the chamber and forcing the projectile down the bore. If there are air gaps between the powder charge and the projectile, the pressure tends to generate outward, rather than forward. This can result in damage to the firearm. For that reason, the ball should be seated firmly against the charge. By doing so, the pressures generated upon ignition are concentrated against the point of least resistance, the ball, forcing it down the barrel.

Another matter to remember is that, after firing a black powder gun, some of the powder residue may smolder for a short time. It's rare, but possible, that the next charge poured into the chamber could ignite. For that reason, the shooter should blow into the empty cylinder to snuff out embers. Individual charges, measured by volume, should be poured into the chamber. Do not pour powder directly from an open flask. If the charge should happen to ignite, the worst that can happen with a measured charge is that the shooter is startled. If the open flask is used and the charge ignites, the person holding it might just as well pull the pin on a live grenade and hold it in the hand. The results can be equally damaging.

Remember, also, to tip the firearm away from you or any bystanders during the charging operation. Should there be a flash, your hands might get a bit sooty, but your face and eyes will be out of the way of direct contact. Naturally, as in any other shooting activity, one should wear glasses to provide that added measure of safety.

Chamber mouths and bore sizes vary slightly among different makes of black powder revolvers, but in general the ball to be used for one of .31 caliber should measure .312 to .319 inches in diameter. For .36 caliber use .375- to .378-inch balls and for the .44s use .454 to .457. A bit of experimentation will help determine which size is correct for your particular handgun.

Black powder firearms require cleaning very soon after the shooting is done. Otherwise, rust and corrosion will begin to damage them within a matter of hours. While it may seem a lot of trouble, it's really quite easy to do and takes only a few minutes. I prefer to do it at the deep sink in the utility room, but a bathtub is a better choice than the usually relatively shallow kitchen or bathroom sink, if a deep sink is unavailable. The reason is that the bore brush may spatter the curtains or wallpaper. That could result in avoidable domestic strife. There's no point in angering one's spouse needlessly.

First, remove the barrel wedge and separate the barrel assembly, cylinder and frame. Then, using ordinary liquid dish washing detergent, very hot water, a bore brush and an old toothbrush, scrub the inside of the barrel, each chamber of the cylinder and all the exposed surfaces, paying particular attention to the area around the nipples of the cylinder. It's usually not necessary to remove the nipples at each cleaning session, but it should be done periodically, to verify that they are in good condition. The entire operation should take less time than doing a few dishes.

Once the powder residue has been cleaned from the revolver, rinse all the components well with boiling water. The hotter the water, the better, because it will evaporate quickly. Then, simply wipe the components down with a good quality gun oil and a soft cloth, being sure to leave a very light coat in the bore and the chambers of the cylinder. A drop or two at the base of the cocked hammer, at the cylinder bolt hole and the slot in the frame for the hand, which rotates the cylinder, should be adequate to keep the lockwork from rusting.

When the revolver has been reassembled, cock and release the mechanism a few times, while holding the hammer to keep it from falling and damaging the nipples. That will coat the internal bearing surfaces with lubricant, so that it works smoothly and internal rust will be inhibited.

The procedure is no more time consuming and only a bit more trouble than properly cleaning and lubricating a conventional revolver. In some respects, it's actually easier, because smokeless powder residues often burn into the steel and may take a substantial amount of scrubbing to remove.

The next time you prepare to shoot the revolver, before loading it, place a cap over each nipple and fire it. This will clear any residual oil from the nipples, so that you will get good ignition.

Shooting these revolvers is fun, easy, and relatively inexpensive. The components cost much less than conventional ammunition, so you may find yourself shooting with greater frequency and enjoying it more.

CHAPTER 5

SHOOTING BLACK POWDER HANDGUNS: A BEGINNER'S GUIDE

Today's shooter takes the self-contained metallic cartridge for granted. But it didn't spring into being like Athena from the head of Zeus. It took decades from the time the basic concept was created until it reached the stage where it resembled the highly developed cartridge with which we have become familiar.

Often as a matter of economy and just as frequently in an effort to improve the performance of our firearms, we take the most expensive part of the cartridge, the brass case, and reload it by replacing primer, powder and bullet. If one were to be more specific, it could be said that those who simply seek economy are "Reloaders." The shooter in search of maximum performance, who doggedly experiments with a variety of components until the formula is found that causes the bullets from his firearm to cluster tightly on target, printing holes one over the other, earns the title, "Handloader."

Our forebears, of necessity, did things somewhat differently. Self-contained metallic cartridges of the more primitive type date all the way back to the 1840s, but it took another three decades before design evolution was sufficiently developed that an individual might profitably make the effort to reuse his fired brass. In the meantime, a large percentage of the world's shooters continued happily stuffing powder and ball down the front of the barrel (or cylinder in the case of revolvers), then charging the pan with a bit more powder or placing a cap on the nipple, depending upon the type of ignition lock one's firearm used. In short, every shooter was a handloader.

Let me be clear about this matter. Given the choice between hunting and shooting targets with muzzleloaders or cartridge firearms, I'll stick with the modern technology, thank you very much. But, happily, I can do both, and so can you.

But why become involved with black powder shooting when using modern firearms is so much easier? For two reasons. First, the experience will give you a greater appreciation of that with which our colonial ancestors had to contend in order to put animal protein on the dinner table and to fight their wars. There will no longer be any question as to why saber and lance, foil and dagger, continued to be the primary military and personal armament until nearly the dawn of the 20th century. Primitive firearms run out of ammunition quickly in battle and in such circumstances are agonizingly slow to reload. The blade is always ready.

The second reason for joining the ranks of the muzzleloading community is much more simple. It's great fun! Whether it's the genuine article, or a modern reproduction, shooting historical firearms can provide a world of enjoyment. The flash, the whoosh-boom of its report, the distinctive smell of the cloud of white smoke from black powder, the ball striking the target at speeds people called fast 125 years ago, but are downright sedate by present standards; these all contribute to the fun.

However, we must in this discussion of shooting pleasures insert a caveat. As noted in a previous chapter, modern smokeless powder is classified as a propellant. That simply means that it burns, rather than explodes. Needless to say, its burning rate is almighty fast, but in order to give an explosive effect, it must be tightly contained, as it is in a cartridge, surrounded by the chamber of a firearm. Black powder, on the other hand, really is an explosive. Handled and stored properly, in small quantities, it is perfectly safe. Far less dangerous, for example, than the gasoline you store in the garage for use in the lawnmower.

Black powder is also a partially organic compound which, after combustion, leaves an ash. For that reason there may sometimes be small burning embers left for a brief time after firing.

Made of charcoal, saltpeter and sulfur, it is the carbon that may be slow to go out. For that reason, as we've said before, one must be sure to reload from a powder measure, rather than pouring loose powder directly from a container. Should the powder from a measure flash, the worst one is likely to suffer is singed eyebrows and a sooty face. Pouring powder directly from the can or from a powder horn into a black powder firearm that hasn't been given a few seconds to allow the embers to burn out can cause the entire contents of the container to ignite. One might just as well play Russian roulette with a grenade. Just attend to normal safety procedures and you'll be perfectly fine.

Using a powder flask to load a black powder revolver is a bit different in that the device has a built-in closure to provide for precise charges of powder. One simply tips the unit down, covering the spout with a finger, draws the spring-loaded lever to one side with the thumb so that the closure can open and the measuring spout can fill, then allows the lever to close before dispensing the powder. The measured charge is then poured into the chamber while taking care that the piece is pointed in a safe direction. The charge is followed by a ball of appropriate size, which is then seated tightly against the powder. Then, grease is smeared over the mouth of the chamber in order to provide lubrication as the ball moves down the barrel on firing. The grease also prevents sparks or flame from one chamber from entering another and creating what is called a chainfire situation with two or more cylinders going off at the same time. A pre-lubricated over-powder wad serves the same purpose and is a bit less messy. Sometimes, if any powder is exposed in adjacent chambers it can be ignited at the same time as the one under the hammer. While this has happened to me and to others I've known, I've never heard of anyone receiving any sort of injury from this phenomenon. Nor, for that matter, any damage being done to the revolver. Nevertheless, it's disconcerting, presents a potential hazard and is easily prevented.

The grease may be something as simple as lard, or a solid vegetable shortening easily found at any grocer's, or one of the specialized products made by the firearms accessory manufacturers, such as Ox-Yoke, Thompson/Center, Lyman, Uncle Mike's and others.

As to projectiles, these are normally made of pure lead. Commercially made conical types are encountered, but rarely. They must almost always be cast by hand. Balls of appropriate size may also be hand-cast, but are available ready made from several sources, including Hornady, Remington and Speer. These have the advantage of being swaged perfectly round, so that they have no sprue marks, as have hand-cast balls. Best results will usually be found using the size that requires a slight press fit into the mouth of the chamber, shaving a tiny amount of lead in the process. Too loose and they are likely to fall out of the cylinder when the revolver is placed in a holster. Too tight and they will be difficult to load and may cause the ramming mechanism to be bent in the process.

Another caveat worthy of mention is that the loading lever must not be raised and lowered rapidly and repeatedly to seat the ball. If the portion of the mechanism that enters the mouth of the cylinder is tight enough to cause friction, sufficient heat may be generated to cause the powder charge to ignite. This phenomenon is rare, but easily avoided by using slow, firm strokes rather than rapid, short ones to seat the projectile.

While we're about it, since most black powder handgun shooters are also likely to shoot muzzle-loading rifles or muskets, it's worth noting that the ramrod should be held in the fingers. It should never be used to push the ball against the powder charge by placing the open palm over the end. If friction were to cause the charge to ignite, severe injury could result.

In general, the Walkers do best with #10 percussion caps and .454 to .457 diameter balls. Charges of 35 to 55 grains of black powder are recommended. The Dragoons use the same components, with charges of 35 to 40 grains of black powder. The 1860 Army revolver is the smallest of the .44's and does best with #11 caps and 25 to 30 grains of powder. The .36 caliber revolvers use the #11 cap and take 15 to 20 grains of black powder behind a .375 to .378 ball. Moving down another size to the .31 caliber, these revolvers use #11 caps with balls of .315 to .320 of an inch.

Chamber mouths and bores tend to vary somewhat in size from one maker's product to the next. To illustrate, one of my 1849 Pocket Model revolvers has a bore measuring .315 inch, while the other measures .319 inch. So, once you've gotten started, you may wish to measure the mouths of your revolver's chamber and bore and, perhaps, experiment with several projectile diameters in order to find the one that suits your particular revolver best.

The correct black powder granulation (grain size) for use in handguns is FFFG, usually referred to as "Three F" or "Triple F." A black powder substitute, such as Pyrodex P may also be used, but the latter is actually a smokeless powder specifically formulated for use in muzzleloaders. When using it, do not weigh the charge. Instead, measure it out by volume. The same measure that gives, for example, 20 grains of black powder will throw an entirely different weight of Pyrodex, but is appropriate for use with that powder. If you weigh the charge, as you would in loading a cartridge with smokeless powder, you could end up with a potentially dangerous overload. Just use the same volume measure with both and you will be all right.

Powder charges may be tailored to some extent to the use for which the revolver will be put. For hunting or for targets placed at 25 yards and beyond, it's best to use full-power loads. With targets to be shot at close range, say 10 to 15 yards, lighter charges of powder may be a better choice.

The loading sequence is as follows: Powder, measured by volume, followed by placing the ball finger-tight into the mouth of the chamber. Then, rotate the cylinder so that chamber is under the loading lever and seat it tightly over the powder charge. Once all the chambers have been loaded, smear grease across the mouth of each one. Be sure to wipe your fingers clean, then press a cap onto each nipple. With that done, you are ready to shoot. If there is to be a delay, place the hammer down on the cylinder between two chambers. This will prevent an accidental discharge. Carried in this manner it is perfectly safe to have all the revolver's chambers loaded. However, in Cowboy Action shooting competition, one chamber is always left empty and the hammer is lowered over it.

Dry firing at a target can be good practice for development of sight alignment and trigger control with some types of handguns, particularly those with rebounding firing pins. This must NEVER be done with original or replica cap-and-ball black powder revolvers. Nipples will quickly be battered beyond usefulness and have to be replaced. However, Ruger's Old Army revolvers are so nicely fitted that they can be dry-fired without battering the nipples, and will still ignite caps with perfect reliability.

Although it's much slower going than using metallic cartridge firearms, one of the nice things about shooting the front loaders is that the cost is comparatively low. You can shoot for hours for a fraction of the expense that a similar amount of time spent with conventional firearms of comparable caliber would require and have just as much fun; maybe more. Just try it and see.

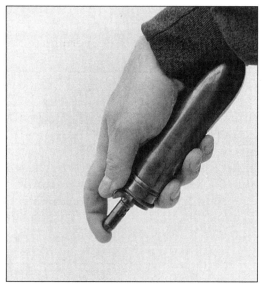

Whichever style or caliber you prefer, select the components best suited to your individual handgun. Match the ball to the size of the revolver's bore and the powder charge to the sort of shooting planned and the range from which it will be done.

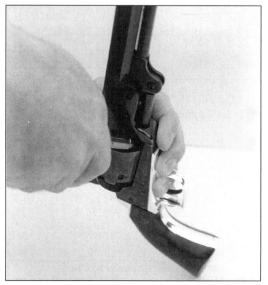

A measured charge of powder, selected to match the range and level of power desired, is poured into each of the revolver's chambers.

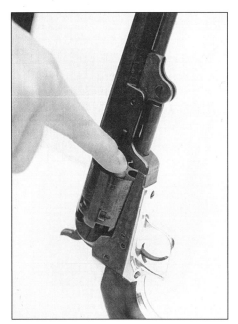

Seat a ball, finger tight, into each chamber. Then, rotate the cylinder to place it under the loading lever

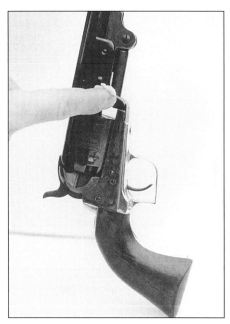

When all the chambers have been loaded with powder and ball, seal the mouth of each one with solid lubricant. Several companies make proprietary compounds for such use, but ordinary vegetable shortening (as used in baking), tallow or lard work well.

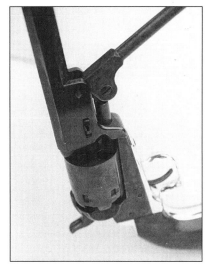

Using the revolver's loading lever, push each ball into the chamber, seating it tightly against the powder charge.

When you are ready to begin shooting, seat a cap onto each nipple.

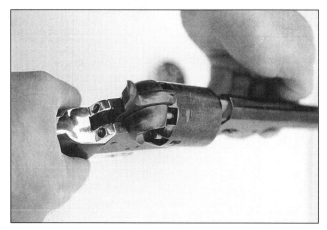

If shooting is to be interrupted or you wish to carry the revolver in a holster, place the hammer at rest between chambers, so that it is out of contact with a capped nipple. Better yet, carry it with the hammer down on a chamber that has been charged, but don't put the nipple in place. If another shot is needed, it can be put in place much more quickly by capping that chamber's nipple than if it had to be reloaded entirely from scratch.

CHAPTER 6

ARMI SAN MARCO'S RICHARDS-TYPE CONVERSION OF COLT'S 1861 NAVY REVOLVER

As brilliant an inventor, entrepreneur and publicist as Sam Colt was, there were some matters about which he was stubbornly short-sighted. One was the double-action revolver mechanism. He regarded those that existed in his day to be hopelessly inaccurate and a blatant waste of good ammunition. Another was the obvious improvement in strength and sighting accuracy afforded by placing a topstrap over the frame of a revolver. To be sure, the Model of 1855 Sidehammer revolver designed by his successor-designate as president of the firm, Elisha Root, demonstrated that he could be talked into some things. But it was not until nine years after Colt's death that the firm began regularly making handguns with that feature.

About one subject Sam Colt was adamant. The self-contained metallic cartridge was, in his estimation, a passing fad, suited only for small revolvers designed for concealment. He felt they lacked power and were unreliable for the serious purposes of military combat and law enforcement that were the primary markets for his big and powerful percussion revolvers.

His former employee, Rollin White, designed a cylinder completely bored through, that would accept such a cartridge, which could be loaded quickly, and allow the used cases to be just as rapidly ejected. All these features allowed the handgun to be fired and reloaded numerous times in a fraction of the time required to recharge a percussion revolver. Colt was not impressed. White had offered him the opportunity to manufacture revolvers based upon his patent and Sam Colt made it perfectly clear that as long as he was in charge, no such inferior technology would be used

to make firearms that bore his name.

Horace Smith and D.B. Wesson, on the other hand, had spent years trying to perfect the Volcanic pistols that were the products of their first partnership. They had extensive experience in the development of fixed metallic cartridges and believed passionately in their potential. They went broke trying to prove it and Oliver Winchester picked up the pieces of their enterprise. Winchester hired B. Tyler Henry, one of the most innovative gunsmiths of the time and together they set about transforming a small and struggling rifle-making firm into what became the legendary giant of the industry, Winchester Repeating Arms Mfg. Co.

When White approached Smith and Wesson, they had no problem understanding the potential worth of a fixed-cartridge revolver system. Their first products using the White patent were little seven-shot revolvers of the very sort that Sam Colt disdained. They chambered a small .22 caliber rimfire cartridge that in later years would come to be known as the .22 Short. Their handguns proved very popular and, with the profits derived from their sales, further research and development allowed them to bring out bigger, more potent revolvers chambered for the .32 Rimfire cartridge.

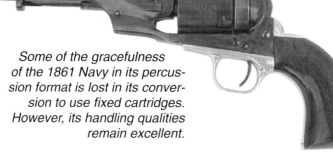

Some of the gracefulness of the 1861 Navy in its percussion format is lost in its conversion to use fixed cartridges. However, its handling qualities remain excellent.

At the same time, in Winchester's factory, bigger, more powerful .44 caliber rimfire cartridges were being made for use in the firm's Henry rifle, a much-modified and more efficient outgrowth of the Volcanic. While neither the rifle nor the cartridge could compare in terms of power or range with the .58 caliber Springfield muskets with which most of the Union forces fought during the American Civil War, the relatively limited use of the Henry rifle during that conflict captured the imagination of the public. It was after all, referred to by some Confederate soldiers as "That damned Yankee rifle you can load on Sunday and shoot all week."

Smith, Wesson and others came to the realization that the Henry cartridge was of a size that could possibly be used in a large service revolver. In the years following the war, there was a lot of experimentation in that direction, so much so that as the year 1873 approached, the subject became a matter of some urgency.

The year is significant, because it was then that the protection afforded the Rollin White patent granted in 1856 would come to an end. From then on, anyone could begin making revolvers with bored-through cylinders. The fixed metallic cartridge had, by that time, proved itself so efficient that the era of cap-and-ball technology for military and law enforcement use was about to die a sudden and permanent death.

Sam Colt died in 1862, but the arms-making enterprise he founded continued to prosper and grow. Colt's management knew that if the firm was to continue successfully in business it would have to face the inevitable and create a cartridge-firing revolver. Their research and development brought forth the 1872 open-top single-action revolver which was quickly replaced by the Model 1873; the legendary Peacemaker. The progression of that revolver's history is well known and endlessly fascinating, but Colt faced other problems as well.

Hundreds of thousands of their cap-and-ball revolvers were in the hands of civilians, lawmen and military forces. A large number of such revolvers also remained in inventory at the factory. For all those handguns to become instantly obsolete would be a devastating economic burden upon all concerned. Many individuals could ill afford to replace their guns outright. Nor would the government purse strings open readily for wholesale replacement of existing arms when so many remained as surplus after the war. In order to make the best of things, Colt's engineers began to develop methods by which the older revolvers could be converted for the use of fixed cartridges.

The first such attempt involved the Thuer system, by which the cartridge was loaded into the front of the revolver's cylinder, seated with the existing rammer and held in place with a boss affixed to the recoil shield at the rear of the frame. This method of loading was relatively slow and the conversion too costly to be practical. To make matters worse, the expended cartridge case was meant to be shaken loose from the chamber, rather than ejected by some manual device. Black powder fouling made that a wholly unsatisfactory proposition.

C.B. Richards developed a system whereby the original cylinder was cut at the rear, creating bored-through chambers. A recoil plate with an integral loading gate was attached at the rear of the frame to take up the missing space. Then, an ejector rod and housing were attached to the right side of the barrel to facilitate removal of fired cartridge cases. The cost of this conversion was a fraction of that of a completely new revolver.

Two additional and excellent features were included. One was an integral, though rudimentary, rear sight made as part of the recoil shield. The other was a spring-loaded rebounding firing pin that was less subject to breakage than one mounted on the hammer. The Richards firing pin had the added benefit of making it less likely that the cartridge head might be ruptured upon firing, thus releasing the pressures generated outside the chamber and endangering the user and bystanders.

William Mason collaborated with Richards on the third conversion method. The Richards-Mason patent improved the loading gate, the ejector and the rotation of the cylinder. However, it placed the firing pin back on the hammer and got rid of the rear sight on the recoil shield, returning it to a notch in the hammer, as had been common to those revolvers in their percussion form. As a cavalry arm, of course,

Based upon the Richards conversion method, the Cimarron Arms/Armi San Marco 1861 Navy .38 Special is certain to attract attention on the range. Its performance was surprisingly good.

even a handgun with the most refined sights is reduced to a point-and-shoot proposition when fired from the back of a moving horse. So, this system was appropriate for its intended use.

The conversions make an interesting study, but their time was short in the historical scheme of things. Until very recently they were all but ignored by most collectors and virtually unknown to shooters, because the ammunition correct for most of them has been difficult, if not impossible, to obtain for a couple of generations. However, with the phenomenal world-wide growth of Cowboy Action Shooting and its participants' interest in authentic dress and shooting gear (within practical limitations), there has developed a small but insistent demand for reproductions of conversion-style revolvers.

Armi San Marco is one of the few makers that has taken up the challenge and is now making revolvers of that kind for several model variants and calibers. Cimarron Arms, which contracted their manufacture, allowed the testing of an 1861 Navy revolver chambered for the ubiquitous .38 Special cartridge.

Made up by the Richards conversion method, it is not historically correct. We can find no evidence that this model was subjected to any but the Thuer and Richards-Mason techniques. While there may have been some, they certainly were not done up in commercial quantities. Nevertheless, the rebounding firing pin and the integral rear sight on the recoil shield probably make it the more practical choice for the modern shooter.

The revolver tested had some superficial faults of fit and finish, but they are not serious and don't affect its shooting and handling qualities. It is a relatively inexpensive revolver as such things go, so it is reasonable to allow for a few minor imperfections.

It should be noted that calling the test revolver a "conversion" is not wholly accurate. These six-guns are made for use with metallic cartridges from the outset, not actually converted from existing percussion revolvers. The term is used here merely to avoid confusion. These revolvers should more correctly be referred to as conversion types.

The test revolver had a delightfully smooth cocking action and trigger pull. The trigger releases the sear with precisely 3 pounds of pressure. The break is very crisp and is certainly a factor in the good grouping the revolver demonstrated. We hardly expected a National Match contender, but we've shot many modern service revolvers chambered for the .38 Special that can't group as well as this one of antique design.

As is the case with nearly all Colt-style single-action revolvers of the period, this one does not shoot to point of aim. The user must hold low and right of the mark with this one to place shots where they belong. Most Cowboy Action Shooting competitors will be familiar with that need. But, once the point of aim is correctly related to the point of impact, it's not difficult to score well.

Modern steels make this a much stronger revolver than the original. Nevertheless, the lack of a topstrap makes the use of high-pressure ammunition designed for hunting, silhouette shooting and law enforcement risky. The revolver is being made specifically for use in action shooting competition and low- to standard-velocity ammunition loaded with the lead bullets mandated for that discipline is all that should ever be used in it. There is a sufficient margin of safety built into the Armi San Marco 1861 Navy conversion to withstand the accidental use of high-power ammunition, should such be inadvertently loaded into the piece. Just as surely, the revolver would shoot loose very quickly and be useless for any meaningful purpose if they were used deliberately. Stick to the light loads and it should give good service.

In keeping with the nature of its intended use, we tested the Armi San Marco 1861 Navy conversion with Black Hills .38 Long Colt and their .38 Special Cowboy load, Federal LRN, Remington's LSW, 3D and Winchester Cowboy loads. All these brands and types use 158-grain lead projectiles factory rated at about 750 fps or less.

Probably as a result of the similarity of projectile weight, material and velocity common to each of the tested loadings, our groups all fell within the same general point of impact. Most groups measured two inches or less from a distance of 15 yards and about 4 to 5 inches at 25

Ammunition from Black Hills, Federal, Remington, 3D and Winchester was tried in the .38 Special Armi San Marco '61 Navy conversion revolver. All of it shot well to approximately the same point of impact.

yards. Clusters of these sizes would be a disappointment from a target grade revolver, but from a piece such as this they are quite acceptable and fully capable of keeping the competitor who wants to use one of these sixguns in contention.

The Armi San Marco 1861 Navy conversion, as made for Cimarron Arms, was put through two range sessions before conclusions were drawn. By that time about 600 rounds of ammunition had gone through it. Often a new firearm requires a significant break-in period before it begins shooting its best groups. In this instance, we had expected accuracy to deteriorate relatively quickly, because of the revolver's inherent weaknesses.

The barrel assembly is held to the frame by a wedge through the cylinder stem, about which the latter part rotates, and by two pins that protrude from the base of the frame into the base of the barrel assembly. We were pleased to see that groups were beginning to get tighter with use.

Encouraging as that may be, it's obvious that it can't continue to be so if the revolver is disassembled and cleaned in the conventional manner. With repeated disassembly the tolerances at the assembly points must begin to deteriorate and the revolver will loosen over time. For this reason we recommend that black powder loads be avoided and that the revolver be cleaned and lubricated without taking it apart. With modern solvents, ammunition of low to standard power levels, and today's lubricants, it can be well-maintained without taking it apart too often, especially if smokeless powder is exclusively used.

It should also be noted that Armi San Marco, through Cimarron Arms, is also making an 1860 Army conversion in .44 caliber. However, the cartridge for which it is chambered is a variant of the original .44 Colt. It might seem that the better

This excellent 10-round group was fired from 15 yards with Remington's standard-velocity LSW load. The X marked low and right of the bull indicates the point of aim.

choice would have been the .44 Special, but that cartridge's dimensions are such that only every other chamber could be charged or that the cylinder be made to have just five chambers. The cylinder's dimensions are such that the .44 Special cartridge cannot otherwise be loaded side by side in all the revolver's chambers.

The .44 Colt ammunition is available from Black Hills Ammunition, in Rapid City, South Dakota. No other major manufacturer is making it. Original revolvers had nominal bore dimensions of .454 inches, but these replicas are made with bores of .429 inches. For that reason, the Black Hills cartridge is made with an inside lubricated bullet, rather than the heel-type of the originals.

The Cowboy Action Shooter in search of something a bit unusual will find the Cimarron Arms/Armi San Marco conversion of the 1861 Navy revolver an interesting alternative to the replicas that dominate the market. It's a surprisingly fine shooter and certain to attract the interest of others on the range.

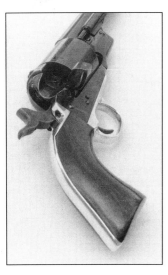

A rebounding firing pin, rudimentary rear sight and loading gate are all integral to the recoil boss attached to the rear of the '61 Navy conversion's frame.

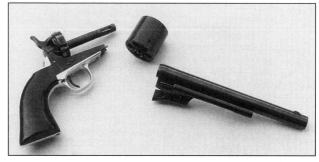

Frequent disassembly is likely to take its toll upon the Cimarron Arms/Armi San Marco '61 Navy's accuracy. The author recommends that the revolver be cleaned and maintained without taking it apart.

CHAPTER 7

THE 19TH CENTURY RIVALS

Given the literary and film references one is likely to encounter regarding the Colt SAA revolver, it might easily be believed that Colt had the market for handguns to itself in the western lands. While they were undoubtedly the most popular products of their kind, there was plenty of competition. Remington, Merwin & Hulbert, Smith & Wesson and a host of other firearms were in frequent evidence. In point of fact, some of these were deliberately chosen by their owners because for one reason or another, they liked them better than the Colts, rather than because that was all that was available, or just what they could afford.

Just as modern shooters may prefer a S&W Sigma over the Glock for its better ergonomics, 19th century handgunners might just as well have preferred the simultaneous extraction of one of the Model #3 S&W variations or the grip design of one of several variations of the Merwin & Hulbert Army revolvers (none of which, by the way, were ever sold under contract to the military in spite of the "Army" portion of their nomenclature), over the SAA Colt. Though very similar to Colt's offerings, those with long fingers might have considered the Remington models of 1875 or 1890 the better choices

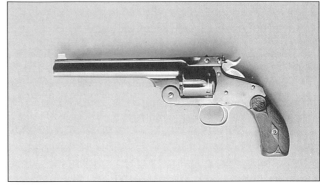

The S&W New Model #3 used in our tests had been factory refinished many years ago. It retains almost 100% of its refurbished blue and its mechanism is as tight as that of a new revolver.

. By the same token, it must be considered that an average working cowboy was making about "a dollar a day and found" during the last quarter of the 19th century. Investing half a month's wages in a handgun was more than many felt they could afford. This was especially so when one considers that ranch work was seasonal. Few cow outfits could afford to keep all their men on during the winter months, when branding, herding, fence mending and droving activities came to a halt as severe winter weather was waited out.

The handgun was a working man's tool, used much more often to shoot the occasional rattlesnake, collect the odd rabbit for the pot, drive off marauding coyotes preying on new calves or to intimidate a steer with a bad attitude than to take on a human adversary. Many a cowboy was perfectly satisfied to carry a Harrington & Richardson, Hopkins & Allen or Forehand & Wadsworth .32

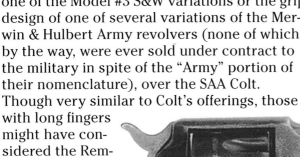

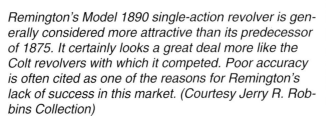

Remington's Model 1890 single-action revolver is generally considered more attractive than its predecessor of 1875. It certainly looks a great deal more like the Colt revolvers with which it competed. Poor accuracy is often cited as one of the reasons for Remington's lack of success in this market. (Courtesy Jerry R. Robbins Collection)

Relatively little is known about the manufacturing history of the Merwin & Hulbert revolvers, but their design and function are unique and, for their time, highly advanced.

caliber revolver in his chaps pocket for such purposes. At a price of about $3, the guns were easy to afford and that was as much money as many felt it necessary to spend for a handgun. Still, a whole lot of the bigger handguns, built to handle more potent cartridges were, indeed, sold to a lot of cowboys, storekeepers, businessmen, and lawmen. Let's take a look at some of the more popular types.

Remington's military-size cartridge revolvers were preceded by a succession of about a dozen percussion revolver variations that began manufacture around 1860. The distinctive feature of these early efforts from their Ilion, N.Y., factory was that, almost unique among handguns of that period, they were made with a topstrap over the cylinder. This provided added strength and a sighting channel down its middle that proved very popular. Some would argue that, had Remington had someone with the promotional acumen of Sam Colt working for them, they might have sold many more revolvers than

Remington's Model 1875 revolvers were good looking and handled well, particularly in big hands. This specimen is engraved and is stocked with beautifully aged ivory. (Courtesy the Ron Ogan Collection)

they did. As it was, they gave the Colonel a pretty good run for his money.

The New Model Army revolver of 1860-1875 vintage was the apparent basis of their Model 1875 cartridge revolver. Similar in profile to the SAA in some respects, it's easily distinguished by the "sail" or "web" found under the barrel. The only purpose for this feature seems to be to stiffen the barrel, making it less subject to barrel whip on firing. It serves no direct mechanical function.

Most of the Model 1875's were fitted with 7-1/2-inch barrels and chambered for the .44 Remington cartridge. A few were made with 5-1/2-inch barrels, but specimens factory-made in that configuration are very rare. Any with that length barrel should be looked upon with suspicion until authentication is obtained in writing from a certified expert on the subject. Later in the revolver's production some were made for the .44-40 cartridge and for the .45 Government round that was used in military issue S&W Schofield and Colt SAA revolvers, but these, too, are scarce and some specimens may be fakes.

The 1875 Remingtons were obviously made in an attempt to compete for the military contracts Colt had won in 1873. But the Hartford products had a long headstart and no U.S. military contracts for the Remingtons have surfaced thus far. However, there were other government sales; most notably, some 1,300 nickel plated specimens that went to the Department of the Interior in 1883. These were intended for use by the Indian Police on a number of western reservations. The only martial contract of note that Remington serviced was for 10,000 revolvers that were sent to Egypt.

Dating Model 1875 Remingtons is difficult, because they were numbered in production batches. For that reason there are duplicate serial numbers, but all are classed as antiques, because production ceased in 1889. In all, there were only about 25,000 of these revolvers made, and surviving numbers can be expected to be substantially fewer than that, so they can all be regarded as rare and desirable.

With their eyes more toward the civilian market which by that time was dominated quite thoroughly by the SAA Colt, Remington redesigned their big service revolver and designated the result the Model 1890 Single Action Army revolver. The chief difference was the elimination of the web under the barrel. All known specimens, which number about 2,000, were originally chambered for the .44-40 cartridge.

Both the Remington SAA's, though mechanically very similar to the Colt revolver, have a somewhat different feel to them. This is because of their slightly elongated-grip design, the back-strap of which is integral with the frame. This makes reaching the trigger and manipulating the hammer with the thumb more difficult for the individual with small hands. Those with long fingers may find it faster and easier than with a Colt. In both instances we have a well made, strong, sturdy revolver that many practical shooters believe to be as good or better than anything else with which it competed for the consumer's dollar in the marketplace.

Smith & Wesson had somewhat greater success in competing with Colt's SAA revolver in both the military and the civilian market. The many versions of their Model Number 3 had much to recommend them. The .45 caliber Schofield was adopted for service use with the Army on the western frontier. The cartridge for which it is chambered is slightly shorter than that of the Colt revolver, which gave rise to the .45 Long Colt nomenclature that has sometimes caused confusion since, officially, there never was a .45 Short Colt round (however, a few cartridges with that nomenclature on their headstamps, made in the early 20th century, have surfaced). The .45 S&W, also known as the .45 Government cartridge, became standard military issue for use in both makes of revolver in order to prevent the inevitable confusion that would have plagued the supply system if both cartridges had been provided. Units armed with the Schofield revolver would, sooner or later, have found themselves with the longer Colt ammo and been unable to use it, because of the shorter cylinder of the S&W handgun.

The nature of the Schofield's design makes it a little slower to shoot than the Colt SAA, but what it lacks in that regard is more than made up in the relative speed with which it can be loaded, shot, and reloaded. As with all the Number 3 frame S&W revolvers, it employs a break-top latching mechanism which, when opened, allows the barrel to be tilted down, while at the same time a spring activates an extractor mechanism that pulls the empty cases out of their chambers. In practice, the revolver should be turned over, so that gravity allows the cases to fall cleanly away from the cylinder. If kept upright, one or more might slip under the extractor and jam the handgun.

A stoppage of that sort is easy enough to clear under ideal circumstances at a target range. However, doing so from the back of a frightened horse, in the heat of a battle with Apache warriors, could turn a minor problem into a permanent setback.

There are two models and a total of six variations of the Schofield that are of interest to the collector. Both the 1st and 2nd Model Schofields include standard military versions and the very rare specimens that were sold commercially (about 35 of the 1st Model and 650 of the 2nd Model).

The "Wells Fargo" variations were purchased as military surplus by Schuyler, Hartley & Graham, of New York, who subsequently sold many of them to Wells Fargo & Co. They were refinished with nickel plating after shortening most of the original 7-inch barrels to 5 inches.

This was a common practice with many long-barreled revolvers during that period, as lack of proper care using blackpowder cartridges, with their corrosive primers, usually affected the barrel near the muzzle worse than at its rear. That's one of the reasons that the so-called "Artillery Model" military issue SAA Colts, some 16,000 of which were called back into service for the war in the Philippines and elsewhere between 1895 and 1903, had their barrels bobbed from their original length of 7-1/2 inches to 5-1/2 inches.

Merwin & Hulbert's offerings were well made and had some interesting design features. Loading them required that the barrel be twisted and pulled forward to gain access to the revolver's cylinder. This movement caused the fired cases to be extracted simultaneously. The most interesting thing about this is that the extraction was selective, so unfired rounds remained in the cylinder. Thus, the user could rid himself of the used cases, close the revolver, then open the gate and insert the replacements, as needed.

The M&H revolver opens by pushing the release latch, twisting the barrel assembly to the right and pulling it forward. The cylinder moves forward with the barrel.

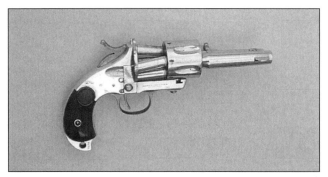

One of the most remarkable features of the Merwin & Hulberts is the ability to selectively extract empty cases, while permitting the remaining loaded rounds to be retained, because they aren't completely removed from the cylinder when the barrel/cylinder assembly is opened.

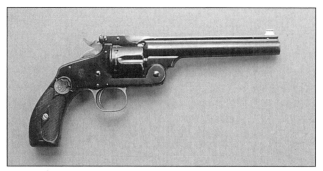

Our test S&W New Model #3 is a target variation. One of the reasons for its precision performance is that it is equipped with a Payne-style bead front sight. Properly used, this type of sight can be exceptionally efficient.

Both of the specimens we had the opportunity to try were chambered for the .44-40 cartridge. The one with the 3 1/2-inch barrel shot reasonably well from a distance of 15 yards, as this group using Hornady's Cowboy Action loads demonstrates.

The long-barreled Merwin & Hulbert delivered a level of accuracy comparable to that of any modern service revolver.

The partners in this enterprise never actually manufactured these revolvers. That was done under contract with Hopkins & Allen, of Norwalk, Connecticut.

Four variations of the M&H Single Action Army revolvers, including a so-called "Pocket Model," were offered in succession from about 1876 to the early 1880s. All were made for .44 caliber cartridges; either the .44-40 or the proprietary .44 M&H round. The latter is similar, but not the same as the .44 S&W American cartridge. While, as noted above, no Merwin & Hulbert revolvers were purchased under military contract, some were bought by the U.S. government for issue to the Border Patrol. These were chambered for the .44-40 cartridge and were still being carried by some members of that organization as late as the 1930s.

Some of the handguns that competed for market share against the Single Action Army were very well made. Specimens of the S&W American, chambered for the .44 Russian round and of the Merwin & Hulberts in .44-40 have demonstrated excellent performance. Actually, a S&W recently tested was found capable of shooting 1-inch groups at 25 yards.

Only the S&W's enjoyed anything close to the popularity of the SAA Colt. As good as the others may have been, the legendary Peacemaker was the sole revolver of the period to develop the mystique that makes this 19th century classic so much appreciated at the dawn of the 21st.

CHAPTER 8

COMPARING SCHOFIELDS: AN ORIGINAL AND UBERTI'S ALMOST-AUTHENTIC REPLICAS

The reason the U.S. Government accepted the Schofield as standard issue to some frontier military posts in the last quarter of the 19th century was the speed with which the revolver could be reloaded. It's operated by pulling back with the thumb of the shooting hand the latch that connects the barrel assembly to the frame, then tipping the barrel assembly, opening it to its full extension. For best results, the rear of the cylinder should be pointed upside down. During the opening process, a star extractor is activated that pulls the fired cases out and permits them to drop free. At the point where the barrel assembly is fully extended, the extractor star is automatically released and a return spring snaps it back into its recess in the cylinder.

When turned upright, a fresh batch of six loaded rounds may be inserted into the chambers and the barrel assembly returned to the locked position. This process takes about a third the time that a practiced handler required for reloading a Colt SAA, using its ejector rod for

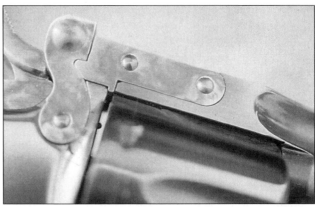

The convex circle on the side of the latch near its top serves no apparent mechanical purpose, but it is a quick way to tell that this is a 2nd Model Schofield. The same area on the latch of a 1st Model is flat.

Top to bottom, Uberti's 2nd Model Schofield in standard military configuration; a Uberti of the "Wells Fargo" type, as reconfigured when the revolvers were sold as surplus; a 19th century original, engraved and nickel-plated, probably long after its use in military service.

The box in which the Uberti revolver comes resembles the packaging used for the originals. Curiously, the revolver illustrated on the label is a 1st Model Schofield.

Yet another detail to give the Uberti an air of originality is the replication of the Schofield patent marks found on the old S&Ws.

removal of the fired cases from each chamber, then rotating the cylinder while inserting one fresh round at a time.

Before we get to the shooting, let's go into the matter of the Schofield replicas being "almost" authentic. The replica revolvers under discussion are Uberti's copies, marketed by Navy Arms. There is another version, made by Armi San Marco. The outward difference between the two is that the Uberti replicates the Second Model, while the ASM revolver is a First Model type. The quickest way to tell the difference is to look at the side of the latch that opens the action. It is located at the rear portion of the top of the frame. The side of that area on a First Model is smooth; the Second Model has a convex circle rising on each side. There seems to be no practical purpose for it; it just is.

The few ASM revolvers that I've had the opportunity to handle have been a bit rough in finish and function, but those were specimens of early manufacture. One I examined recently, a

Wells Fargo version, nickel plated with 5-inch barrel, was nicely finished.

To be fair, the first of the Uberti replicas to leave Italy were less than mechanically perfect. However, it seems that the problems attendant to the fit, finish and mechanical operation of these relatively complicated frontier period handguns have been resolved. Recent production lots have them looking good and working as they should.

Not having an ASM version before me, I can't comment in detail, but the Uberti has several differences from the originals that would make it difficult for an unscrupulous person to pass it off to a knowledgeable collector as an authentic antique. The screws, of course, are threaded metrically, so originals cannot interchange. The grip escutcheons are of a different style. The cylinder is longer, so that the modern revolver will accept .45 Colt ammunition. The latch on an

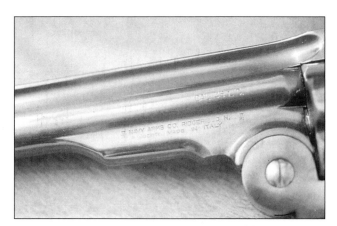

The distributor's mark on the right side of the Uberti Schofield makes it obvious that the revolver is a replica.

The U.S. marking found on the heel of the revolver's butt adds one more measure of authenticity to its appearance. Still, it would be difficult to pass a Uberti replica off as an original Schofield.

original has diamond knurling, while the Ubertis have straight horizontal grooves. Likewise the hammer spur. The rifling of the bore of an original has a left-hand twist. The Uberti's rifling twists to the right. Grips are marked with replicated cartouches of inspectors that worked when the Schofields were first made, 120 years ago, but the marks are those of the wrong inspectors for these revolvers.

There are a number of other differences, but they are more subtle and many are internal. Suffice it to say that only the most inept buyer would mistake one of the replicas for an original.

Those who want it so can also have the Schofield chambered for the .44-40 cartridge. Industry rumors have it that it may soon be made to chamber the .44 Special, too. Neither cartridge, of course, was chambered in the originals. But some buyers will choose one or the other of them to match the caliber of the rifles they use in Cowboy Action competitions.

Most Cowboy Action ammunition is loaded to modest velocities, so recoil control is of little concern. The original load used in the 19th century Schofields featured a 230-grain bullet and 28 grains of black powder and is also easily controlled. However, most modern users are inclined to shoot handguns with wrist and elbow locked. The shape of the Schofield's gripframe is such that it is better handled in the 19th century manner, aiming with wrist and elbow bent. But, even with the most potent of .45 Colt ammunition the pruning-saw shape of the revolver's gripframe merely slides under the hand, rather than slamming it in the way a modern revolver that recoils heavily might.

Several manufacturers catering to the Cowboy Action competitor offer a broad selection of popular calibers, but Black Hills Ammunition offers the shooter an especially comprehensive listing of factory loads in calibers of interest to those who shoot the old sixguns and rifles. Many are, at the time of this writing, commercially unavailable elsewhere. All their Cowboy Action loads are specifically made to duplicate the ballistic performance of black powder ammunition of the late 19th century, albeit with cleaner burning and non-corrosive smokeless powder.

Much of Black Hills Cowboy Action ammunition is loaded with Starline Brass, which can be purchased from the case maker as a separate component. It's also made by Bertram Bullet Co., of Victoria, Australia, and imported to the U.S. by Dangerous Dave, The Old Western Scrounger, of

This Schofield, made by S&W in the 1870s, was engraved later in the same style as used by the artisans employed by the distributors, Schuyler, Hartley & Graham. It still functions well, but its accuracy is substandard.

Montague, California. If you don't have dies made specifically for the Schofield, satisfactory handloads can be constructed by trimming .45 Colt brass to Schofield case length of 1.10 inches, sizing in a .45 Colt die, then decapping, belling, seating and crimping using .45 ACP dies.

Among Black Hills offerings is the Schofield cartridge, using a 230-grain bullet closely duplicating the ballistic performance of the originals. And, in response to the specific requests of many competitors, another load featuring a 180-grain bullet meant to provide velocities sufficient for meeting standard Single Action Shooting Society (SASS) criteria, but with much reduced recoil, has also been added to their catalog.

This is significant because, in the process of preparing this chapter, I had an opportunity to compare my own blued, 7-inch barreled Uberti's performance with a genuine original, which of course, is not capable of shooting the full-length .45 Colt cartridge for which the replicas are made.

The original Schofield functioned well, but its accuracy was poor. By military standards it may have been acceptable, but this specimen would not be a good choice for today's sports competitions.

The number "36" stamped on top of the backstrap of this revolver indicates that it is probably one of those sent to the San Francisco police for use in dealing with the Sandlot Riots. Most of those revolvers were later sent to the California Militia.

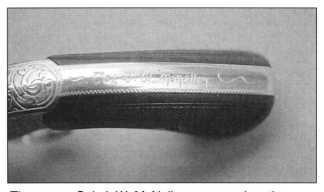

The name, Col. J. W. McNelley, engraved on the backstrap of the S&W Schofield, is believed to be that of an officer who served in the California Militia, during the last quarter of the 19th century.

The original Schofield, belonging to my old friend, Peter Stebbins, is a nickel-plated and engraved 2nd Model. The engraving is in the New York style, typical of that provided by 19th century firearms distributors, Schuyler, Hartley & Graham. However, the engraving appears to have been rendered to the revolver long after it was made. Its character makes it appear likely that it was done some time in the first half of the 20th century.

Examination under a magnifying glass reveals that, while its bore and the chambers of its cylinder remain in excellent condition, the original finish was probably poor. There is distinct evidence of rust pitting, which the engraving and nickel plating have disguised. It's been speculated that a descendant of one of the revolver's owners had it embellished, either to improve its appearance or as a tribute to the ancestor, maybe both.

Of particular interest is that the top of the backstrap bears the number 36, indicating that it was one of those that were said to have been consigned to the San Francisco Police Department for their use during a series of incidents known as the Sandlot Riots. Later, those revolvers were turned over to the California Militia. The name, Col. J.W. McNelley, engraved on the revolver's backstrap, is thought to be that of an officer of the state militia of that period. But that hasn't been verified.

A third revolver was included in our tests for good measure. Another Uberti, it was provided by Tom Eiben, another friend of long standing. It's one of the nickel-plated, 5-inch barrel, "Wells Fargo" variety. However, this specimen has no Wells Fargo markings as do some of the replicas of that configuration. The use of all three handguns to evaluate handling and functional characteristics and the performance of the

ammunition used for the tests would give us exceptional insight into the practical worth of the Schofield in general, and the modern replicas, in particular.

Tests of the three revolvers were conducted during a visit to Peter Stebbins' home in Vermont, where he has range facilities out to 100 yards. Targets were placed at a distance of 15 yards from the firing line and the shooting was done with a two-handed modified Weaver stance. The time and place did not permit the usual bench rest and sandbags evaluation we would have preferred. The original revolver tended to string its shots vertically, and was not especially accurate, providing groups of 4.5 and 5 inches with the 230-grain and 180-grain loads, respectively. For practical purposes, each bullet weight shot about as well as the other.

The Ubertis did very nicely with both the .45 Colt and the 230-grain Schofield loads, with

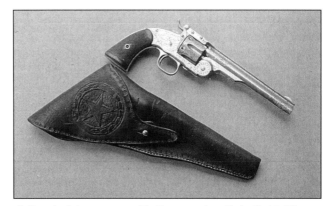

A flap holster came with the genuine Schofield. There is no maker's name on it, nor is it military issue, but it is meant to be worn in the same reverse-draw fashion as the original military type. It certainly adds character to the revolver.

The Wells Fargo-style Uberti Schofield proved to be an excellent performer on target. Black Hills 230-grain loading, which compares well ballistically with the original black powder load, shot particularly well in this revolver.

most groups measuring 1.5 to 2 inches. The 180-grain loads were also good, shooting slightly larger 2- to 2.5-inch groups during these tests. They demonstrated the performance potential for practical use of these revolvers nicely, but they told nothing of the potential for the pure accuracy of which they might be capable. For that evaluation more comprehensive tests were done after returning home.

Using the blued Uberti replica over sandbags from 25 yards, 10 different loads from five makers were tested. The Norfolk County Rifle Range's indoor facility, with its fluorescent lighting allowed for shooting comfort, without contending with environmental variations caused by wind, changing light conditions and temperature.

The ammo used included the three Black Hills variants listed above, plus their conventional .45 Colt load using the 255-grain LSWC bullet. In addition, we tested Hornady's Frontier brand Cowboy Action load with 255-grain LFP bullet; Remington's conventional 225-grain LSWC and 250-grain LRN; 3D's Cowboy Action 255-grain LRN and Winchester's conventional 255-grain LRN load and their Cowboy Action 250-grain lead flat point load. Results are shown in the accompanying table.

Throughout the tests of the Schofields, original and replica, recoil was very modest and easily controlled. Even the heavier .45 Colt loads were pleasant to shoot. The handling qualities of the replicas are essentially identical to the original and the speed with which they may be unloaded and reloaded may actually provide a bit of an advantage in some competitive events.

I wouldn't trade my SAA Colts and their clones in favor of exclusive use of the replica Schofield, but the Uberti Schofield is being used a lot. The S&W clone provides surprisingly good accuracy and is just as much fun to shoot as the more frequently seen SAA types. If you're tired of the same old thing, and looking for something different to use in competition, a Schofield replica might be just the thing to fill your holster.

TABLE OF UBERTI SCHOFIELD ACCURACY

Five groups of five rounds each were fired from the bench at 25 yards. The revolver was secured within the folds of an Uncle Bud's Bulls Bag rest.

Brand	WT/Type	Smallest group	Largest group	Average
Black Hills	180 Schof.	2.6 in.	4 in.	3.5 in.
Black Hills	230 Schof.	1.88 in.	3.75 in.	2.74 in.
Black Hills	250 LRNFP	1.5 in.	2.75 in.	2.13 in.
Black Hills	255 LSWC	2.4 in.	3.8 in.	3.1 in.
Hornady	255 LFP	2.8 in.	4.5 in.	3.65 in.
Remington	225 LSWC	3.2 in.	4.5 in.	3.85 in.
Remington	250 LRN	3.0 in.	5 in.	4.0 in.
3D	255 LFP	3.4 in.	5.2 in.	4.3 in.
Winchester	255 LRN	2.7 in.	4.75 in.	3.73 in.
Winchester	250 LFP	1.9 in.	3.2 in.	2.55 in.

CHAPTER 9

SLAPPING LEATHER - HOLLYWOOD STYLE

About 40 years ago the television phenomenon known as the "Adult Western" spawned a nearly decade-long fascination among a large segment of the public with a facet of the shooting sports known as "Fast Draw."

Some of the more serious bull's-eye shooters considered the whole thing pretty silly, given the distinctly Hollywood flavor of the thing, but for those of us who were there, it was a lot of fun and something of an adventure.

Professional shootists of the Old West were probably meticulous in the care of their firearms. These guns were the tools of their craft and essential, not just to their livelihoods, but to their very lives. Modifications to internal and external parts, however, were very rarely performed. The extended fanning hammers and slip hammers meant to be rolled off the thumb while the trigger was held or tied back are products of 20th century innovators, not 19th century gunfighters.

In those "good old days" of the 1950s and '60s, the emphasis was on achieving maximum speed while looking as much like one's favorite TV cowboy hero as possible. Those oft-emulated television personalities frequently got into the act themselves, by participating in some of

Ready to fire, but how long did it take for him to get there? Check out the photo sequence at the end of the chapter.

the "Walk and Draw" competitions and by making claims regarding the level of their skills that prompted minor feuds that were, I suspect, largely contrived for the benefit of the publicity it generated.

In the very earliest stages of the sport's development many of those intrepid participants used live ammunition. The number whose trigger fingers got ahead of their hands and shot themselves in the foot or leg (or worse) was significant. It wasn't long before live ammunition wasn't just discouraged, it was absolutely prohibited. In some circumstances wax bullet loads were employed to demonstrate accuracy at extreme close range, but the potential for accidental discharge, with its attendant danger of injury or death, made the use of conventional ammunition too great a risk to be tolerated. To be certain that none was inadvertently loaded into a sixgun contestants went so far as to fill the cartridge loops on their gunbelts with dummy rounds. Sometimes those dummies were actually glued into place to be certain a live round couldn't be introduced into the competitions.

Today's Cowboy Action shooting places greater emphasis upon authenticity of arms, accouterments and costume. But the greatest concern remains that of safety. While these contests involve timed events that require the use of live ammunition, the fast draw is prohibited. Some scenarios may require that the firearm to be employed in a given event be in the hand. When drawn from the leather, the revolver is removed quickly, but deliberately, not with high speed and the hammer must not be cocked until it is at least 45 degrees out from the body and pointed downrange. That is not to say that the fast draw is no longer practiced at all, it certainly is. But blanks are always used, as in those events of decades ago, and it is now a minor aspect of most Cowboy Action competitions, with the Fast Draw competitions pretty much a separate, though active, entity. Still, it remains a fun and interesting part of the game and shouldn't be ignored.

The low slung, forward raked speed holster of the late cinematic Western is a modern contrivance that was unknown in the 19th century. Then, as now, people who carried handguns for serious use usually wore them high and tight, on the hip. This was in consideration of both security and convenience. A firearm is and was an expensive investment; particularly for the worker who must rely on it as a tool of his livelihood. The typical "top hand" cowboy of the 1880s earned about "$30 a month and found." The cost of a Colt Single Action Army, a comparable Remington revolver or a variation of the Model #3 S&W represented about half a month's wages. If it were one of the short-barreled types it was normally worn behind the strong side hip, convenient to reach, but enough out of the way to permit freedom of movement to the arms and hands. While the holster he used in most of his later movies was

That's fast, but is it fast enough?

actually of fairly recent design, the method described above was very well illustrated by "The Duke," himself, in the John Wayne westerns of the 1960s and '70s.

If the user chose one of the longer barreled revolvers for regular use it was frequently carried in cross-draw fashion, often at a severe angle. This permitted quicker access, with less strain than would be required to get a long barreled handgun into action from behind the hip, especially from horseback.

The speed rigs of such makers as Arvo Ojala and Andy Anderson that were so common a few decades ago would not have been so popular in a time and place where one's occupation required the daily commute to work be done on horseback. Wearing a speed rig in such work, especially if it is done with a tie-down thong, is inconvenient, uncomfortable and insecure. Just try riding a horse at full gallop while wearing such an outfit. You're unlikely to do it twice, as the tie will chafe your thigh raw and the revolver's butt will slap your leg black and blue. If you have any doubts, just look at the way such rigs bounce around in reruns of some of the more popular TV Westerns of the '50s and '60s.

Anyone who works with livestock can attest that there are circumstances when a horse or cow must be put down, so firearms are as important a tool of such a trade today as they were in the last century. I once had the unhappy occasion to have a horse I was riding gored in the abdomen by a recalcitrant steer. I had to walk nearly 5 miles back to the ranch house to get a fresh mount and fetch a gun with which to dispatch the suffering animal. It was the last time I undertook such a job without having a suitable firearm with me at the start.

The holsters of the Old West were often made of thin, soft, leather which tended to grip the revolver, inhibiting the attempt to make a fast draw. A few gunfighters were said to overcome this inconvenience by lubricating the inside of the holster with bear grease. This might have helped getting the gun out in a hurry, but it would attract dust, dirt and grime. It was also more likely that the gun might fall from the holster unnoticed when one's attention was turned to other things. Others are said to have used corset stays, made of whale bone, to allow their revolvers to be removed freely.

Then, as now, professionals knew well that the action rarely starts from the leather. It was widely believed that the best bet was to have the gun in hand when the action commenced. That's not a bad philosophy, but it isn't altogether true, either. Reaction time being what it is, believe it or not, it is possible for an expert to draw and fire a single-action revolver from the holster so quickly that the shot is fired faster than an opponent, with revolver drawn, cocked and ready, can pull the trigger.

To the uninitiated this may sound incredible, but a fast draw artist who has learned his craft well can start the action, clear leather and drop the hammer in less than 20/100ths of a second. Some few, in much less time. On the other hand, average reaction time is about 25/100ths of a second. Ergo, the individual with the holstered gun wins. To be sure, in a real-life confrontation the victory will be Pyrrhic, but I've demonstrated this in survival training classes for peace officers many times in order to illustrate the potential to turn the tables on an opponent in a situation that may appear hopeless. After all, if you're going to get it anyway, you might as well go down fighting. With a bit of luck, you may prevail in the end.

Speed with a handgun is best accomplished in stages. The first step is to select the belt and holster. If one is working for maximum speed and period authenticity is of no concern, the Hollywood-style rigs are the ones to use. For a period-style holster, carried high, the rig should have about a 10 degree butt forward cant. Carried low, the speed rig should have a 15 degree muzzle forward cant. As compared to a butt forward cant or a vertical draw, having the muzzle forward at that angle when using a low slung holster can increase speed by as much as 20%.

The best position for the revolver's handle to be in relation to the gun hand is subjective, but most find that with the arms and hands relaxed at the sides, the position they like best is for the butt to be 2 to 3 inches above the wrist. The novice will often reason that he'll do best if the revolver's grip is right next to the hand, but this doesn't prove out in practice. In that position the hand tends to grasp first, then the arm moves up to pull the gun from its sheath. This is wasted motion and economy of motion is critical to development of speed. Worn slightly higher, the hand and arm work in concert to grasp and draw at the same time.

The fingers of the hand should be held in a normal position, which means their natural curve. Held straight out or with claw-like tension, the grasp is often missed.

Most of the practitioners of this craft cock the revolver as it is lifted from the holster. As the muzzle clears leather the gun is thrust forward and the trigger slapped to fire the shot. This method works, but can appear relatively slow to the observer. When your purpose is to fool the eye, rather than to beat the clock, the trick is to let the revolver do the work for you. Instead of making the arm lift it to the horizontal, let the thumb do it.

The draw is started with feet apart, left leg slightly forward and hands relaxed. The revolver is a well tuned SAA Colt .45, with 5-1/2-inch barrel.

The thumb...??!? - I thought that might get your attention.

Before we get into that, a few words regarding proper stance are in order. The feet should be about shoulder-width apart, with the weak side leg slightly forward. It is important that the knees be slightly flexed.

The draw is started in the conventional manner, but the thumb is placed over the hammer. The cocking action is not begun until the muzzle clears the forward lip of the holster. At that point the natural tendency is for the muzzle to swing slightly behind. At that moment the ham-

draw seems faster to the onlooker if the hand's approach to it starts slowly, then finishes with all possible speed.

Don't expect to become an expert overnight. The key to development of the fast draw is the same as with any other shooting discipline; start slow in order to develop muscle memory and, as the techniques become natural movement, build speed.

An excellent test of one's skill is the trick known as, "Drop-the-Dollar." It was originally done with a silver dollar, but those are getting scarce and too valuable to allow to be dinged by

The handle is grasped while the thumb moves to cover the hammer...

The muzzle is just clearing leather...

mer is brought sharply down by the thumb while the index finger enters the trigger guard, rotates upward and the two digits acting in concert swing the revolver level. At the moment it reaches that position the trigger is slapped and the blank charge is fired. By this method the hammer acts as a lever, while the index finger serves as a fulcrum, bringing the gun level with minimal muscular effort, rather than the gross effort required to raise the entire forearm. If the gun handler wants to appear even quicker, the

dropping. Any similar size coin or a poker chip will do. Place it on the back of the hand and extend the arm full length at shoulder height. When ready, simply go for the gun, draw and fire. If you do it fast enough that the blank charge explodes before the object hits the ground, you can count yourself a pretty good gunslinger.

When you get really good at it, try starting with the upper arm straight down and the forearm and hand at a 45-degree angle. If you can do it from that position, you're really fast on the draw.

As the arm starts to move forward, the muzzle tilts slightly backward...

Speed starts to increase as the hammer begins to act as a lever against the trigger finger's fulcrum...

the index finger enters the trigger guard, pushing up against the frame, while the hammer begins to come back, starting the revolver's forward motion.

the hammer comes to full-cock as the muzzle begins to rise...

With the muzzle nearly level, the thumb slides off the hammer...

An instant later the revolver is pointed at the target and the hammer has dropped...

There's a variation of the "Drop-the-Dollar" that, if you can master it, can give an audience the impression that you're truly a sixgun wizard. Actually, that assessment isn't far off the mark, but only because it takes precision movement, not the accuracy it seems to illustrate. The object is to draw so quickly that the barrel of the revolver strikes the object as it falls and fire the blank at the same instant. The coin will spin off in some unpredictable direction, leaving the audience with the impression that it has been shot out of the air. When you can do that one, take a bow. You will have earned it.

While the practice of fast draw in this context is strictly an exercise in showmanship, and is not to be considered with live ammunition, the real life use of speed with handguns as tools of law enforcement and personal protection in the Old West and beyond may best be exemplified by an answer Wyatt Earp is said to have given to a question from his biographer, Stuart Lake, in researching his work, *Wyatt Earp, Frontier Marshall*. Lake asked, "How is it that in a career that spanned more than 40 years and 80 gunfights (the number actually documented is a small fraction of that figure), how is it that you managed to win them all and come away unscathed? What is the secret to your skill with a sixshooter?" Whatever the reality of his life as compared to the legend, or the truth behind Lake's telling of the story, Earp's supposed reply is a worthy motto for those who form the "thin blue line" against the criminal element of any era, and not a bad practice for the fast draw hobbyist to consider, as well: "Take your time - FAST!"

The belt and holster are by Backwoods Custom Leather, 3022 Tyre Neck Rd., Portsmouth, VA 23703. These photos in this chapter were taken using a motor drive with the lens set at f5.6 and a shutter speed of 1/125th of a second.

CHAPTER 10

FINE TUNING COLT-STYLE SINGLE ACTION REVOLVERS

Within 10 years of its introduction in 1873 the Colt Single Action Army revolver was no longer state-of-the-art, but it not only continued in military service for another decade and more, it remained in production for civilian consumers until the dawn of World War II. Moreover, public demand for it continued to be so great that by 1955 Colt had been pressured into returning it to market again.

The Colt SAA is a particularly expensive handgun, partly because it requires a lot of handwork in construction and assembly. This has made the original Hartford-built product extraordinarily expensive for the consumer. The high cost of labor is a part of the equation but, so is the brand name. The hands-on work required also leads to erratic performance on target, because it can vary in quality and detail from one to another, depending upon the skill of the machinist and assembler. Some revolvers do very nicely, but others seem incapable of firing a decent group.

Colt likes to regard even the standard production SAA as a collectible of sorts, discouraging its use as a shooting tool. This also seems to affect the price. The gun is more than 10 times more expensive than the $125 it commanded when it was reintroduced in 1955; far above what normal inflationary change would indicate it ought to be. Compare the price changes of Ruger's Blackhawk and S&W's Military & Police revolver since that time and you will see what I mean.

This has encouraged the replica makers to produce copies of it; something that has actually been going on for more than 30 years. But, in the past decade, sales of the mostly Italian-

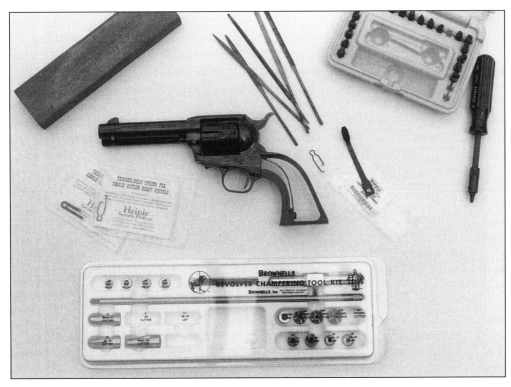

Most improvements and repairs are a simple matter for the knowledgeable owner of a Colt-style single-action revolver. It's always a good idea to keep a few spare parts on hand. A good screw driver set, polishing stones and set of quality files are basic. The more advanced hobbyist may find the revolver chamfering kit very helpful, but its use is usually best left to a professional gunsmith.

made handguns have increased exponentially, largely in order to keep up with the demand generated by Cowboy Action shooting. Their overhead costs are not quite as high, nor is there a surcharge for the brand. The quality of the products varies somewhat, but is generally quite good and often superb. Yet, the accuracy of single action revolvers, both American and European, is erratic.

What level of accuracy can this 19th century revolver design deliver? In a word; Excellent! Properly tuned, using compatible ammunition, most can be made to hold 25-yard groups of 2 inches or less. Some specimens can deliver accuracy comparable to the finest target revolvers, literally placing one shot after another through the same ragged hole at distances of 25 yards and more. Some years ago, while still on active duty and shooting for a Navy team, I demonstrated my faith in the SAA's accuracy potential by shooting a practice National Match course with my 5-1/2-inch nickel SAA .45 with its .45 ACP auxiliary cylinder in place. When the smoke cleared, my score was a respectable 270 out of 300 points possible. Not a bad showing, at all.

How we go about achieving such accuracy is not just a matter of making the action lighter and smoother, it frequently involves critical adjustments to a number of the revolver's component parts and often requires tailoring ammunition to the individual handgun. Let's examine the matter step by step.

Because barrel dimensions vary considerably among SAA revolvers of the same caliber, projectile compatibility is an especially critical factor in development of premium accuracy. The Single Action Shooting Society (SASS), governing body for sanctioned Cowboy Action Shooting world-wide, mandates the use of lead projectile ammunition only and it must not exceed 1,000 fps from a handgun. Much of the shooting in the sport requires rapid repeat shots so, in practice, most competitors strive to use either handloads or factory loads that provide modest recoil and little muzzle flash. Most of the ammunition used is more likely to deliver velocities in the range of 700 to 750 fps than to try to push the 1,000 fps level. On the opposite end of the scale, the minimum velocity permitted is 650 fps.

While single-action revolvers are often used for hunting, it's rare these days for them to be employed for personal protection or law enforcement. Their primary use is as a tool of competition, a circumstance in which power is

of little consequence. This is actually an important advantage to the shooter, because it allows greater leeway in tailoring the cartridge to the gun. The need for this latitude will become more clear as we progress.

The cylinder bolt and bolt spring are the two parts most subject to breakage from metal fatigue. Assuming the locking notches in the cylinder are in good condition, the pressure applied on it by the spring pushing the bolt into place can tighten it substantially, providing greater stability and better, more consistent accuracy. All that's needed is to tweak the leg that contacts the bolt slightly, so that it places more pressure on the bolt, seating it more firmly into its recess in the cylinder. However, this can reduce the already relatively short life of the spring.

The pointed angle of the cylinder bolt is pushed against the bolt spring during the cocking maneuver. It is usually at that contact point or at its rearmost that the spring breaks. By dressing the point of the cylinder bolt with a file, rounding it just slightly (not flattening it), the life of the spring can be greatly extended. You can eliminate this problem entirely by replacing the flat leaf bolt spring with a music wire spring made by Heine Specialty Products, available from Brownells, Inc. Very much worthy of note is that by the simple expedient of replacing the original with a wire Heine spring, the revolver's trigger pull may be reduced by as much as 2 pounds.

Most new SAA revolvers come from the factories well timed, with their cylinders indexing properly. Adjustment, should it be required, starts with determining where the fault lies. It will usually be either the hand (pawl), which reaches out and rises to turn the cylinder as the hammer is cocked, or the cylinder bolt, one leg of which cams over a stud on the lower right side of the hammer, near the notches cut into

With the Heine bolt spring in place the SAA revolver's reliability is greatly improved and a remarkable improvement of the weight of pull of the trigger is often achieved.

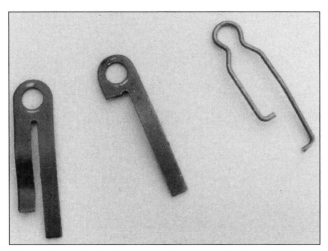

The bolt spring is the most frequently broken SAA part. A Heine bolt spring (R) may be used to replace the flat original (L). Made of music wire, it should last for the life of the revolver.

its face. Filing and polishing either the bolt or the hand, whichever is the culprit part, is a simple enough procedure for any competent gunsmith or knowledgeable hobbyist.

The slot at the rear of the frame, through which the hand protrudes, may be too narrow or rough. This can add drag to the lockwork. Polishing the slot can make a surprising difference to the smoothness of the cocking action. Brownells offers a set of stones especially designed for this operation.

Rarely, the ratchet teeth at the rear of the cylinder, sometimes called the star, are found to be damaged. This may require as simple a measure as light de-burring with a stone or file or, in the case of severe damage, completely welding and recutting them. Unless the revolver is a rare variation or chambered for a scarce cartridge, it is usually more cost effective to simply discard it and install a replacement if the cylinder is that bad.

Generally, 1st and 2nd generation cylinders interchange with little or no problem. Some

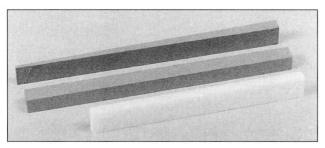

Stoning the hand slot can make a remarkable difference in the smoothness of the revolver's action. A set of stones specially designed for that purpose is available from Brownells.

adjustment of the cylinder bushing may be needed, but the two variants are alike. Third generation cylinders have ratchet teeth that are quite different in shape and will work only if the hand is also changed.

The gap between the face of the cylinder and barrel is best held at .002 to .003 inches. Reasonable accuracy may still be achieved if the gap is as much as .008 inches, but it's unlikely that one with tolerances that poor will shoot really tight groups.

Assuming that its mechanical operation is correct and the gap is within reasonable tolerances, the key ingredient in accuracy refinement is the diameter of the mouth of the chamber. Too tight and the bullet may be swaged down so much that it cannot properly engage the bore of the barrel. Too loose and the bullet may enter at an angle and become sufficiently distorted to ruin its concentricity, making its flight erratic. Ideally, bullets should barely hang up on their bearing bands at the mouth, if dropped into the rear of the cylinder, but be easy to push through using a pencil or other sort of push rod. Usually, a chamber mouth .001 inches larger than the bullet diameter is perfect. If the chamber mouths are too tight, a reamer can be used to open them to an appropriate diameter. If it drops out freely it may be possible to improve matters by using cast bullets of larger than standard diameter.

This is where the relatively low velocities and attendant reduced pressures of the loads used in Cowboy Action matches makes things more flexible. For example, we've encountered some revolvers chambered for the .45 Colt with bores as tight as .451 inches that have cylinder mouths as wide open as .456 inches. It's possible to use soft cast bullets of that diameter with mild, "starting load," charges of powder that will greatly improve accuracy while keeping pressures low and safe.

By the same token, the Italian-made .44-40 clones are usually made with bores that measure .429 to .430 inches. This is in keeping with the standard for modern .44 Special and .44 Magnum ammo. But the .44-40 cartridge was originally made to be used with cast bullets of .427 diameter. Worthy of note is that pre-war rifles from the major makers were made with bores of .425 inches and jacketed bullets loaded in factory ammo were sized to match. By handloading, using an expander ball of proper size from a .44 Special or Magnum die in the .44-40 die in order

The tension of a factory hammer spring can easily be reduced by placing a spacer between it and the frontstrap. Spacers made of Neoprene are now available, but a simple piece of leather cut from an old belt will do.

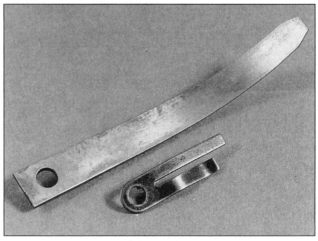

The Wisner reduced power spring kit is designed to lessen the force required to cock the Colt-style revolver. Properly used, these parts should not affect the revolver's reliability.

to open the neck of the case to proper dimensions, and using the larger diameter bullet, one can often get such a revolver with modern bore dimensions to shoot excellent groups.

While grinding, then polishing the mainspring in order to lighten the force required to cock the hammer works well and is an effective method, it is easily overdone. A simpler, yet very effective technique, used successfully since the SAA was first designed, is to punch a hole in a piece of leather about 1/8th inch thick, pass the mainspring screw through that part, then the leather and secure it to the gripframe. A piece from an old belt used in this manner usually works very nicely to reduce the weight of cocking force needed, without compromising the reliability of ignition. However, stiff leather should be used. If it's too soft, cocking the hammer will feel mushy. Again, Brownells can eliminate the need to alter factory parts. They have reduced weight hammer springs and spring spacers in stock.

Barrel dimensions can vary considerably among SAA revolvers of all vintages and types. This is especially true of first generation Colts and the Italian replicas. Ideally, the lead bullet used should be .001 to .002 inches greater in diameter than the bore in order to properly engage the rifling and fly true. But that's not always possible to do. For example, many 1st generation .38-40 revolvers are found with bores as wide as .410. Since the proper bullet size for this caliber is .401 to .403 inches, it's impossible to make such a revolver shoot well without sleeving it or installing a different barrel of correct diameter. Such a handgun should be traded off to a col-

lector who won't be interested in shooting it.

One of the problems often encountered with SAA revolver barrels is a forcing cone that is either improperly cut or cut at an incorrect angle. In some cases the forcing cone may actually be non-existent. In most instances this can be easily corrected by recutting it with a forcing cone reamer, also readily available from Brownells. An angle of 11 degrees is just about perfect for the revolver to deliver premium accuracy.

Before attempting to adjust the fixed sights of an SAA revolver one should first determine the load that will be used in it for competitive or practical shooting. Whether it's a factory load or a handload, the ammo that shoots the tightest groups should be used to the exclusion of all others in any given revolver. Once that's been established, we can break out the files.

Generally, SAAs shoot low more often than high. Raising elevation is simply a matter of trimming the front sight an appropriate amount with a file, then freshening the resulting bare metal with a quality cold blue. If it shoots too high, using a lighter weight bullet is the easiest way to drop groups into the black. If that fails, installing a new front sight and trimming it to an appropriate height is often the easier alternative to welding additional metal onto the existing one.

This should, of course, never be done to an original pre-war Colt.

Windage errors may be corrected by bending the front sight with padded pliers. Remember to move it in the direction opposite that in which you want the shot to strike the target. Alternatively, one can make the rear sight channel wider, but this will make the finish look unsightly and, on a revolver with a case hardened frame, cutting will be difficult. This should only be done if you're planning to refinish the revolver. Probably the best method of all is to turn the barrel within the frame, in or out, as required. However, this may be a problem with 3rd generation Colt revolvers, because the barrel threads are sometimes crush fitted and the frame may be twisted in the process.

As with other handguns, one of the most critical aspects of accurizing the SAA is adjustment of the trigger release so it is short and crisp. Typically, weight of pull from the factory is about 6 or 7 pounds and offers a lot of creep. For best results the weight of pull should be adjusted to between 3 and 4 pounds. Sometimes an even lighter pull can be achieved, but the engagement of the trigger's sear to the hammer's notch must always be such that they engage without slipping. Too aggressive a job of stoning can easily cause the sear to slip when the revolver is brought to full cock. This could result in an unintentional discharge. If, when you have adjusted the weight of pull and the character of the trigger to the level you seek, you can push against the fully cocked hammer without making it fall, the trigger can be regarded as safe. The best means to accomplish this with consistent results is to use a jig designed for the purpose.

An often overlooked aspect of smoothing the action of an SAA revolver is the roughness of the internal portions of the frame. By stoning these areas, the parts that bear against the frame, such as the hand and the hammer, will move more freely. Most of the Colts we've encountered have had no need of this treatment, but some of the Italian copies do.

For more information about tuning single action revolvers Mike Venturino's book, *Shooting Colt Single Actions/ In All Styles, Calibers and Generations*, is highly recommended.

Most of the adjustments required to improve the performance of SAA revolvers on target can easily be accomplished with a quality set of screwdrivers, appropriate files, stones and a pair of padded-locking pliers. In some instances a drill press or lathe may be necessary. Still, a lot can be accomplished by careful load development. Whatever the needs of your individual handgun, many single-action revolvers can be made to shoot close to the level of a high-grade target pistol. The design may be old, but it can still be bold.

CHAPTER 11

DOES YOUR SAA COLT HAVE A HISTORY?

Most of the First Generation SAA Colts you can expect to encounter were originally purchased by perfectly ordinary people of no great historical note. Still, a documented history of its ownership can increase its value, even if it belonged to a shopkeeper. If the piece belonged to a lawman, a cowboy or was purchased by a railroad, a bank, a shipping company, a ranch or a government agency, such information can add greatly to collector interest. If it was owned by a person of some fame or notoriety it might prove very valuable.

There is, for example, the well-known story of the 4-5/8-inch barreled .45 caliber revolver ordered by Bat Masterson, on Longbranch Saloon stationery (one of several he was known to have purchased directly), that a lucky collector had verified by the Colt historian some years ago. Directly associated with a famous gunfighter of the Old West, its well worn finish permitted only modest value as an antique, but that was raised significantly by its verified link to such a famous person. Other such treasures are out there, waiting to be

found. All it takes is a check, a letter to the office of Colt's historian, and a little luck.

Most of us are curious to know when our six-guns were made and where they went. That information will, at least, give us some idea of what role they might have played in history. A letter from the Colt historian will also give as

Ron Wagner was employed by Colt for 54 years, from 1918-1972. He served as Colt's historian from the 1950s until his retirement.

Marty Huber, right, succeeded Wagner as historian, holding that post until his retirement in 1993. By then, he had devoted 56 years of service to Colt. He often consulted with Colt's Custom Shop Supervisor, Al DeJohn, left.

much information as the records can provide as to the original caliber, barrel length and any special features the gun may originally have possessed. This will go far in determining whether an item in question remains as original or has been altered in some fashion. This, in turn, can make all the difference in its value.

The letter will also tell the owner when it was shipped and to whom. Not all the records are as complete as one might hope, but if they are available for the revolver in question, they may describe the gun's finish, possibly the type of grips provided and any other special features, such as engraving, or other modifications that might have been custom ordered.

Sometimes this will mean disappointment, because the revolver will prove to have been altered since leaving the factory, which usually lowers its value. At other times it may confirm its originality and, once in a great while, such a letter will verify its having been shipped to some well-known person. This turns an otherwise ordinary antique handgun into an historical artifact.

By its serial number one may quickly determine the year in which a Colt SAA revolver was made. That, however, says nothing of when it might have been shipped. There are numerous instances in Colt's records wherein such a revolver was held in inventory for years before leaving the factory. An example listed in the chapter on Sheriff's Models shows one revolver was sold 27 years after it was made.

Just after World War II, John E. Parsons, one of the pioneer researchers of Colt's history, published his seminal work, *The Peacemaker and its Rivals*. In it, he provided a detailed list of Colt SAA production figures by serial number and year of manufacture. In addition, he listed the volume of manufacture of SAA's and Bisley models by caliber. The latter figures provide the collector with the information needed to determine the relative rarity of any given chambering.

However, these figures are not entirely reliable, because they are based upon shipping records, not production lists. Some of the records are incomplete and some of the listings are erroneous. This should come as no surprise in a circumstance wherein human frailties might come into play.

All the records were kept by clerks writing longhand in their ledgers and some were more meticulous about their entries than others. It appears, for example, that when Parsons encountered an entry that simply listed the caliber as .44, he seems to have assumed that the round meant was .44-40. There has long been speculation that in some instances it might just as well have actually been .44 Russian or .44 Special. A tired clerk, or one too lazy or disinterested to do his work properly might very well have failed to differentiate.

It could also be that he really didn't know the difference. It is easy for us to take for granted that someone who works for a gun company should know something about the product, but these were not gunsmiths or assemblers; they were office workers. Their knowledge of and interest in guns might vary considerably. When one considers that Parsons lists five varieties of .32 caliber SAAs and seven each of .38, .44 and .45, there is little wonder that non-shooters might not understand the differences. So the accuracy of the records might sometimes suffer.

All of this would account for there seeming to be altogether too many pre-war .44 Specials out there. Only 506 of the standard configuration and one of the target variety are supposed to have been made. Yet, though scarce and highly desirable, the standard versions don't seem to be as rare as these figures would indicate. To be sure, many were certainly converted to that chambering, but the numbers of them that are encountered still don't quite seem right.

In the 1980s, R.L. Wilson compiled a listing of 1st, 2nd and 3rd Generation Colt SAAs by serial

Kathy Hoyt took the historian's chair when Marty Huber retired. At the time she assumed the title she had more than 25 years with Colt and much of that time had been spent in the Custom Shop. Her computer and organizational skills, coupled with a thorough knowledge of the product line made her an ideal choice for the post.

number and date of manufacture. These are to be found in his books, *Colt Heritage*, and *Colt-An American Legend*. In the same period, Don Wilkerson researched the production figures of the 2nd and 3rd Generation pieces by caliber. His efforts are entitled, *The Post-War Single Action Revolver 1955-1975*, and *The Post-War Single Action Revolver*. The titles are similar, but each of Wilkerson's books is different. It must be noted that 3rd Generation production has continued, so none of the listings in that category can be complete in any source.

With the exception of a few presentation pieces and some that may be associated with well known personalities, not many 2nd and 3rd Generation SAAs are likely to be classified as "historical." Few, in the last half of the 20th century, have served their owners as arms of law enforcement or military service. But, who's to say that 50 years from now collectors might not have just as much interest in them as those of today have in the 1st Generation SAAs. Sixguns owned by well-known writers, like Skeeter Skelton, Mike Venturino, Phil Spangenberger and John Taffin, for example, might bring a premium. So might the guns of well known Cowboy Action Shooting competitors or some of our modern exhibition shooters, fast-draw champions and television or movie actors.

The price of a letter from the Colt historian, as this is written, is $100 (subject to change). Some may wonder if it is worth the cost. To be sure, it may not be for most post-war revolvers, but it can be considered cheap insurance if an expensive, allegedly rare piece one contemplates purchasing turns out to be a fake. By the same token, if the revolver has been altered, knowing how it was configured when it left the factory may allow the owner to restore it to its original specifications. There are lots of pleasant surprises still to be found out there, as well. If it confirms the revolver to be a genuine rarity, or to have been sent to some well-known historical figure, the letter that verifies the fact will make the sixgun worth many times what its price might otherwise be. Even if it turns out to be just one of many thousands of ordinary SAAs, a letter that verifies its originality is reassuring and the price for that knowledge alone is usually recouped on resale.

However, it must also be acknowledged that some of the letters alleged to have come from the Colt historian's office are forgeries. In any case, where the revolver is presented as a rarity it is worth the trouble and expense to get a new letter. In any such instance the buyer should also make the finality of the sale contingent upon the new letter's verification of authenticity. This can save some serious anxiety and, quite possibly, legal consequences down the road.

Marty Huber was often accused of having been with Colt so long that he knew Sam Colt personally. Australian collector, Neil Speed, left, dressed the part of the company founder when he attended the annual meeting and Gun Show of the Colt Collectors Association in 1992.

Colt collector Bill Dascher and his wife, Beryl, pose with Marty Huber, right, next to the Rampant Colt that stood atop the Colt factory dome for generations. The statue had been removed at that time while the dome was under renovation.

CHAPTER 12

COLT'S SHERIFF'S MODEL: THE SNUBNOSE AND EJECTORLESS SINGLE-ACTIONS

One afternoon in 1963, I gazed longingly into a gun dealer's showcase at one of the last of the Sheriff's Model revolvers that Centennial Arms had contracted Colt to manufacture a couple of years before. The 3-inch barreled .45 I was looking at was one of 25 nickel-plated guns among that order. The price tag threaded through the trigger guard was marked $125. It had been discounted from the original suggested retail price of $140. Nevertheless, the $88 a month that the Navy paid me in those days couldn't be stretched quite enough for me to afford it, so I left with my desires unfulfilled.

In the intervening years, those snub-nosed Peacemakers have managed to remain beyond the reach of my bank balance. In new condition, their value has outstripped the rate of inflation substantially. As this is written, *The Standard Catalog of Firearms*, by Ned Schwing, one of the best price guides on the market, declares that a new-in-the-box standard revolver, blued with case hardened colored frame is worth $2,500. Any of the 25 nickel-plated models, if authenticated,

would, according to Schwing bring, " ...a substantial premium."

Slow movers, at first, those 2nd Generation sixguns took about three years to sell out. Their 1st Generation predecessors are so rare that few collectors in those days recognized the historical background of the new revolvers. Some sales may have been stimulated by the appearance of a nickel-plated Sheriff's Model in the holster of the Bat Masterson character played by actor Gene Barry on the TV series based (very loosely) on the life of the Old West lawman.

It may be of interest to some that actor David Carradine of *Kung Fu* fame, used an identical nickeled Sheriff's Model in the title role of the short-lived TV series, *Shane*, which was broadcast during the first half of the 1966 season.

There were gun writers during that time who expressed the opinion that the large, heavy frame, combined with short sight radius and no attached ejector system made the guns impractical, an opinion apparently shared by many of our 19th century forebears, but one with which I don't happen to agree.

The growth of interest in shooting and collecting, along with greater interest in things nostalgic, make the short-barreled variations some of the most popular of the current crop of Colt Single Action Army revolvers. Their excellent investment potential hasn't hurt, either. The 3rd Generation Sheriff's Models available through the Colt Custom Shop in recent years are meant to be collectibles, but they make great shooters, too. There are more than a dozen variations,

Ejectorless Model 1877s, such as this, and similarly made Model 1878s are fairly common. Single Action Army revolvers originally made without ejectors are rare and valuable.

Third Generation Sheriff's Models like this .44 Special are desirable to collectors, but many more of them were made than the 2nd Generation .45s.

with 2-1/2-, 3-, 3-1/2-, 4- and 5-1/2-inch barrels in calibers .44 Special, .44-40 and .45 Colt and with finishes available in blue with case-hardened colors, full royal blue and nickel plating. Frames have been made in both standard and black powder styles.

The first SAA Sheriff's Model appears to have been made in 1881 and shipped the following year. At least 85 were produced before Colt's catalog began listing this option in 1888. Similar guns, short-barreled, without ejector rod housings, had long been available in Colt's double-action models of 1877 and 1878. Those are quite common.

The term, "Sheriff's Model," appears to be a mid-20th century term. Until recently the factory has referred to them by a variety of names, including: Pocket Pistol, House Pistol, Ejectorless and Storekeeper's Model, but they were never, as far as I've been able to determine, called Sheriff's Models until after World War II. Nevertheless, the name has stuck and it is a good one, conjuring up the image of hard-bitten lawmen bringing in the bad guys.

Defining the Sheriff's Model is a bit tricky. It is usually understood to be a Single Action Army revolver of shorter than standard barrel length, without an ejector rod assembly. To confuse matters, a few 1st Generation guns were made without an ejector assembly in standard and odd barrel lengths. To carry the matter further, a few have been made with shorter than standard barrels, but retain the ejector rod assembly. Some of these have ejector rods so short as to be useless, because they cannot reach far enough to tap the base of the cartridge to make it easy to remove from the chamber. What constitutes a Sheriff's Model may then include any ejectorless SAA or

one with a barrel length shorter than standard, even if it does have an ejector.

To make matters even more confusing, Colt began making ejectorless SAAs with 4-inch barrels in the 1980s and labeled them the Storekeeper's Model. Most of us called them Sheriff's Models, nevertheless.

Standard SAAs have often been the subject of outright fakery, although a few examples have been seen that were clearly altered at the factory. One such is an early post-war .38 Special, bearing serial number 4408SA, which was shipped from the factory on June 21, 1956, to a Hartford, Connecticut, dealer. Originally fitted with a 5-1/2-inch barrel, it allegedly found its way to a Pennsylvania deputy sheriff who had returned it to the factory, where it was shortened to 3-1/4 inches, retaining and shortening the ejector rod and its housing. Eventually, it ended up in the hands of a Vermont collector, Peter Stebbins, who carried it regularly for more than 20 years. Just long enough for the ejector to be functional, the revolver is fast, accurate and comfortable to carry - an ideal "kit gun" for the outdoor sportsman.

Altered guns are not necessarily fakes. Some are worked over in order to improve handling characteristics. The late Jerry Klufas was a master craftsman who created works of functional art in steel, using SAA revolvers of recent manufacture or early models that had their collector value compromised by the ravages of time, poor care or earlier alteration. He was an avid student of the history of the Old West and a skilled fast-draw enthusiast. Jerry cared for the old classics and would not make alterations to guns with historical or collector value. Actually, he extended the useful life of many pieces that would otherwise have ended up as junkers.

Jerry Klufas made just nine Sheriff's Models like this one before his untimely death. They feature a bird's-head gripframe, Bisley-style hammer and trigger and a front sight made from a 19th century dime, cut in half.

His favorite means of modification was to install a Bisley-type hammer and trigger, alter the gripframe to bird's-head configuration and work over the action for smoothness and precision. He then finished the piece by re-case hardening the frame, and finely polishing the other parts to take a deep, lustrous blue. The products of his craftsmanship were the stuff of which an Old West gunfighter's dreams might have been made. Unfortunately, Jerry died some years ago, but Colt made his trademark bird's-head grip styling an available option for a time and, with a bit of ingenuity, it is possible for a good gunsmith to modify such a piece to use the Bisley-style hammer and trigger. Such a revolver would be close, but the Klufas touch would be hard to duplicate.

Outright fakery of Sheriff's Models is a problem for collectors. When it is done, a 4-5/8-inch barreled gun is usually chosen, because the two-line address on its top surface allows for relocation of the front sight without damaging markings. Frames have the ejector rod fitting ground off and, if these steps are done well, it is next to impossible to detect the changes.

Another factor to consider is that there are two types of Sheriff's Model frames. The first is the type originally made in that format, with the frame contours matching on both sides. The second involves revolvers that were factory altered, starting with standard frames, then grinding off the fitting for the ejector rod housing. These are referred to as "scalloped" frames and were usually done over using ordinary SAA revolvers from stock when a customer order was received and no regular Sheriff's Model frames were on hand.

A factory letter is essential to verify the authenticity of a pre-war Sheriff's Model. It is

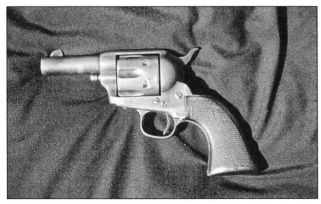

Bearing the serial number 154062, this is a fairly well executed fake. It replicates an original of the same number, barrel length and finish.

One of only 32 1st Generation Sheriff's Models verified to have been factory nickel plated, this specimen, with a 4-inch barrel, retains its original eagle grips of gutta percha (hard rubber). In remarkably good condition, it was made in 1884.

simply too easy to be fooled. Honorable dealers will guarantee their merchandise and allow returns if a piece is proved to be spurious. However, some flim-flam artists will go so far as to alter the serial numbers to match those of a genuine specimen. Such is the case with a gun bearing the serial number 154062. Close inspection shows that the front sight has been relocated. The shape of the frame where it was altered is slightly distorted, but the factory letter obtainable for that number lends authenticity to the fake one. Unfortunately, those aware of the fake may now suspect the genuine piece when it is offered for sale. Thus, it is important that sellers be completely honest and aboveboard when offering an altered piece and should be the first to point out its faults. Such a sale should be made on the basis of its value as a curio, rather than as an antique.

The real thing, as exemplified by #108382, can be lovely to behold. One of only 32 pre-war Sheriff's Models verified to have left the factory with nickel-plated finish, it remains in excellent condition after more than 100 years. Chambered for the .44-40 cartridge, it has a 4-inch barrel and still retains its original gutta percha (hard rubber) American Eagle grips.

The Sheriff's Model seems to have had limited appeal in the 19th century, but is a coveted prize for today's collectors. One dedicated student of colonial and frontier Americana, Mr. Peter Liddy, a magistrate from Adelaide, South Australia, had determined that he would one day own a consecutively numbered pair of black powder era Colt SAA revolvers, with the same barrel length, finish and grips. To that end,

The only firearm Howard Dove ever did with an acorn and oak leaf motif; this is a silver-plated, ivory-stocked 2nd Generation .45.

in the late 1970s, he began subscribing to the catalogs and lists of about 100 antique and arms dealers in the United States.

For more than a decade, Liddy examined, recorded and collated the offerings of these dealers and, in 1989, he hit paydirt. The pair, serial #108400 and #108401 had been shipped in April and May, respectively, of 1884. Both are .45 caliber, factory nickel-plated and have 4-inch barrels: # 108400 was factory furnished with one-piece ivory grips: # 108401 was originally shipped with gutta percha grips, but Liddy replaced them with a period set made of ivory, to match those of the companion revolver. Independently, both had been renickeled at some time in their history. A unique find that was the culmination of a long search, the pair were purchased and exported to Australia where, subsequently, they were the subject of a cover story in the July, 1989 edition of *Australian Shooter's Journal.*

There were some guns that stayed in factory inventory for many years before being sold. For example, the revolver bearing serial number 123309 was made in 1887 but, as noted earlier,

was not shipped from the factory until 27 years later, in 1914. It is one of those that was factory altered from its original 5-1/2-inch barrel length to be made into a 3-1/2-inch Sheriff's Model.

The table found in Appendix II lists the pre-war revolvers that have thus far been verified as to authenticity by factory records or expert opinion. Included are some that are known to have been reworked; appropriate notations accompany these. It is also known that some of the factory records are incomplete and it is certain that other legitimate guns exist, some of which unfortunately cannot be lettered. A close examination of the list demonstrates that there were several large groups of Sheriff's Models in the same general serial number range. In some instances there are several consecutive serial numbers with, here and there, a gap. Some of these gaps may be filled with heretofore unconfirmed Sheriff's Models.

No one knows precisely how many of the 1st Generation SAAs were made up as Sheriff's Models, but it is certain that they are very rare. Second and Third Generation production has been far greater. In spite of their increased numbers, these revolvers hold a promising future for collectors.

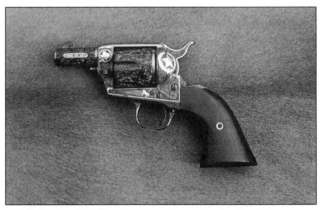

Howard Dove engraved this Sheriff's Model commemorating the state of Texas.

CHAPTER 13

COLT'S BISLEY MODEL

When Colt introduced its Single Action Army to the public in 1873, it caused a world-wide sensation in shooting circles. The revolver was rugged enough to stand the abuse of regular use in the most inhospitable places on earth, strong enough for the most powerful handgun cartridges of its day and so accurate as to attract the interest of the best marksmen in the business.

The old Peacemaker and similar revolvers, such as Ruger's Blackhawk and Vaquero series, the Freedom Arms revolvers and the excellent Colt copies from Uberti and Armi San Marco, remain among the world's most popular handguns.

Target shooters in the late 1800s knew full well that the old thumb buster had faults when it came to the kind of precision shooting they were doing. As intrinsically accurate as it was, and still is, fast repeat shots were difficult, if not impossible to accomplish with the accuracy of the first to be fired. Hollywood's depiction of fast draw and fanning techniques are nothing but celluloid fantasy.

The SAA's plow-handle grip absorbs recoil well, partly because of the revolver's tendency to slide in the hand under recoil. This makes it very comfortable to shoot, but requires the revolver to be shifted in the hand to regain the proper grip. As any serious target shooter will

Ruger's Bisley Model revolvers borrow heavily from the Colt design, but good as they are in their own right, they don't have the same feel as the originals.

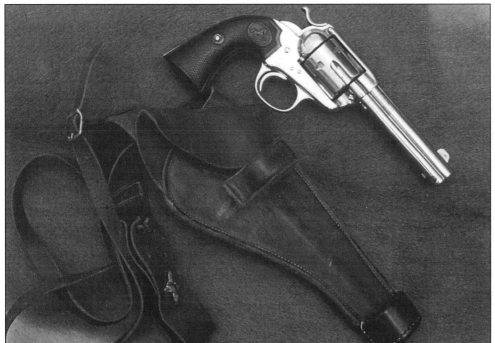

One of the most common of the Bisley barrel and caliber configurations, this .38-40 is a scarce variation because few of them were factory nickel plated. The holster is a scarce clip-spring type made by Heiser.

attest, a change in the position of the hand on a gun's gripframe will result in a shift of the point of impact of the next round to be fired. This phenomenon often causes rapid-fire scores to fall.

By the same token, trigger control is a fundamental aspect of good marksmanship. The target disciplines set minimum standards for weight of pull, as much for the sake of safety as for the limits of fairness in competition. A crisp, uniform let-off is more important than the weight of pull. Also, a heavier than optimum pull can be made to feel lighter when the face of the trigger is wide.

These factors were not lost upon the leading marksmen of the 1880s. Colt was approached and a good deal of research and development went into design modifications that would satisfy the most demanding targeteers on the line. Over time, these changes resulted in a modified version of the SAA that gave the revolver a somewhat different outward appearance, but varied little from the standard SAA internally.

The first of these revolvers were made in 1894 and 24 of them, all with flat-top frames and adjustable sights, were shipped to Colt's London agency on May 15th of that year, to be tested in England's National Matches. They were chambered for the .450 and .455 Eley British service cartridges and were made without provision for ejector rods.

The 19th century rifleman regarded the Creedmoor range on New York's Long Island to be the world's finest. Pistol shooters looked to

Bisley, England for their version of Mecca. In an era when sport shooting was as popular as football and racing cars are today, the mention of either range could evoke visions of glory in the mind of a competitive shooter. Moreover, it's worth noting that then, as now, it's a much safer sport for participants and spectators alike.

Creedmoor is long gone, the victim of suburban sprawl. But, Bisley remains among the finest shooting facilities to be found anywhere. Unfortunately, Britain's near total ban of handguns, enacted in 1997, may mean its death.

The Holland & Holland catalog of 1895 listed the new Colt offering as the "*Target Revolver - Model of 1895.*" By the following year it was called the Bisley Model, so named for the range in that town, and so it was officially labeled in the H&H catalog in 1898 and forever after.

The new revolver had a long, curved gripframe that was slightly underslung; a low, wide hammer spur and a deeply curved wide trigger. The frame itself was slightly higher from top to bottom than on the standard SAA revolver to allow for the minor difference in the mode of attachment of the backstrap.

The gripframe was designed to cause the revolver to recoil as nearly straight back into the hand as possible, reducing the tendency to slide under the shooter's palm. The low mounted hammer spur could be reached for subsequent shots by simply rolling the thumb over and back without moving the rest of the hand. More importantly, it did not obscure the sights when at rest against the frame, so that the shooter could maintain proper sight picture and follow-through during the firing sequence. The trigger design allowed for a greater measure of control and a subjectively lighter weight of pull. All these attributes combined to make it the premier target revolver of its time.

Whereas a mere 30 years before there had been bloody conflict, at the close of the 19th and the beginning of the 20th centuries most of the world's frontier territories were well on the road to civilization. Nevertheless, there remained, as now, some places where prudent men and women went about their daily business armed. Carrying a gun was less for the sake of protection from renegades and outlaws, though there were those with whom to contend. More often the need was for defense against carnivorous animals, poisonous reptiles and for food gathering.

The days of the western gunfighter were all but gone. There were, to be sure, such hangers-

Using one of the author's pet handloads, which incorporates Lyman's long discontinued #401452 semiwadcutter bullet, this nonagenarian revolver demonstrates a level of accuracy comparable to some of the best modern handguns. Many Bisleys are extraordinarily fine shooters.

on as Tom Horn, Butch Cassidy and his partner, the Sundance Kid. Hold-overs from the wild days, such as Bill Tilghman, Tom Threepersons and Frank Hamer continued to serve the law in the west well into the 20th century. But fast shooting was no longer as important (if it ever was) as precise shooting. The greater control a revolver like the Bisley offered was not lost upon the sensibilities of many shooters more interested in practical application than competitive challenge.

Some 976 of these revolvers were done up in various calibers for target shooting during the 17 years of Bisley Model production. But 44,350 were made with the standard fixed-sight frame for the same general uses to which an outdoorsman might put any handgun. These numbers take on a clearer picture when it is considered that in the years during which the Bisleys were produced they amounted to more than 36 percent of total single-action revolver production at Colt and that serial numbers on the Bisleys are concurrent with their more common stable-mates.

The double-action revolvers and semi-automatic pistols were refined to such a degree that they began to supplant the popularity of the single-action designs in the early 1900s. Motion pictures and Wild West shows continued to stimulate some sales for many more years. But, by that time competitors on the firing line were doing better with their Officers Model and New Service target-grade revolvers and similar offerings from Smith & Wesson and others. The Bisley was dropped from Colt's catalog after 1912 and the last of them was shipped from the factory on November 18, 1919. By then, the SAA was also beginning its long decline into practical obsolescence.

As this is written, eight decades have passed since the door was closed on Colt Bisley production. Still, the influence of that design continues to be felt. A close look at the grip frames of all but the most recent double-action revolvers in Colt's line reveals a distinctly Bisley-like silhouette. Ruger introduced a variation of it based on their Blackhawk line of single-action revolvers in 1986. And the small custom revolver maker, Texas Longhorn Arms, makes a mirror image duplicate of Elmer Keith's version of the design that he called the No. 5. EMF's Dakota line of inexpensive single-action revolvers included a Bisley Model during the 1980s. In 1997 Uberti began making a fairly close clone, followed by Armi San Marco's even more Colt-like copy of

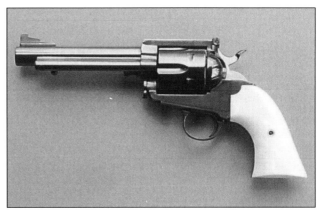

Texas Longhorn Arms made duplicates of Elmer Keith's No.5 experimental variation. The gripframe combines the modified backstrap of the Bisley with the trigger guard of the SAA. Adding features of their own, TLA made the ejector rod and loading gate on the left side of the revolver, so that a right-handed shooter doesn't have to shift it to the left to load and eject cartridges.

this classic variation. As fine handling shooters as these later variations are, my personal favorite of the lot is Colt's original design.

By far the most popular caliber among the original Bisleys was the .32-20, a reflection of their common use for small game hunting and varmint control, as opposed to personal protection. Second in production volume was the .38-40, a perfect ballistic twin to the modern .40 S&W cartridge. It was often the choice of gun-wise lawmen, many of whom regarded it as the most accurate and hard-hitting bad-guy medicine available in its day. Next in order of popularity in this model were the .45 Colt, .44-40 and .41 Long Colt.

Figuratively speaking, I cut my shooting teeth on a Bisley Model with a 4-5/8-inch barrel, back in the early 1960s. For a time, I modified it slightly for fast draw work, by altering and fitting a standard SAA hammer in it. The Bisley's long handle made it easier to grasp than a standard SAA during the fast draw, while the longer hammer spur was quicker to cock than the low slung original. It was a remarkably fast handling sixgun for the first shot. But the hammer's height made follow-up shots slower and less accurate, so the original was re-installed.

That old Colt was responsible for my introduction to Sheriff Fischer. He was past 80, a retired lawman, when we met. I was in my early twenties, in my senior year of college. One Saturday afternoon I was plinking at a row of tin cans along the north bank of the Yellowstone river, near Pompey's Pillar, a few miles east of Billings, Montana. I'd fired the last round in the handgun and began to eject the empty cartridge cases to reload, when I felt something pressed to the middle of my back and heard a voice say, "Bang, you're dead!"

I turned to see an elderly man with a grin on his face and a twinkle in his eye. The object at my back had been his forefinger. He'd injuned up on me without making a sound. He then added that it was a big mistake to let your gun run dry like that, then finished by complimenting my shooting. He also mentioned that he liked my taste in guns. It was then that I noticed the Bisley Model revolver riding high on his belt, just behind his right hip.

His was a .32-20 with a 5-1/2-inch barrel that he'd carried throughout his 50-year career as sheriff of a sparsely populated northern Montana county. He had by then been retired for several years and was living nearby with one of his sons and his family. Despite the difference in our ages, or maybe because of it, we hit it off well and became fast friends. In the brief time I knew him before he died, he taught me more about handling a sixgun than I could have learned in a lifetime on my own.

Among the things I learned about him was that in all those years behind the badge, he'd had to draw his Bisley just once against another man. When he did so, it was to hit the criminal over the head with it. That incident precipitated the only time he ever got into trouble with his constituents. It seems the man was so evil that the community was overwhelmingly of the opinion that he should have shot the man dead. A jury convicted the man of his crimes and the judge seems to have concurred with popular opinion. He ordered the man hanged, headache and all.

The old man told me this tale to emphasize that when a lawman really knows how to handle his gun, the people who most need to know of his skill become aware of it. Thus, it usually becomes unnecessary to prove his prowess.

I'd like to say that fine old gentleman left me his .32-20 Bisley, but it remained in his family; as it should. However, he gave me some things of much greater value; an increased measure of maturity and a greater appreciation of the Bisley's virtues. As relatively rare as Bisleys are, compared to pre-World War II SAAs of standard configuration, they have never enjoyed the interest of collectors that the more common version has always commanded. As a result, prices for good specimens are generally lower, but that doesn't make them cheap. Part of the difference is certainly the relative lack of public recognition. For example, Model No. 3 S&Ws and Colt's Models of 1877 and 1878 double-action revolvers have been more often seen on both the small and large screens. Sharp-eyed movie buffs and televi-

Mechanically sound, but with little original finish remaining, an SAA of standard configuration would command a price several hundred dollars greater in most markets than this Bisley .45 in the same condition. In all likelihood the Bisley will shoot better.

sion watchers may recall Raymond Hatton, a classically trained actor who became one of the regular sidekicks in the Republic and Monogram grade-B Westerns of the 1930s and '40s, carrying an ivory-handled .32-20 Bisley with a 7-1/2-inch barrel. Carroll O'Connor carried one in the Western comedy, "*Water Hole Number 3*." Richard Farnsworth used a Bisley .45 in the fact-based film, "*The Grey Fox*." There are certainly other instances of its use on screen, but unlike the prominence with which Bat Masterson's (Gene Barry) nickel-plated Sheriff's Model and Wyatt Earp's (Hugh O'Brien) Buntline Special were displayed in those long ago TV Westerns, leading to their return to the marketplace, the Bisleys on film have been strictly low profile.

The world of literature has given it even less recognition. Probably the best known work in which a Bisley figures prominently is the late, great, Louis L'Amour's book *The Broken Gun*. Unfortunately, the master story teller made a

This Ruger Bisley started out as a 7.5-inch .357 Magnum. The barrel was bobbed to 5 inches and it was rechambered and bored by Cliff La Bounty of Maple Falls, Washington to use the .38-40

gross historical error by placing its use about 20 years too soon. Oh well, it's still a good yarn, in spite of that faux pas.

Original Bisleys have come to the stage where they are too valuable as collectibles to carry afield. I like mine well enough to shoot it often, but it's packed in a pistol rug when it leaves the house and is carefully cleaned and stored between range sessions.

It's nice to have something of the same general feel to carry on wilderness treks without being concerned about the wear and tear such use would cause. Several years ago I had a gunsmith cut the barrel of a Ruger Bisley to 5 inches. He rebored and rechambered it from . 357 Magnum to .38-40 caliber. It's a little bigger and heavier than the Colt, but it gives me nearly the same feel as the older gun in the same caliber, and provides the utility I want afield. Moreover, it's one of the most accurate revolvers I've ever fired, being capable of groups of just over of an 3/4ths of an inch from a distance of 25 yards, when using the loads it likes best. While it lacks the charm and grace of the older Colt, the converted Ruger is a fine revolver in its own right and it can be enjoyed for itself.

Before WWII Bisleys drew almost no collector interest. They were thought of as merely commonplace shooters of an all but obsolete style. Experimenters thought nothing of subjecting them to all manner of custom modifications. The aforementioned revisions by Elmer Keith are good examples, but some shooters wanted something more from them. A few (no one knows exactly how many) are known to have been returned to the factory in the late 1930s for conversion to .357 Magnum.

Each of those revolvers was stripped of its case hardening, the frames were made over to flat-top configuration and fitted with 7-1/2-inch barrels. The revolvers were then equipped with target sights and new stocks of nicely figured walnut with a fleur-de-lis checkering pattern and silver colored medallions. They were finished in full (civilian) blue. These are truly handsome revolvers and the one specimen I've been privileged to handle is a beautifully crafted, superbly accurate shooting machine that remains in near mint condition.

One of the most interesting things about these revolvers is that the barrels are rollmarked on the left side to read "Frontier Six-Shooter." That marking was generally believed to have been reserved exclusively for use on revolvers chambered for the .44-40 cartridge. So much for rules.

For several years I encouraged the importers of SAA-style replica firearms to commission the manufacturers to make revolvers with authentic Bisley features. I don't know how much my efforts may have contributed, but both Uberti and Armi San Marco began shipping them in 1997. As this is written, they are only just beginning to make their way into the Cowboy Action shooting scene.

Some users seem to feel that the Bisley Model is an acquired taste, like olives or brussels sprouts. Once tried, most shooters seem to like them and find they wouldn't want to be without one. They're just that much a pleasure to shoot.

CHAPTER 14

COLT'S BUNTLINE SPECIAL

During the late 1950s and early '60s a strange phenomenon occurred on television in America and, ultimately, throughout the world. It was known as "The Adult Western." Vestiges of this genre continued into the 1970s, but by that time the market had been thoroughly saturated and the network studios began to turn back to films about private investigators.

Copycat series have been a fact of life in the television industry for as long as the medium has been with us. One of the factors common to nearly every Western of that era was the gimmick gun. Yancey Derringer had numerous four-barreled Sharps pistols concealed about his person, which he employed with amazing speed and a level of accuracy that could only be achieved with special effects wizardry.

In the Johnny Ringo series, the title character was played as a lawman, rather than the drunkard, ne'r-do-well petty criminal that history records. In the TV version of the story, he carried the usual Colt Single Action Army, modified to fire a seventh round, a .410 shotgun cartridge. The revolver was reminiscent of the Le Mat revolvers of the Civil War. The power of the shotgun barrel was greatly exaggerated when it was used on screen.

Chuck Conners, in The Rifleman, carried a Model 1892 Winchester with a loop lever which he spun cleverly, either left- or right-handed, with equal dexterity. It could be made to fire as rapidly as a modern semi-automatic rifle with the set screw, a dangerous accessory that could be used to fire around each time the lever was cycled.

One such series that fascinated me during its brief run was

called Wichita Town. It starred Joel McCrea, one of the greats of the Silver Screen, even if this series was not one of his best efforts. His gimmick was an otherwise standard Colt SAA that had no trigger. It was fired by simply slipshooting the hammer out from under the thumb in the manner of the John Newman technique, explained in detail by Elmer Keith in his classic tome, *Sixguns*. The only difference was that McCrea's gun was without the alteration of the hammer that was Newman's trademark.

Nearly all of the gimmick guns were either impractical or impossible, but the best known of the lot was that used in Hugh O'Brien's series, *The Life and Legend of Wyatt Earp*, which was based on Stuart Lake's biography, *Wyatt Earp, Frontier Marshall*. The series followed the events in Earp's life fairly faithfully, at least to the book. As to the accuracy of many of the incidents described, there is great doubt.

Earp was the subject of nearly as much controversy during his lifetime as after. Some of this surrounds the long-barreled Colt SAA, said to have been presented to him by Edward C.Z. Judson, a pulp fiction writer and newspaperman, better known by his pen name, Ned Buntline.

The story has it that Buntline presented one of these revolvers to each of the members of the, so called, "Dodge City Peace Commission," which included Earp and lawmen, Neal Brown, Charlie Bassett, Bat Masterson and Bill Tilghman. Some sources have said that the revolvers were originally fitted with 18-inch barrels, but

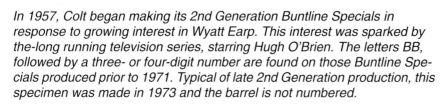

In 1957, Colt began making its 2nd Generation Buntline Specials in response to growing interest in Wyatt Earp. This interest was sparked by the-long running television series, starring Hugh O'Brien. The letters BB, followed by a three- or four-digit number are found on those Buntline Specials produced prior to 1971. Typical of late 2nd Generation production, this specimen was made in 1973 and the barrel is not numbered.

The inspiration for the Indian's head inlay on the recoil shield of this revolver should be familiar to most Americans. It's an almost exact duplicate to the one found on a buffalo nickel coin. (Engraved by Howard Dove)

Attention to detail is the mark of good inlay work. This eagle has feathers so realistic that it looks almost as though it could fly off the revolver. (Engraved by Howard Dove)

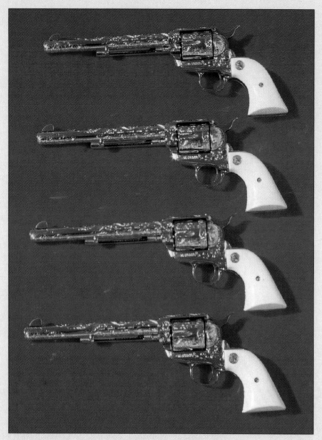

Only one order for a quartet of consecutively numbered SAA revolvers has ever been filled by Colt.

Genuine Colt Sheriff's Model revolvers of any generation are too valuable to shoot. The two shown here with staghorn handles saw some use in their early years, but have long been retired. The early 3rd Generation Sheriff's Model, on the bottom, remains unfired after more than two decades.

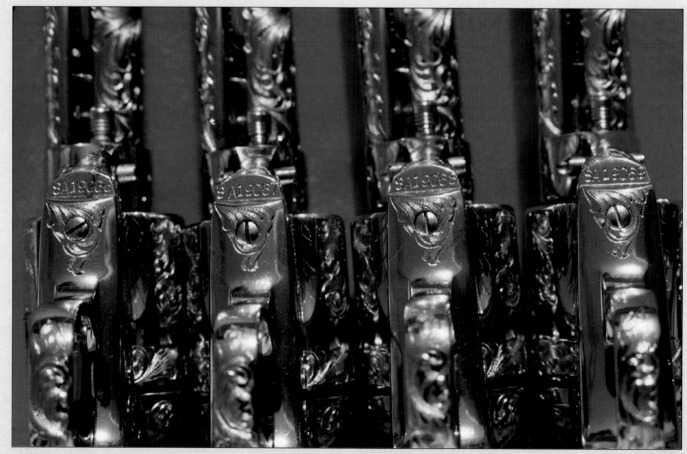

These revolvers are so nearly identical that only the serial numbers and the slight differences in the grain of the ivory stocks makes them individually identifiable.

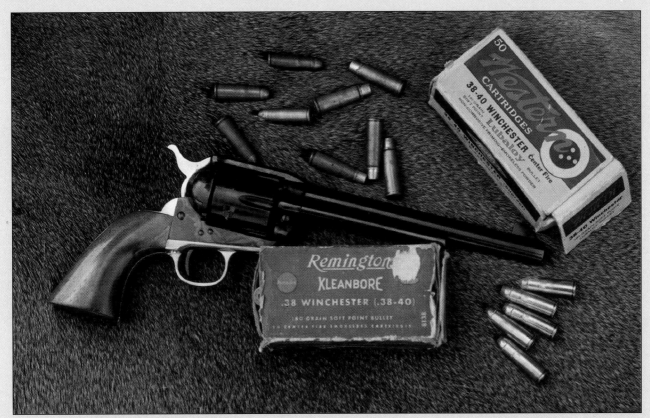

EMF, along with several other manufacturers and distributors, began early to fill a market niche with close copies of the SAA produced in Europe at much less than the cost for a genuine Colt.

Adjusting the cylinder's headspace made a lot of difference on the target. Accuracy for a revolver of this type went from poor to excellent.

Using Federal's 148-grain wadcutter loads, this group was shot offhand just as the gun's first owner, Ed McGivern, might have done, albeit much more slowly, from a distance of 20 feet. The flyer was called (some very nasty names).

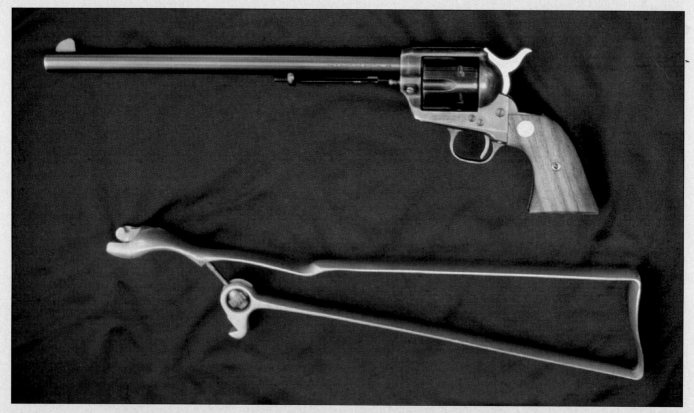

In the 19th century, skeleton stocks were a common accessory. Since 1934, U.S. law has required that the barrel be at least 16 inches in length if a stock is to be attached. Otherwise, a $200 transfer tax must be paid. It is legal to own both gun and stock if the extended hammer screw necessary to attach them is not in place.

Collectible SAA Colts come plain and fancy and don't have to be original to be interesting or valuable.

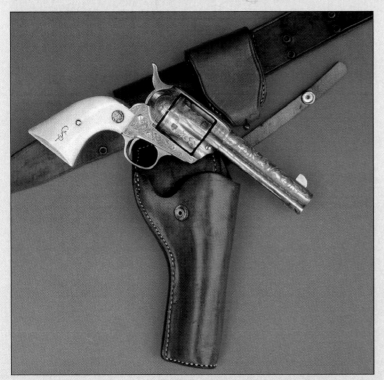

Horacio Acevedo duplicated General George S. Patton's revolver to perfection. The belt and holster were made by El Paso Saddlery, which made Patton's original in 1916.

Fired from 15 yards, this group made with the author's .45 Colt handloads, using a Keith-style bullet, demonstrates that the Uberti Cimarron revolvers have the potential to deliver near target-level accuracy.

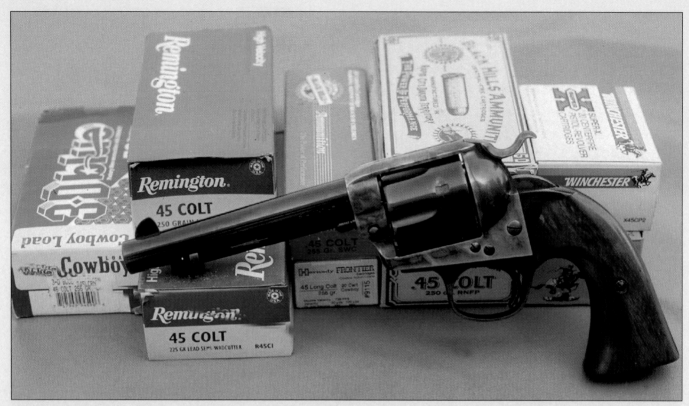

Nine different factory loads, both standard and Cowboy Action types were tried in the Uberti Bisley. All did well, with groups measuring less than 3 inches; some measured much less.

Decades after his passing John Wayne remains an American icon. The detail evident in the gold inlay portrait of the actor, by Howard Dove, is so striking that it seems as though he might actually speak.

Adding a set of stocks made of an exotic material, such as these made of staghorn, is the quickest and easiest way to personalize your sixgun.

This 2nd Generation .38 Special SAA left the factory in 1956 with a 5 1/2-inch barrel. Although the source of its modification is unsure, it appears to have been returned to the maker and made over with a 3 1/4-inch barrel and barely functional ejector. A .357 Magnum auxiliary cylinder was fitted to it later.

Most original Colt internal parts worked well in the EMF Bisley, but the firing pin on the Colt hammer is the wrong shape for the hole in the recoil plate. The Colt cylinder wouldn't fit at all. Note the extra step that works as a safety mechanism on the EMF cylinder pin.

One of the most prized items of Colt memorabilia, this Tex & Patches lithograph, by Western artist Frank Schoonover is one of thousands that were shipped to Colt firearms dealers and distributors as a promotional premium from 1926 to 1932. Very few originals survive.

Lavishly engraved and fitted with staghorn grips, these sixguns were used in his films by "B" Western hero, Lash LaRue.

The last Bisley was shipped from the factory on November 18, 1919, so one might be forgiven for believing this .357 Magnum Bisley is a fake, but according to Colt's Historian Emeritus, Marty Huber, several of the old flat-top Bisleys were converted in this manner at the factory during the late 1930s.

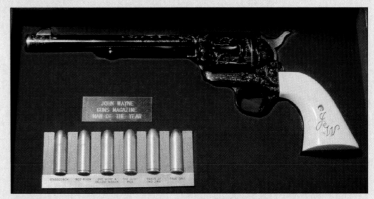

Guns Magazine chose John Wayne as its "Man of the year" and presented him with this ivory-stocked SAA Colt with "C" coverage engraving. Below the cartridges, the brass plate lists half a dozen of his greatest movies.

To demonstrate the accuracy of the SAA and New Frontier revolvers, this composite 100—round group was shot from a distance of 25 yards using all three Colts and the S&W Model 25. Both .45 LC and .45 ACP cylinders were used with the Colts.

Loads using 5 grains of Hodgdon's Clays powder with both the 200-grain semi-wadcutter and the more commonly available 180-grain LRNFP cast bullets produced these excellent groups.

Its handling qualities are the reason many knowledgeable shooters chose the Bisley Model. With good ammunition it helps the user deliver groups that would do a modern target pistol proud.

Its break-top action and simultaneous extraction makes the Schofield revolver very fast to load and reload. Cavalry soldiers often found this a particular advantage.

Using Black Hills' new .44 Russian ammunition, four of five rounds went into one ragged hole from a distance of 15 yards. The flyer was called and entirely the author's fault, not that of either the handgun or the ammunition. Premium accuracy such as this proves that our great-grandfathers had some fine equipment at their disposal.

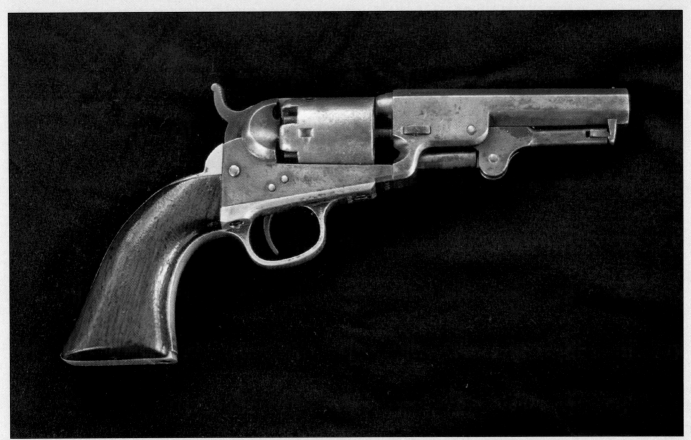

By far the most popular handgun during the California Gold Rush was Colt's Model 1849 Pocket revolver.
This one has seen hard use, but can still be fired nearly 150 years after it was made.

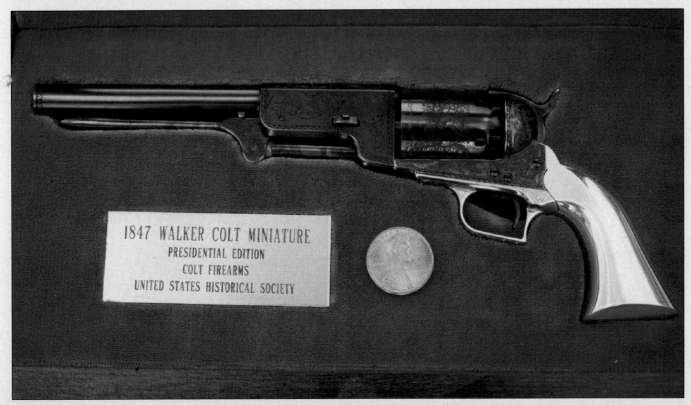

1847 WALKER COLT MINIATURE
PRESIDENTIAL EDITION
COLT FIREARMS
UNITED STATES HISTORICAL SOCIETY

If it were not for the penny next to it, one would be hard pressed to identify this Walker as a miniature. The US
Historical Society was licensed to produce these tiny handguns under the Colt name.

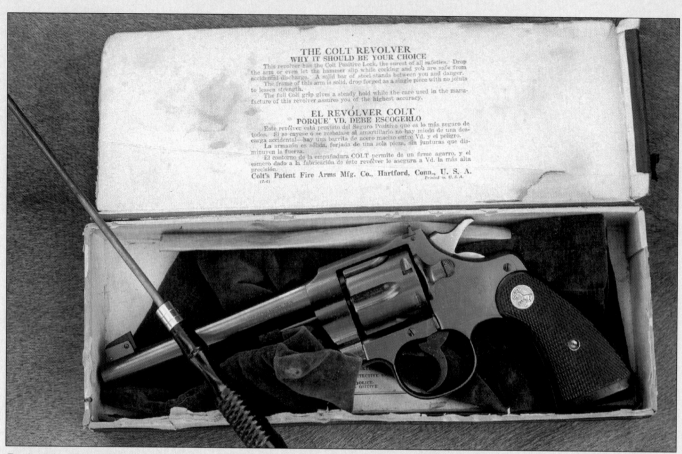

During the depression years of the 1930s SAA production came to a virtual standstill. Those who could afford new revolvers usually chose more practical, less expensive products like the Officer's Model Match, shown here, or Colt's more basic Official Police and S&W's M&P models.

Only one consecutively numbered pair of SAA revolvers chambered for the .357 Magnum cartridge was made prior to WWII. In the midst of the depression, they were an extravagant purchase.

Anecdotes of the War, by Frank Moore, is one of the best books of the reconstruction period to offer the reader an understanding of the realities of the Civil War as seen by its participants on both sides. But the feel of it begins to really sink in when one handles the firearms of the period.

A brace of blued Officer's Model Colt .38 Special revolvers, these were sometimes used in movies, but more often worn by actor Tom Mix for trick shooting exhibitions. The stocks are scrimshawed ivory.

Horace Smith's portrait on the recoil shield, D.B. Wesson's on the left ivory stock panel and S&W's logo in place of the Rampant Colt on the frame would certainly elicit suspicion as to this revolver's true origins, if one knew nothing of firearms.

With three extra cylinders fitted to it the author's .38-40/10mm can also use .40 S&W and the potent .401 Herter's Powermag cartridges. One more cylinder converted and it will be able to shoot .41 Long Colt ammo, too. Now, there's a multi-purpose revolver.

The military-style Uberti Schofield did well with all three of Black Hills loads made for Cowboy Action competition. Just as the short-barreled revolver had done, it shot especially well with the 230-grain loading.

Most Ruger Blackhawk revolvers deliver good accuracy, as demonstrated by this 25-yard group using .32 S&W Long cartridges, loaded with wadcutter bullets. With good handload development or carefully selected factory loads, many will provide near match-grade performance.

These revolvers were crafted entirely of wood. Even the springs are wooden and make them fully functional mechanically. They could be used to shoot a cartridge, but to do so would turn these exquisite replicas into splinters.

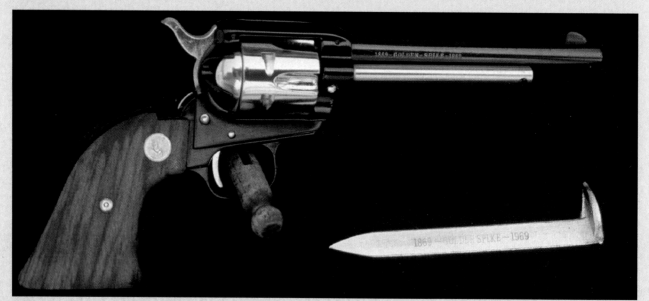

Standard variations of Colt's Frontier Scout offer little variety to interest the collector. However, they have been the vehicle for more than 60 Commemoratives, like this Golden Spike Centennial, made to celebrate historical events, well-known personalities and anniversaries.

In recent years gold bands at the muzzle, the rear of the barrel and on the cylinder have become very popular. On a blued revolver, with a case hardened colored frame, they add a distinctive accent that enhances the darker colors.

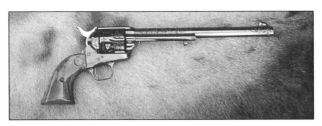

Colt's 150th Anniversary Commemorative revolver, issued in 1986, harkened back to the 19th century Buntline production, when the most common extra length order was for a barrel of 10 inches. These were produced with A-style engraving of the barrel and cylinder. The frame is blued, rather than having the usual case hardened colors.

that Earp cut his to a more manageable 12 inches, and that the others cut them back to one of the more usual lengths; each to suit his own taste. Earp, according to Lake, says the guns were presented with 12-inch barrels.

No factory records of an order for such revolvers exist, but that is not to say that it isn't possible that barrels of extraordinary length might have been fitted by one of Colt's distributors, or for that matter, any competent gunsmith, after leaving the factory. For their part, Colt's refused to get involved with the controversy during the pre-war years. In spite of this, after the appearance of Lake's book, all SAA's of greater than standard barrel length came to be called, "Buntlines."

Whether these revolvers actually existed, or were the product of either Earp's or Lake's fertile imagination, is speculative. Earp, allegedly, told Lake that, while he was working as a bartender in Nome, Alaska, the revolver was loaned to a friend who lost it overboard from his small boat during a storm and that it now lies at the bottom of the Bering Sea. How convenient.

It is known that Lake made attempts to contact some of the other lawmen who were still alive when he worked with Earp and were supposed to have been the recipients of Buntline's largess. There is no record of any response or any independent confirmation of the existence of those extraordinarily long-barreled sixguns.

In the late 19th century Colt would make up revolvers with barrels longer than 7-1/2 inches upon customer request. The cost was $1 per inch over the normal price of the handgun. Their records make mention of revolvers with barrels of 8, 8-1/2, 9, 10, 10-1/2, 12, 14 and 16 inches. None with a length of 18 inches is noted in their ledgers and the same records show that the lone specimen of 12-inch length was chambered for the .44-40 car-

tridge. That one is of particular interest, because it was ordered by a Tombstone, Arizona bartender who witnessed the fight at the O.K. Corral and testified at the inquest that followed that the revolver Earp used seemed to have a barrel a foot long. Perhaps in the midst of a gunfight, the bartender only thought the barrel looked that long.

The first group of long-barreled SAA Colts was made up in 1876. The serial numbers of the guns fall into range 28,800 to 28,830. However, they were not shipped until December 1, 1877 and some specimens fall outside this serial number range. The earliest known specimen bears serial number 25,922. Many of these revolvers had included in their shipment, flap holsters and skeleton stocks that were fitted to an extended hammer screw and had a hook-shaped toe, designed to be snugged up against the forward end of the bottom of the grip-frame by means of a thumb screw nut. Globe front sights are common to this variation and, with the stock attached, it makes for a very serviceable little carbine. A revolver of this description, from the John S. du Mont collection is shown in John E. Parson's work, *The Peacemaker and Its Rivals*. One feature common to all the known Buntline Specials of the frontier period is that every specimen has a flat top frame and a folding ladder rear sight.

It's worth noting that barrels of greater than standard length were known to have been produced during the percussion era as well. I've seen an 1851 Navy Model Colt, that is known to be authentic, with a 12-inch barrel.

The truth of the matter regarding Earp and his associates having Buntline Specials will probably

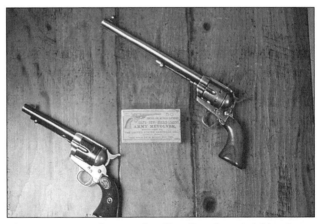

A very rare 1st Generation Buntline Special, it's chambered for the .44 Colt cartridge. As is typical, it carries a globe front sight and adjustable ladder rear sight. The companion revolver in this photo is chambered for the same cartridge.

be debated long into the 21st century. But most historians seem to have concluded that the story is pure fiction. The lack of any corroboration by Earp's contemporaries seems to support this view. But there is no doubt that the revolver featured in the Wyatt Earp television series so fascinated the shooting public that, by popular demand, Colt began producing them in 1957 as a regular addition to their line of SAA revolvers, and continued to do so until 1974. A total of about 4,000 were made in the usual blue with case hardened colors. An additional 65 were nickel plated during the second generation period of production.

All but a few experimental pieces that were never offered to the public, were chambered for the .45 Colt cartridge. A reliable informant has told me that he saw one such revolver at the factory in the 1960s that was chambered for the .357 Magnum cartridge. I've also heard of one chambered in .256 Winchester Magnum, but cannot confirm the existence of either. However, both chamberings were listed in a flyer issued by Colt.

Among the Third Generation SAA revolvers, Buntline Special production resumed in 1981. These are a bit more versatile in terms of caliber, as the .44 Special and .44-40 were made readily available, as well as the usual .45 L.C.

Over the years, many gun writers, some of whom are otherwise enamored of the SAA revolver, have looked down their noses at Buntlines as being completely impractical. With all due respect, I must disagree.

My own experience with this variation dates back to 1963. At that time I tried desperately to effect a trade with a canny old Yankee gunshop owner in Vermont who simply wanted too much for the specimen he had. It was in near-new condition and fascinated me from the first moment that I hefted its 43 ounces of plow-handle shaped, wood-stocked gripframe and gorgeous case hardened frame set off by blued steel. It

One of the great rarities of the modern Buntline Special production is the New Frontier Model, with flat-top frame and adjustable target sight. The exact number produced is not known, but may be as few as 72.

was hard to believe that such an ungainly looking revolver could feel so right in my hand. However, we couldn't reach a mutually agreeable compromise and I went away without that fascinating firearm. Nevertheless, I made up my mind that I would one day own one like it.

Two years later in the town of Hasty, Colorado, I found a gun shop. I spent a lot of time there; more time than money, being on a tight budget. I came by an 1898 vintage SAA that had a new 4-5/8-inch barrel and cylinder of current manufacture. It shot well, just as it was, and I liked it, but a glimmer of an idea grew in my mind until it became a compulsion. I had it shipped to Colt to have a Buntline Special barrel installed and to be nickel plated.

The entire project cost me a whopping $80 and included a complete rebuilding of the innards. Considering that I had an income of about $125 a month at that time, it really was an extravagance, but I'd had a couple of good swaps on guns I was able to sell, so most of the cash outlay was in found money. A new one from the factory would have set me back nearly twice as much.

The result of Colt's labors was a wonder to behold. It might have made a purist collector lose his lunch, but the revolver was clean, crisp and shot like a dream. It became my virtual trademark during the course of the next 13 years of my proprietorship. I used it frequently for both hunting and plinking, and learned a lot about shooting and handloading with it.

Dozens of small game animals and pests, including porcupines, badgers, weasels, grouse, jackrabbits and coyotes fell to its bark. On two occasions it was used to collect mule deer. Not once was a second shot required to finish any animal upon which I laid its sights.

Many years later I was made an offer for that revolver that I couldn't refuse. I felt a sense of regret from the moment I handed it over, but the fellow who got it had a lot more money than sense and, as luck would have it, a few years later that same gentleman came up with a new-in-the-box, case hardened and blued Buntline and we made another deal. This time I was the one who walked away with the Buntline, but I had gotten it for a price I could afford. Actually, less than the price received for the first one.

This time I had a real collector's item. Second Generation Buntlines bring a premium price; somewhat more than I had needed to invest. However, I was more interested in its shooting qualities than its monetary worth. Like most 2nd Generation Buntlines, it proved to be very accurate.

The only disadvantage I've found with the Buntline is carrying it afield. Commercial leather for such a revolver is difficult to find. Even if a holster company lists it in its catalog, few dealers feel it worthwhile to stock such an item, so it must be special ordered. A few years ago I found a left-handed Bucheimer Model PM-25, which had been ordered for a customer who never took delivery. In spite of the fact that I'm right-handed, it has worked well for me, because it is carried out of the way, behind the back. Sometimes I rig it within easy reach to the outside of my backpack; readily accessible when needed.

Generally, I experiment with handloads. When it comes to the .45 Colt, such experimentation has been unnecessary. I've found no load to beat 8 grains of Alliance (formerly Hercules) Unique powder behind a hard cast Lyman #454424 Keith-type semi-wadcutter bullet weighing about 250 grains.

Modern revolvers chambered for this round have groove diameters of .451 to .452 of an inch. Pre-war revolvers have a .454-inch diameter. Ammunition makers have followed suit with bullet diameters changing when the transition was made in the guns. My cast bullets are routinely sized .454 and lubricated with Alox. With linotype alloy, depending upon the mold in use, these bullets may weigh as little as 240-grains. In practice, this has not affected accuracy adversely. Actually, quite the opposite has been true. Nor has there been any indication of excessive pressure with such loads, because the 8-grain charge of Unique is a full 2 grains below the maximum recommended in most

manuals. What's more, there has never been any problem with leading using these bullets.

Usually, a Magnum primer is used, because it gives more uniform ignition and more complete burning of the powder. This handload has proved accurate in each of more than a dozen revolvers in which it's been tried over the years. Its velocity is about 825 to 850 feet per second in standard-length barrels. In the Buntline, it chronographs just under 1,000 fps. That's certainly adequate for most sporting applications and still within the limits set for SASS competition.

While on the subject of this cartridge, it's worth mentioning that there is some controversy over its nomenclature. There are those who refer to it simply as the .45 Colt. Currently, ammunition manufacturers label it thus. This is a relatively recent change. As discussed in Chapter 7, it was originally called the .45 Long Colt to distinguish it from the U.S. military cartridge which was designed to be used in the shorter cylinders of Smith & Wesson's military issue Schofield revolvers. But both terms are correct. Dinosaur that I am, I simply prefer the older appellation.

By whichever name it is called, it is, and always has been, a useful and powerful cartridge. It is capable of taking game, within its limitations, and is a suitable man-stopper; the purpose for which it was originally designed. In most revolvers it is capable of accuracy levels of less than 2 inches at 25 yards. With the right gun and load in the right hands, it is capable of shooting into one ragged hole at the same distance. The long sight radius of the Buntline not only allows it to shoot tighter groups in the hands of a good shot, but the higher velocity and flatter trajectory from the 12-inch barrel extends its useful range from around 60 yards in the shorter barrel lengths to about 100 yards.

When engaging closer targets, the Buntline makes consistent hits easy. Its extra length makes point shooting, quite literally, as easy and accurate as pointing one's finger. Whether plinking at targets of opportunity or shooting tight groups on paper, it's almost like shooting a short rifle. Its report is also more rifle-like, eliciting a more high-pitched cracking sound than a deep throated boom, as do most handguns of this caliber.

One has to make allowances to carry it conveniently and it certainly isn't for everyone. Yet, I've found the Buntline Special very useful afield and on the range. Certainly, it's a gimmick gun, but so what? It's a lot of fun to shoot and having fun is what shooting is all about, isn't it?

Finding a good holster for the Buntline Special is difficult. This one, of Western style by Backwoods Leather, is a handsome and efficient rig in which to carry the long-barreled revolver. In spite of the long barrel, the Buntline Special maintains the graceful lines and natural handling characteristics for which the Single Action Army is so justly famous.

CHAPTER 15

COLT'S NEW FRONTIER REVOLVERS

It is one of the great ironies of modern American history that John F. Kennedy, whose assassination incited intense anti-gun sentiment in some quarters was, at least in his public pronouncements, one of the most pro-gun politicians of the post-World War II era. It was his reference during his inaugural address to America's challenges in social and scientific achievement being a "new frontier" that inspired the marketing people at Colt to apply that name to the modern reincarnation of their flat-top target Single Action Army revolver. To compound the irony, an exquisitely engraved New Frontier revolver had been completed and was to have been presented to Kennedy, but after his murder the revolver was simply put away, eventually to be sold to a private collector.

The New Frontier revolver is one of those variations, like Bisley Models and Buntline Specials, that Single Action Army buffs seem either to love or to hate. Personally, I've never encountered a SAA of any vintage, caliber or style in which I couldn't find some merit. I like them all, but I'm especially fond of the New Frontier revolvers, because every one I've ever encountered has exhibited fine workmanship and every one of the many I've shot has proved capable of match-grade accuracy on target.

Because of its refined target sights, it falls into the Modern Class at Cowboy Action matches, right along with such 20th century revolvers as the Ruger Blackhawks. However, the parts used in its lockwork are no different from those of any standard SAA Colt revolver. There is, however, some difference in the manner in which they are assembled. There seems to have been greater attention paid to the fit, finish and function of the New Frontiers than the standard SAA's of the same period.

Colt's Royal Blue is the standard finish found on the New Frontiers, usually contrasted with especially colorful case hardening of the frame. A few, however, were nickel plated. The most common caliber is .45 Colt, but some were chambered for .38 Special, .357 Magnum, .44 Special and .44-40. Any such revolver chambered for a cartridge other than .45 Colt can be regarded as scarce.

The most common barrel length is 7-1/2 inches, but specimens with barrels of 12, 5-1/2 and 4-5/8 inches were also made. Again, any with barrel lengths other than 7-1/2 inches can be regarded as scarce. There were even a couple of special order

A flat-top frame, fully adjustable Eliason rear sight and prominent ramp front sight are universal characteristics of Colt's New Frontier revolvers. The vast majority were made, as this specimen was, for the .45 Colt cartridge, with a 7.5-inch barrel, finished in royal blue, with case-hardened colors.

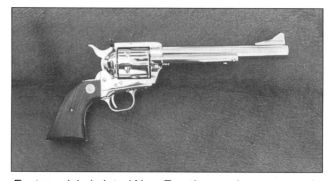

Factory nickel plated New Frontier revolvers are rarely encountered. The exact number produced is unclear, but may be as few as 10.

New Frontier revolvers chambered for calibers other than .45 Colt are very scarce. Only 39 .38 Specials were made with 5-1/2-inch barrels. Just 10 were made with 7-1/2-inch barrels.

revolvers from Colt that were made up as the "Charter Oak" commemoratives engraved by A.A. White. Stocks and a French fitted case derived of wood from the "offspring" of the State of Connecticut's historic Charter Oak tree (trees grown from that particular tree's acorns) and barrels just two inches long are features of these ejectorless Sheriff's Model New Frontiers.

As originally conceived, the SAA revolver was designed for military combat. Standard issue to the U.S. Armed Forces for most of the last quarter of the 19th century, it continued in some measure in such service for another generation thereafter. Its military utility carried over to the civilian sector, in law enforcement and personal protection, just as such handguns as the Government Model semi-auto, and a variety of military issue double-action revolvers, like the Model 1917 New Service have done.

Generally, it was employed at distances from arms length to 50 yards. Much beyond that a rifle would normally be called into service. From the beginning, it was recognized as a fairly accurate handgun, but the crude fixed sights built into it limited its capacity for precision.

That's where the early flat-tops and the modern New Frontier come into their own. Good adjustable sights permit a handgun to more efficiently use a greater variety of ammunition. Cartridges of differing brands and bullet weights shoot to different points of aim. If the handgun is equipped with fixed sights one must shift point of aim to accommodate. Adjustable sights allow the shooter to maintain normal point of aim with any ammunition.

Colt's Eliason rear sight, fully adjustable for elevation and windage, is mounted to the New Frontier with a roll pin through the topstrap of the frame to secure it in place. Its adjustment blade moves from side to side within a mounting assembly that protects it from damage and permits little extraneous reflected light to distract the shooter's eye. The front sight is a solid ramp upon a ramp, both well serrated to eliminate reflection. The result is a Baughman-like profile providing a classic patridge-style sight picture, ideal for the 6 o'clock hold preferred by most target shooters, but easily adapted to the dead-on center of mass hold most outdoorsmen like.

Typical of the tuning found on most of these handguns is one of my favorite revolvers, a New Frontier chambered for .45 Colt and fitted with a 4-5/8-inch barrel. It indexes perfectly and the sear releases the hammer with just 2.5 pounds of pressure. There is no creep and it lets off so crisply that what little over-travel there is goes entirely unnoticed. While it would certainly be possible to install a set-screw to eliminate the over-travel, no practical purpose would be accomplished by such an alteration.

Its capacity for precise shot placement is such that this is the revolver I use as a control to test the potential accuracy of factory loads and handloads of .45 caliber. A non-fluted .45 ACP cylinder has been fitted to it, so that

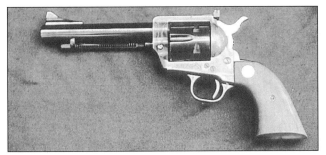

More common than the .38 Special., but still quite rare, only 120 with 5-1/2-inch barrels were made to shoot the .44 Special. There were 135 made with 7-1/2-inch barrels.

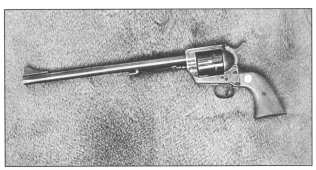

Buntline Special New Frontier revolvers are another great rarity. There were only 72 of them produced by the Colt factory.

Engraved New Frontiers have seldom been ordered. Author Don Wilkerson records only 30 having been made.

One of the author's favorite revolvers is this New Frontier .45 with 4-3/4-inch barrel and unfluted auxiliary cylinder for the .45 ACP cartridge. Superbly accurate, it's one of just 81 made with a barrel of this length.

round can also be tested. If a given load shoots well from this New Frontier, the performance of another handgun with the same ammunition can be better evaluated. If that gun doesn't group well, the fault may be placed on the gun being tested, rather than the load. I've yet to encounter an ammunition variant of either cartridge that shot poorly from that particular New Frontier and did well in a different revolver.

If you're more interested in performance than tradition in your single-action shooting activities, the New Frontier revolvers offer some of the best shooting available. Even at that, there's still a large enough measure of the traditional in them to satisfy your cowboy heart.

CHAPTER 16

SHOOTING ED MCGIVERN'S COLT

Fifty years ago there probably wasn't a dedicated shooter anywhere in the world who didn't know the name, Ed McGivern. But today, only the most avid students of sixgunnery perk up their ears when they hear his name. That's probably the reason my friend, Bill Dascher, asked if I knew about him when he called me on the phone that momentous evening.

"Sure," I replied, "he was the fastest man with a sixgun who ever lived. His book, *Fast and Fancy Revolver Shooting*, is a classic."

This established my bona fides on the subject, making it unnecessary to explain the whys and wherefores of the speedy old sign painter (that's how McGivern earned his living when he wasn't amazing people with his skills or teaching them to shoot). Bill went on to tell me, "Well, I just bought one of his guns."

It took a few seconds for me to respond to that, because the lump in my throat was a little hard to talk around. I think the first thing I said was. "I want to photograph it." I didn't have to ask what kind of handgun it was. Knowing Dascher as I do, it was unlikely to be anything other than an SAA Colt. He's collected them for more than 35 years.

The only words I respond to as quickly as an "I love you" from my wife are the words, "Single Action Army Colt." When he finally got around to specifics, I learned that it was a .357 Magnum with a 5-1/2-inch barrel, blued, with case hardened colors and wearing a set of factory two-piece ivory stocks with silver medallions. Condition was described as excellent. Considering that the revolver was more than 60 years old and the use to which it had certainly been put by its original owner, that would prove to be an understatement.

Only 525 SAA's chambered for the .357 Magnum left the factory before our fracas with the Axis powers began in 1941. The serial number

McGivern's book, Fast and Fancy Revolver Shooting, *is one of the early classics of firearms literature. He was often the subject of magazine articles such as the cover story in the October, 1974, issue of* The American Rifleman. *The target shown was shot from 25 yards over sandbags, using Winchester's 145-grain .357 Magnum loads.*

Ed McGivern was a portly, rather ordinary looking man, but his shooting skills were legendary. Law enforcement agencies and military authorities often sought his counsel for training their personnel in the use of the handgun.

One that demonstrates McGivern's reputation in the community concerns a robber who came into town to hold up the bank. Someone who had happened to glance through the window and seen the thief at his work called the local authorities but, when the robber was confronted, he had a number of hostages in the building and refused to surrender. McGivern heard about the goings on and appeared on the scene wearing a Buscadero rig with a pair of double-action S&W .38's.

The senior officer on site used a bullhorn to inform the criminal that McGivern was there and if he didn't surrender immediately, the six-gun wizard would go in after him. Ed McGivern's reputation was such that the miscreant surrendered right quick and without further incident.

In many ways, McGivern was an artist and artists often have patrons to support their work. A Philadelphia businessman by the name of Walter Groff was fascinated by his skills and accomplishments. Groff became McGivern's patron and made certain that he never lacked for ammunition or any firearm with which he might wish to experiment. His shooting activities left McGivern no time for handloading, so he worked with factory loads, exclusively. Groff had caseloads of the stuff shipped to him, directly from the ammunition manufacturers.

When the Master Sixgunner died in 1957, the 16 handguns that were a part of his legacy were willed to Groff. When Groff, himself, went on to the big shooting range in the sky, his will specified that 14 of the McGivern handguns were to be donated to the NRA. The remaining two were passed to Groff's long-time friend and fellow shooting enthusiast, Henry Stewart, of Wynnewood, PA. In the succeeding years the .357 SAA that was one of the two Stewart inherited was passed from one hand to another several times. It even left the country to spend some time in the hands of a noted Canadian collector. Eventually, Bill got it and provided me with the opportunity to handle this significant piece of shooting history.

There's a factory letter to attest to the revolver's authenticity. However, there is no mention in the document of the checkered backstrap, trigger guard and the wider than standard trigger on the gun. Judging by other pieces, previously observed, that are known to have been done at the factory, these features appear to be original to the revolver, although it's certainly possible that they are aftermarket additions.

The mechanical qualities of the revolver are superb. The timing of its lockwork is on a par

on this one indicated that it had been made in 1936. It was shipped from the factory on August 7, 1937. All that makes the piece a great rarity in its own right. Its association with such a legendary figure makes it even more rare.

Ed McGivern was university educated, but never achieved greatness in any conventional academic pursuit. His passion was "Gunocology." He was one of the first independent experimenters to bring into the shooting game a true measure of science by applying to his ballistic explorations the subjects of mathematics, physics, anatomy, physiology, psychology and electronics.

Back in the late 1960s, I lived about 100 miles from McGivern's home town of Lewistown, Montana. Such distances are considered little more than a drive around the block in that part of the country. My wife and I shopped there fairly often. Stories about the old sign painter were often told at the town's gun shop and at the general store.

with that of a fine Swiss watch. An RCBS trigger gauge demonstrated that the weight of pull was a near perfect, crisp, 3-1/4 pounds.

In the course of discussing the revolver, I made the off-hand remark that I'd sure like to shoot it. When Bill replied that he thought that was a great idea, I was stunned. He's an advanced collector with a passion for the history of the guns he collects, but Bill is not a shooter. Nevertheless, he was just as curious to trot out the old Colt and put it through its paces as I.

In all likelihood, the revolver had not been fired since some time before McGivern's death. But there was no doubt that it had seen some serious use before that. Valuable as it is, there would be no harm in using it with quality factory ammunition as long as it were properly cleaned and lubed after it was shot. Of course,

Shown here, shooting what may be the very revolver the author had the opportunity to test, Ed McGivern demonstrates his fanning technique. Fanning isn't for amateurs. Note that his arm is tucked tightly against his body to minimize the movement of the gun as the palm of his other hand sweeps across the sixgun's hammer.

shooting it was limited to slow fire over sandbags. No attempt would be made to shoot for speed or from a holster.

In keeping with McGivern's methods, groups of five shots were fired; in this instance, from a distance of 25 yards. A .357 Magnum factory load, using Winchester's 145-grain Silvertips and .38's from Federal, loaded with 148-grain wadcutters, were used to fire five groups of five shots, each. With the .357 Magnum loads the clusters of holes in the target averaged 1.4 inch. The largest was 2.1 inches and the smallest measured only .94 inch. Switching to the wadcutters, the largest group measured 1.2 inch and the smallest a mere 3/4 of an inch.

As a control, a 4-inch barreled S&W Highway Patrolman of proven superior accuracy was used to demonstrate comparative performance. The S&W did very well, but the old Colt demonstrated slightly better precision.

The McGivern Colt has a non-standard front sight. There's a small, L-shaped, cut made in its rear face, with a dimple and a dot of white paint to fill it, to provide the appearance of a bead front sight. McGivern was known to favor bead or dot front sights and this one probably had a bead at one time, but it has been lost over the years and the paint applied in its place. The revolver's sights are regulated to strike point of aim at 25 yards using a dead-on hold.

As I finished the accuracy tests, Bill reminded me that McGivern had done most of his exhibition shooting from a distance of 15 or 20 feet; typical of the distances at which gunfights occur. At this juncture all we'd proved was that this fine old sixgun is accurate when fired from a rest. Bill wanted to see if it would do as well off-hand, at the distances McGivern, himself, had probably used it. From the 20-foot mark, holes made by four rounds of the Federal wadcutters touched, stringing across 3/4 of an inch in the 10-ring. The fifth round was a called flyer that expanded the group to 1-1/2 inches, with that hole just touching the 10-ring line at about 5 o'clock. Not bad. Of course, the group was shot in careful slow fire, rather than with the speed with which McGivern might have fired it.

Shooting that old Colt was one of the great thrills of my life. Although I think anthropomorphism is silly, anyone who's ever sweet-talked an ailing automobile into the nearest service station can relate to this thought - perhaps, that classic old Colt from a bygone era, that once belonged to one of the greats, might have enjoyed performing as much as I enjoyed its performance.

CHAPTER 17

TEXAS COOPER'S COLTS

With his passing at age 87, in 1951, the Hollywood community and the entertainment industry at large, lost a showman who had actually played a first-hand part in the unfolding of the real history of the Old West. When the West became a little less wild, around the turn of the century, he became a performer in rodeos, Wild West shows and motion pictures. Texas Cooper

Texas Cooper, who billed himself as "The Oldest Cowboy in the Movies," was the genuine article. As lawman and showman, in real life and "reel" life, he portrayed the best of the West. It would be nice to know the story behind the Colt Lightning rifle he's holding in this photo.

was a featured player, a bit player and dress extra in various aspects of show business for almost as long as stories of western adventure had been portrayed on stage and screen to an excited audience.

As his name suggests, Cooper was born in the Lone Star State. The year was 1864. During the closing days of the Civil War, the Confederate States were in serious economic trouble and the prospects for the coming Federal occupation during the years of Reconstruction promised even harder times to come. His parents sought a better and safer life for their infant son and, in a covered wagon, moved the family north to the Indian Territory, that would become The State of Oklahoma. There, they were less likely to encounter the Union troops and carpetbaggers that would cause such hardship to the occupied South in the years ahead.

In early manhood, Texas Cooper became a Deputy U.S. Marshal. But, when the wild and wooly days became more tame, he heard the siren call of the stage and found employment, first as a sharpshooter, later as an announcer, for such entertainment entrepreneurs as Buffalo Bill Cody, Pawnee Bill and the Miller Brothers 101 Ranch Wild West shows.

It was during the time he spent with the 101 Ranch outfit that Cooper placed an order with Colt for a very special pair of revolvers. On May 5, 1913, the custom-made sixguns he'd purchased were shipped, and in short order he took delivery of a pair of exquisitely engraved and silver plated, .45 caliber, Single Action Army revolvers fitted with 5.5-inch barrels. That the pair was engraved is enough to make them noteworthy collectibles, but the silver plating is also an extremely rare finish option. To make them even more unique and desirable, these revolvers were made with smooth bores, to facilitate their intended purpose of shooting shot cartridges at thrown targets. With such revolvers, seemingly uncanny feats of marksmanship were possible.

It would seem that, in spite of the use of shot cartridges, he really was a gunslick, because the Indians who performed with him in the 101 Ranch Show gave Cooper a nickname that testified to his abilities with a sixgun. They called him "Old Centershooter." Unconfirmed evidence of his prowess is seen on the silver dollar that was among his belongings. There is a dent in it, just off center. It's alleged that a bullet struck the tossed coin when he shot it from the air. There's a second silver dollar that he's said to have kept to remind him not to accept things at face value. That coin is gold plated and is said to have been passed to him in lieu of a "double eagle" $20 gold piece, during a poker game.

At the same time as the motion picture industry was beginning to blossom, the Wild West Shows went into decline and, eventually, folded. From the very first, Westerns were among the most popular films, so it seemed natural that Cooper would be drawn to them. In the succeeding decades Cooper appeared in more than 100 "B" Westerns. He was often seen in crowd scenes and sometimes, while wearing a black frock coat and black hat, he played the part of a judge. He's not hard to spot, because his lean frame and exceptional height of more than 6 feet, 6 inches made him stand head and shoulders above most of the other cast members.

With his shoulder length white hair, handlebar mustache and goatee, he resembled Buffalo Bill Cody. In a few films where the character of Cody was a small, ancillary part, he appeared in that role. He made frequent personal appearances at hospitals, orphanages and children's homes playing the same part.

Cooper was often seen with his movie cronies in the Gower Gulch area. Now long gone, that was the part of Hollywood where the wranglers, extras, bit players and character actors whose

Cooper's brass cigarette case is clearly engraved with his name. Most of the accessories that accompany the remaining revolver are similarly identifiable as his belongings.

work was centered about making the old "Oaters" could usually be found. When a casting call went out or a hand was needed to work stock, the studios looked there for the people they needed.

Sometimes he could be observed walking along Hollywood Boulevard with his wife, Nona, who was a midget. The contrast of this exceptionally tall gentleman with the diminutive lady at his side, made the couple hard to miss. Usually dressed in a tan suit of western cut, 10-gallon hat and boots, his outfit was accented with a distinctive silver belt buckle, with matching billet and tip. These items, taken together with his heavy silver pocket watch and brass colored cigarette case, are indicative of the lifestyle of this showman who, after performing in so many films was, near the close of his life, billed as the "The Oldest Cowboy in the Movies."

The dimple just off center on the silver dollar is alleged to have been caused when Cooper shot it in mid-air. A gold-plated silver dollar among the performer's possessions was supposedly passed to him in a poker game, in lieu of a $20 gold piece.

It would appear that Texas Cooper acquired his heavy silver cased pocket watch during his time with the Miller Brothers 101 Ranch Wild West Show.

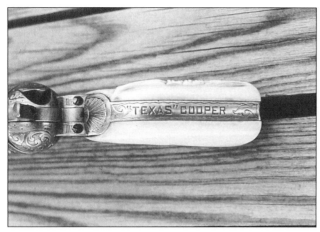

No doubt surrounds the original ownership of the Cooper Colt. It will be just as easy to recognize its missing mate, because his name stands out as prominently on the revolver as the man did in the motion picture scenes in which he played.

Its smoothbore barrel, for shooting shot cartridges at aerial targets, the beautifully executed engraving and very rare silver plate finish would make Texas Cooper's revolver a valuable and desirable collectible, even if its original owner were unknown. That the performer's other belongings remain with it makes it even more interesting.

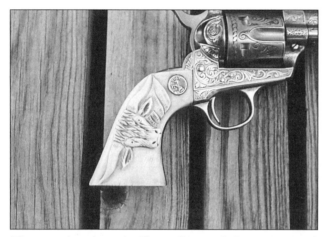

The steer heads on the Texas Cooper Colts were carved on opposite grip panels, so that they could both be seen when worn with a double rig. This was an unusual feature, not often found on matching pairs of revolvers. This one, with its carving on the right, was obviously intended to be worn in the holster on that side.

The name, Texas Cooper, was engraved on the backstrap of each of his revolvers in raised block letters. On their butts, in the same fashion, each is marked, "101 Ranch." The ivory stocks, which have turned a pale golden hue with age, had a carved steerhead on the right grip panel of one revolver and, as the factory records attest, on the left panel of the other. Setting them off nicely are silver colored medallions, set extra deep into the stocks, as was the custom of the period.

The name of the original owner is engraved on the backstrap of both revolvers and the position of the carved steerhead on the left grip panel of one is important. That half of the pair is missing, but will be instantly recognized, even without referring to the serial number, 326962, because of the position of the carving. The gun disappeared from among his effects after Cooper died and it has yet to be discovered. As distinctive as the handgun is, it seems certain to surface one day. The one bearing serial number 326965 is in a private collection, along with the other items belonging to Cooper that remain with it as complimentary accessories. It would be nice to see these lovely old Peacemakers reunited.

CHAPTER 18

THE GUNS OF JOHN WAYNE

Much of the popular view of the Old West centers about the cowboy, the trail drives, and the immigrant wagon trains. The Indian Wars, the Army on the frontier and the legendary lawmen and gunfighters are a part the image, too. But it is the cowboy that dominates the imagination. The National Cowboy Hall of Fame and Western Heritage Center in Oklahoma City captures this spirit, and more, within its walls and its spacious grounds. No one I can think of better represents the image of the American cowboy than John Wayne. And rightfully, he has a wing in this museum that is all his own.

When I visited the place, on the lower level of the main building there was a life-size exhibit of vehicles common to the Old West, such as buggies, a chuck wagon, a stagecoach and a sheepherder's wagon. Several full-size model horses, made of fiberglass, are present to display the saddles and harnesses typical of the frontier. From the sight of the pinto Indian pony picketed on the outskirts, one is given the impression of walking into a town with a curved street.

The lighting suggests that the setting is early evening. Inside the homes and shops the furnishings, utensils and merchandise are, for the most part, from the post-Civil War period. A saloon, newspaper office, doctor's office, general store and the town Marshall's office are among typical establishments represented. Although one can only look from behind rails or glass, it appears almost as though these "premises" are actually in use. But the "gunshop" contains a display of many varieties of rifles and handguns in a more museum-like setting, so that they might be more closely examined by the visitor.

At the end of the "street," a gallery of contemporary paintings hangs in the Western Performers Hall of Fame. Portraits in oil of such motion picture and television favorites as James Arness and the entire cast of Gunsmoke, Gary Cooper, Glenn Ford, Randolph Scott, Joel McCrea, Roy Rogers and Dale Evans, Gene Autry and others greet the eye like a gathering of familiar friends. But there was one missing and conspicuous by his absence; John Wayne.

Leaving that gallery and looking across to the far wall, a portrait of "The Duke," in the Western garb with which he is so closely associated in the minds of his millions of fans, smiles back at the observer. It is mounted at the entrance to a small gallery dedicated solely to the memory of this man, a former trustee of the institution, whose motion picture roles, no matter which

A portrait of John Wayne, as he is best remembered, the All-American cowboy, can be seen hanging at the entrance to the gallery displaying memorabilia of his life and career.

period of history they depicted, typify the concept of the self-reliant rugged individualist, who seeks justice for all.

Many items of John Wayne memorabilia are on display in glass-faced cabinets. The saddle in which he sat so tall, a couple of bowie knives, some personal books on western themes and small bronze sculptures are included. And, of course, there are the guns. A pair of matched flintlock pistols, George Washington Commemoratives, that were a birthday gift from his son, Michael, hung on the wall protected by the glass. Below, on the floor of the cabinet rest a cased pair of ivory-stocked single-action revolvers that look like Colts, but were actually made by the Great Western Arms Company, which went out of business more than 25 years ago. They appear to be the revolvers presented to him by Bill Wilson, the president of the company that made them, in 1954. The museum staff believes them to be those used in John Wayne's final cinematic role, that of the dying gunfighter, J.B. Books, in *The Shootist*.

On the opposite wall of that cabinet are several more items from Wayne's personal firearms collection, including a fine pepperbox and a four-barreled Sharps pistol. A rare revolving rifle of Mexican manufacture has a featured

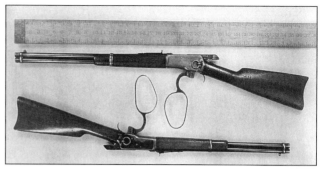

John Wayne used several Model 1892 Winchester rifles with large-bow levers during the course of his film career. Both of these have had their barrels shortened. The top one is 17.25 inches long, while the one below is 19.25 inches in length. Their barrels were shortened from the their original length of 20 inches so they could be spin-cocked with one hand without the barrel striking him in the shoulder as they came around.

place in the display. But the pieces that attract the greatest attention are the .44 caliber Model 92 Winchester carbine with the large loop lever and the ivory stocked SAA Colt .45 revolver, nestled securely in its holster. He wore this rig in so many films that it become Wayne's trademark during the last decades of his film career.

Actually, there are two Winchester carbines on display. One of which is shown separately, in its own case. The Center's Curator of History, Richard Rattenbury, who is the author of the definitive work on Western gunleather, *Packing Iron*, and was gracious enough to allow me to view some of the Center's collection to which the general public doesn't yet have access, told me that there are believed to have been several such rifles used in the course of The Duke's long film career. At least one more is known to be in the Stembridge Armory, a supplier of firearms to the motion picture industry.

One of the reasons for the expansion program under construction during my visit was that there simply wasn't room enough to display all the pieces in the collection. Of Wayne's personal firearms, only a few family gifts and the pieces best known to be associated with him in his public persona were on exhibit. In the Center's storerooms are thousands of artifacts, firearms and works of art representative of the entire history of the West, old and new, that deserve to be shown. It is there that a couple of dozen rifles, shotguns and handguns that John Wayne owned and, in many instances, used for hunting and recreation are stored, awaiting a time when they can be properly exhibited.

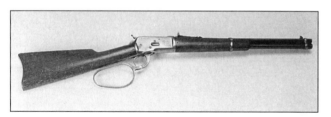

There has been some controversy about the caliber of the rifles Wayne used in his movies. Both of those in the gallery devoted to his memory at the National Cowboy Hall of Fame are chambered for the .44-40 cartridge.

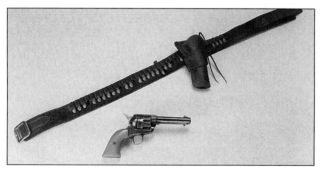

This two-piece ivory-stocked .45 caliber SAA Colt and its much-copied holster, crafted by Arvo Ojala, were worn by John Wayne in most of the Westerns in which he appeared during the last 20 years of his career.

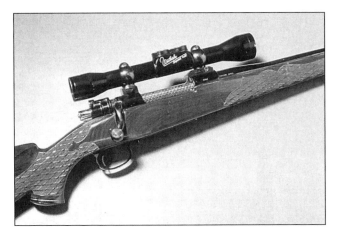

John Wayne's .300 Weatherby Magnum was not for show. It bears evidence of hard use, but good care. This rifle put meat on the table.

During its first year of publication, *Guns Magazine* had a regular feature entitled, "My Favorite Gun." Entertainers, sports and political personalities were featured with their photographs and a brief description of the guns they liked best. John Wayne was among the first invited to participate and, in the October 1955 edition, was quoted as telling the interviewer, "I can say without hesitation that my favorite is my .300 Weatherby Magnum rifle. There are several reasons for this. First, it's the flattest shooting and most accurate hunting rifle I've ever seen. And when it comes to killing power, it's pure dynamite. The workmanship and beauty of my Weatherby make it one of my most prized possessions." In the course of his career it was the only firearm of which I'm aware that John Wayne officially endorsed in advertisements.

In the process of photographing The Duke's guns, his .300 Weatherby was one of several that I had the opportunity to handle personally. It's an early one, made up on a Mauser action, with a claw extractor. It shows the effects of honest wear, but good care. It's clear from examining it that the gun is no wall-hanger. That rifle put meat on the table.

Just as obviously, that was not the case with an Omega III rifle chambered for the 7mm Remington Magnum cartridge, on which a Leupold scope is mounted. The rifle is profusely engraved and inlaid in gold. There are some who would consider taking such a rifle afield, but it seems that John Wayne was not among them. It remains as new.

A couple of Browning shotguns caught my attention. One is a 12-gauge Auto-5 that's seen long, hard use. The other is a fine Superposed

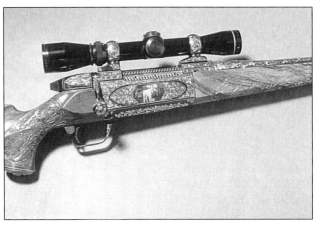

A gift to John Wayne, this richly embellished Omega II rifle is chambered for the 7mm Remington Magnum cartridge and topped with a Leupold scope. It's a worthy tribute. However, the hand-carved stock, engraving and gold inlay make it too valuable to take afield.

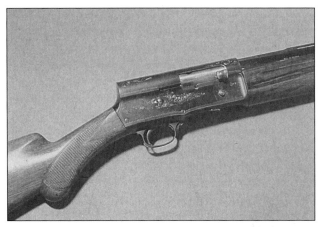

John Wayne's Browning A-5 shotgun has been well cared for. But with close examination, you can tell that it's spent many long hours in a duck or goose blind.

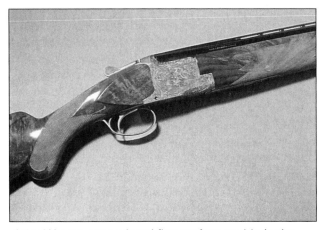

John Wayne appreciated fine craftsmanship in the firearms he chose for his own use. This Browning Superposed shotgun is indicative of how seriously he took his upland game shooting.

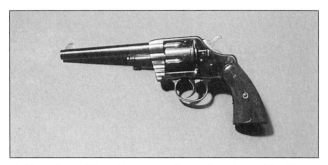

A New Army/New Navy revolver, chambered for the .38 Long Colt cartridge, this piece from the Wayne collection is very unusual. It has a superb set of Fleur-de-Lis checkered rosewood stocks and a bead front sight that appear to be original.

Full coverage engraving adorns this single-action revolver from the John Wayne collection, but it's a copy made in the 1950's by Great Western, not a Colt.

Over/Under. Both are Belgian made. From their condition, it's clear that Wayne took his wing-shooting seriously.

There are a number of commemorative handguns in the collection, many of which were presented to him by individuals and groups. One of the nicest is a .45 caliber Colt SAA with 7-1/2-inch barrel, engraved, ivory-stocked, with dual gold band inlays at the muzzle and a single one at the rear of the cylinder. It was presented to him near the end of his career by *Guns Magazine*, honoring him as its "Man of the Year." It's in a ruby red plush fabric lined display case. Below it within the case, are six cartridges, lined up in a row, beneath which are the titles of some of the movies for which John Wayne is best remembered, engraved on a brass plate. They include: *Stagecoach, Red River, She Wore a Yellow Ribbon, The Quiet Man, Sands of Iwo Jima* and *True Grit*.

Other handguns include a cased 3-gun set of Browning Renaissance pistols and a New Army/New Navy Colt revolver chambered for the .38 Long Colt cartridge that wears a beautiful set of

A rare, flat-top target SAA chambered for the .44 Russian cartridge, it has what appears to be a replacement barrel, because it is marked, (BISLEY MODEL). It's another one of many firearms presented to John Wayne during his career.

original fleur-de-lis checkered rosewood grips and has a bead front sight of the Paine-type.

One of the most curious pieces in the collection is a scarce flat-top target SAA with full civilian blue, ivory stocks with a carved eagle and shield and 7-1/2-inch barrel. What's unusual about it is that the revolver has a standard grip-frame, but the barrel is made for the .44 Russian cartridge and is clearly rollmarked in the fashion of the period, (BISLEY MODEL). It's unlikely, but possible, that the barrel is original to the handgun.

A visit to The National Cowboy Hall of Fame and Western Heritage Center is worth doing for its own sake. The art, the history, the weapons, the tools of every day life, the grandeur of the landscape and the people who are a part of the heritage of the West all come together in this one remarkable place. But, John Wayne has become an American icon and the opportunity to see the guns and other belongings associated with him in his personal life and movie career are certain to be the subjects of greatest interest to many.

My own love of all things Western began when I was a child, living in El Paso, Texas, in the early 1940s. Back then, cowboys - real working cowboys - were a part of everyday life and I was fascinated by everything about them. Nearly six decades later that interest is in no way diminished. If anything, it has expanded to include all facets of the history and settlement of the Old West. My perspective is certainly now more realistic; partially as a result of study of its history and in some measure from having spent much of my youth and early adult life living in many places throughout the west, working on several ranches and competing in rodeos.

The history of the settlement of the American West is reckoned by most people as the period following the end of the American Civil War until the end of the 19th century. Actually, it began with the early Spanish explorers and the transition into the modern world wasn't complete until about 1930.

The romantic view of the Old West, nurtured at the bosom of decades of dime novels, followed in succession by Hollywood movies, radio dramas and, later, by television, is not entirely without historical foundation. To be sure, the Old West had its share of opportunists, cheats, thieves and villains. But in contrast, many of its settlers were peaceful, honorable people with an idealistic view of the world. These were fiercely independent men and women who believed in principled behavior and would not tolerate the dishonorable actions of the lawless element. It was a time and place where justice was swift and a man's word was his bond. To this day, many western folk do without legal contracts in business, relying on a man's handshake as all the guarantee needed in their dealings. It was and is a way of life many people would love to preserve.

To do so, the late Kansas City businessman, Chester A. Reynolds, envisioned the heritage center. The idea came to him during a visit to the Will Rogers Museum at Claremore, Oklahoma, in 1956. The cowboy entertainer had been one of the most popular humorists of his generation, but there was so much more to be told of the story of the West. By 1958, Reynolds' idea had begun to blossom. A private, non-profit organization had been established and it was declared a National Memorial. The institution opened to the public in 1965.

Located a few blocks from Exit 143 off Interstate 40 in the northern part of Oklahoma City, in nearly the geographical center of the United States, its sprawling complex of grounds and buildings house some of the finest examples of period and contemporary western art and artifacts. It includes galleries devoted to subjects such as the myth and reality of the American West, rodeo sports, Native American art and culture, exhibits of old and modern western photographs and, of course, the firearms of the Old West.

Naturally, it was the latter that attracted my greatest attention. The quality and variety of firearms and associated equipment and accessories to go with them is truly impressive. Included are representative specimens of civilian and military firearms dating from the first explorations of the Rockies by the Mountain Men who trapped beaver, to the Texas War for Independence and the U.S. War with Mexico that followed. Those of the Civil War, the westward migration, the cattle drives the range wars, Indian wars and the gunfighters and lawmen are also prominently displayed.

Arms, uniforms and equipment used by the military during and after the Civil War are contrasted with items that saw action in the hands of the Plains Indian Tribes that defended their way of life against a steadily increasing encroachment of settlers on their lands.

The products of most of the firearms manufacturers of the period are on display. Many were actually the property of some of the historical figures we remember well, today. Nearly all are excellent representative examples of their type. Given the treatment of the subject by Hollywood, it's easy to gather the impression that there were only two makers whose firearms saw service of any note on the western frontier, Colt and Winchester. The products of both manufacturers were, of course, very popular. But those of Marlin, Merwin & Hulbert, Remington, Smith & Wesson and many others were there in the thousands.

Colt Single Action Army revolvers get most of the attention on the screen, but there are many examples of double-action handguns being chosen in their place. And, as the 19th century gave way to the 20th, semi-automatics began to come into vogue.

Lever-action repeating rifles would seem to have been the universal choice of westerners, but single shots from Remington, Springfield Armory, Sharps and others were just as likely to be chosen. By the 1880s, there were some slide-action repeaters available, too. And, as the new century dawned, semi-automatic rifles became popular with many shooters.

Then, of course, there is the leather. The means by which a man carried his rifle on horseback or his handgun on his person are more diverse than the firearms themselves. There are slings and saddle scabbards; hip holsters, shoulder holsters and pommel holsters to be carried across a saddle. Some are military issue, others were mass made in great quantity in eastern factories. There are also those made by private leather craftsmen in small shops throughout the west. A few were home-made leather goods crafted by the men who carried those guns. They are all interesting and worthy of your time.

This place is a shrine to the cowboy way and anyone with even a remote interest in the legends of the Old West should schedule a visit.

Chapter 19

THE MYSTERY OF THE LONG-FLUTE TREASURE

When production of Colt's Double Action Army Model of 1878 ended in 1905, the company was left with about 1,500 surplus cylinders. At some time during the next decade some bright person realized that by simply milling the appropriate notches into their sides they could be installed in the still popular Single Action Army Model P. The necessary work was accomplished and it was made so. This resulted in a considerable savings in manufacturing costs, for which I hope the individual responsible was suitably rewarded.

The recycled M-1878 cylinders began appearing on newly made Peacemakers in 1915, but at that time no one paid attention to this minor change from the norm. However, succeeding generations of Colt collectors have been provided with a rare, interesting and valuable variation as a result. The flutes milled into the sides of the discontinued revolvers were 5/16 of an inch longer than those of the usual SAA Army.

On October 21, 1918, Colt SAA revolver number 331092 was shipped from the Hartford plant to the Imperial Valley Hardware Company of Los Angeles, California, for their customer, the William Hoegee Company. It may be the most decorated of the "long flute" Peacemakers ever made.

This beautiful six-

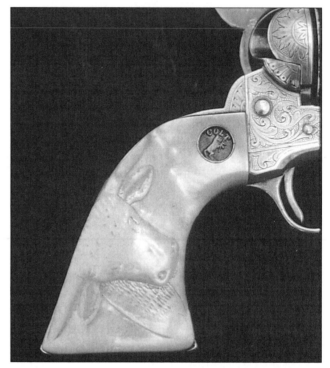

An ox head was hand-carved into the Long Flute Treasure's right stock panel. Mother-of-pearl is very fragile and seldom survives intact as long as this specimen has.

gun is chambered for the .45 Colt cartridge, as are most of the long flute SAAs, and has a barrel length of 4-5/8 inches. One of the rarest of finish materials, silver plating, covers it. Elegantly engraved in the style of Cuno Helfricht, there is every reason to believe that it was embellished by the hand of that master craftsman, himself.

Mother-of-pearl stocks, with gold colored medallions are the crowning glory of this exquisite revolver. The right panel sports a hand-carved ox head.

Beautiful to behold, this exquisitely engraved long flute SAA, silver plated and stocked with hand-carved mother-of-pearl, was obviously intended to be presented to someone held in high esteem.

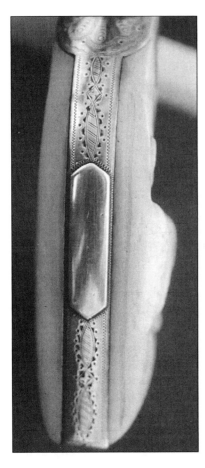

The inscription plate remains blank. The reason for this will probably remain forever a mystery.

The blend of scrollwork, stippling and crosshatch engraving found on this revolver are characteristic of the work of Cuno Helfricht's shop. Often, in establishments such as his, an employee did most, if not all the work under the guidance of the master. In this instance the work was so well executed that it was probably done by the meistergraver, himself.

In the early 1970s, the Imperial Valley Hardware Company was contacted in an effort to learn more about the revolver's origins. But, according to a company spokesman, the firm had no record of it, nor could they shed any light on William Hoegee Co. or its personnel. Neither firm is listed in the current edition of the Los Angeles Yellow Pages. Even if either or both firms remained in business there is no reason to expect that they would have kept the records pertaining to that transaction for more than 80 years.

It's unfortunate that so little is known of this very special revolver's history, because the raised presentation plate on its backstrap was never inscribed. Factory records add nothing to our knowledge of its intended recipient. We can only speculate as to whom that may have been. Perhaps it was intended for the personal use of the one who ordered it, but if so, why was it not marked?

If it was to be a gift, the same question arises. Could it have been an oversight? That seems hardly likely in view of the care that must have been taken in ordering it. Might it have been intended for an early silent movie cowboy star fallen from the good graces of the studio? Perhaps an "idol" to whom it was to be presented was found to have "feet of clay." Could the person have died before receiving this award? No one knows.

The revolver remains unfired after more than 80 years. It stands as mute testimony to the craftsman's art and the esteem in which its intended recipient was held. The identity of that person is lost in the mists of time and will probably remain forever a mystery.

CHAPTER 20

THE CONCEPTION OF THE COLT SCOUT

Following World War II Colt decided to shelve the Single Action Army revolver, but within a decade the success of Ruger's Blackhawk series had convinced the Colt hierarchy that there was, indeed, a market for their old handgun. When it was reintroduced to the marketplace in 1956 the reception for the 2nd Generation SAA was overwhelming.

In addition, Ruger's Single Six, chambered for the ubiquitous .22 Long Rifle cartridge, was so popular that the powers at Hartford felt a need to enter the fray with a single-action .22 of their own. In the physical development stages as early as 1955, Colt's Frontier Scout

This Frontier Scout revolver remains in excellent original condition. Most have seen hard use. They aren't target revolvers, but they can be lots of fun to shoot and some are surprisingly accurate.

became a reality to the shooting public in 1957. However, this is not the beginning of the story.

Several years ago I found a 3-ring loose-leaf binder at a gun show that was labeled with the familiar Rampant Colt and bore the title, Colt Marketing Methods. Picking it up, I began to look through it and discovered it to be the personal notebook of a Colt employee of the wartime era, one E.P. Colbath. The mimeographed notes and memos within revealed some of the innermost secrets of Colt's wartime corporate history, so I bought it.

A few days later I phoned Marty Huber, who was still Colt's Historian at the time. He remembered Mr. Colbath well. I was told that he was the firm's Chief Inspector during the World War II period. No one would have been in a better position than he to know what was going on in the firm during those busy days.

Among the memoranda in the binder was one dated June 5, 1943, that described in intricate detail a proposal for the manufacture of a .22 caliber version of the Single Action Army revolver. There was, even then, nothing new about a .22 Peacemaker. As early as 1883 Colt had chambered the full-sized SAA for the diminutive round. Mr. Colbath noted that he had seen, literally, hundreds of requests for such a revolver from the shooting public since the late 1920s.

As it was described in this memorandum, the new revolver was to be built as far as possible along the lines of the existing SAA in order to economize on new tooling and to cater to the sentimental attachment the shooting public had toward the Peacemaker.

No attempt was to be made to turn this into a target handgun. It was to be a working gun for the outdoorsman, farmer or rancher who would carry it on a regular basis. Fixed sights were considered appropriate for such a revolver.

Some versions of the standard Frontier Scout revolver were furnished with plastic imitation staghorn grips. The earliest serious consideration was for an imitation ivory stock with a steer head or other Western-style motif to be molded into it.

Investment casting was recommended for the frame, while a 6-inch barrel length was to be standard. The hammer was to be made with a lower profile, similar to that of the Bisley Model revolver. The only finish to be available on the new .22 was to have been nickel plating.

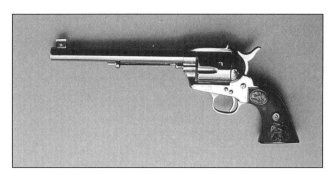

Colt Single Action Army revolvers were made in .22 caliber as far back as 1883. This specimen was made in 1884 and has been expertly restored to original condition.

The box in which it would be packaged was to have a scene reminiscent of the Old West printed on it. A name, such as Frontier or Peacemaker, associating it with that period of history was to be applied to the handgun.

It's interesting that there was additional consideration given to the possibility of chambering it for a centerfire cartridge; namely, the .22 Hornet (5.6X35R). The reason for this is that there are times when a farmer or rancher working from horseback or the seat of a tractor may need to eliminate such animals as badgers or coyotes. Such species are sometimes better taken with a round more potent than the .22 long rifle. Although a centerfire Scout was never made, many were provided with an auxiliary cylinder chambered for the .22 Winchester Magnum Rimfire round, which was meant to serve the same purpose as the originally proposed .22 Hornet.

The revolver, as it was actually made, is not very different from the one that was under consideration more than a decade before. But it ended up, for the most part, as an inexpensive version of the SAA for people who wanted to play cowboy, during the era of the "Adult Westerns" that dominated television in the late 1950s and early '60s. It made for a good informal target revolver and something the would-be Wyatt Earp or "Wild Bill" Hickok could play with; but it never quite qualified as a working gun for most outdoorsmen.

There are six basic variations with four barrel length options, so the basic .22 Scout/Peacemaker/New Frontier variations don't present much of a challenge to the collector in their standard versions. But there were at least 60 Commemorative variations of the Scout revolver available that can provide that challenge and make for an attractive display.

CHAPTER 21

THE GUNS OF TOM MIX

I was probably about 9 or 10 years of age when I found out that Tom Mix had died. When I later learned that it had happened about a year before I was born, it didn't seem to help much. I still mourned him. I'd read Tom Mix comic books and seen some of his movies on after-school TV. One of the local stations showed the old "B" Westerns of the 1930s and early '40s every weekday afternoon, and some of Mix's later films appeared often. He ranked right up there with Gene Autry, Roy Rogers and Hopalong Cassidy in the hearts and minds of the kids in my neighborhood.

That's the way it had been for the more than 30 years of his movie career, and his popularity continued for many years after his tragic death in an automobile accident, in 1940. It happened as he was driving his 1937 Cord (sic) automobile through Arizona, on his way to Hollywood. The crash occurred when he encountered a road crew near the town of Florence. Swerving to avoid the workmen, he crashed into an embankment. A piece of his heavy metal luggage, stacked in the back seat, flew forward, striking him in the back of the head and breaking his neck. He was dead in moments, but he continued to live on for years in the memories of millions of his fans.

A lot of hyperbole from the Hollywood press led the public to believe that Mix was a true Western hero, born in a log cabin near El Paso, Texas (an area singularly devoid of trees suited for making such a structure) and had been a hero of the Spanish-American War, the Boxer Rebellion in China and the Philippine Insurrec-

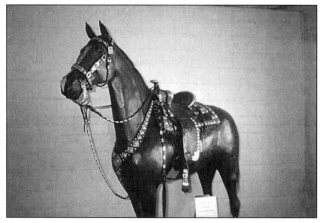

Tony, Tom Mix's horse, was nearly as popular with audiences as the actor. A full-size fiberglass model of the animal, outfitted with a parade saddle, bridle, chest strap and martingale all adorned with silver, has a prominent place at the entrance to the Tom Mix Museum in Dewey, Oklahoma.

Nickel plated and stocked with genuine mother-of-pearl, this pair of Colt Official Police .38 Special revolvers was frequently worn by Mix in his movies. The metal and the stocks show a lot of wear and scuff marks from hard use during filming.

tion. He was even supposed to have seen action during the Boer War (on both sides). There were further claims that he'd been a Sheriff in Colorado, a Texas Ranger and a U.S. Marshall.

The truth of the matter is a bit less melodramatic. He was actually born in the East, in 1880, near a place called Mix Run, in the area of DuBois, Pennsylvania. His Army career had been exemplary. He earned First Sergeant's stripes during his four years of service, which began in 1898, but his assignments had been in Delaware and he saw no combat.

He was discharged from the Army in 1902 and, by 1904, Mix had fulfilled a life-long ambition and moved on to Oklahoma. In Guthrie and Oklahoma City he worked as a bartender, a prize fighter and athletic coach. By 1912 he was in Dewey, Oklahoma and became a Deputy Town Marshall. That was the extent of his law enforcement career. The Texas Ranger and U.S. Marshall's commissions that bear his name were honorary and presented during the height of his film career. The closest he ever came to getting involved in a real gunfight occurred in 1924, when his fourth wife, Victoria Forde, shot him during a domestic squabble.

One of the skills for which Mix was best known was his horsemanship. His father had been a coachman and he grew up riding and training horses. He used those skills as a performer with the Mulhall and the Miller Brothers 101 Ranch Wild West Shows. He was spotted by a movie company filming in the area around Dewey and was hired to wrangle stock for the film crew. He did some stunt work, then a few walk-on parts followed. His chiseled features and superb horsemanship led to featured roles and, eventually, his popularity began to overshadow that of the reigning king of movie cowboy heroes, William S. Hart.

Much of the reason that he became so popular was that he was a consummate showman. While Hart was striving for realism, Tom Mix used fancy tricks and flashy clothes to catch the attention of his audience. It worked. Hand-tooled saddles, bridles and gunbelts graced Mix and his horse, Tony. His clothes were so fancy that no working cowboy or self-respecting lawman of the Old West would have worn such flamboyant gear, but he set the tone for a generation of cowboy heroes to come. He was there to entertain, not to teach history.

Although his personal life was fraught with the excesses for which Hollywood is infamous, his screen persona stressed moral, upright behavior. For more than 30 years he put out the message to millions of kids that good guys don't smoke, swear or drink liquor. Yet, he did all of that and more. He was also married five times.

You can't tell it from watching his films, but Tom Mix appears to have known something of shooting and had a genuine appreciation for fine firearms. He seems, also, to have begun collecting them long before it became common practice. There are several that are known to have belonged to him in the museum that honors his memory in Dewey. On film, his sixgun handling looks more like chopping kindling with a hatchet than something one might do with a handgun to hit a target.

If you watch closely, it appears that he often used Single Action Army Colts, the traditional Western movie sixguns, for close-ups, but switched to double-action revolvers for the action scenes. That way he could shoot faster, alternating fire from one hand to another. It's

Tom Mix is said to have had difficulty operating single-action revolvers as quickly as a movie hero would be expected to do, so he substituted double-action Colts, like the Official Police revolver he's using in this film still.

been suggested that he simply didn't have the manual dexterity to use the single-action revolvers as quickly as his audiences would expect. He was one of the original Hollywood two-gun men, as well. Because he usually did his own stunts, until age began to make that a bit more challenging, he was also one of the first to carry rubber guns in his holsters during fight scenes and when jumping off horses. They didn't hurt as much as the real ones when he fell on one.

There's no provenance to go with any of the guns in the Mix collection. So, how they were acquired and what personal significance some of them may have had is pure speculation. But we do know something about a few of them. There are two matched pairs of nickel-plated, mother-of-pearl stocked, .38 Special Colt Official Police revolvers, with 6-inch barrels. One set, apparently used for personal appearances, has factory medallions inset in the mother-of-pearl stocks. The other pair has plain pearl stocks and the guns are well scarred and scuffed. These seem to have been used hard during actual filming.

A third pair of DA Colts is a set of blued Officer's Model Match revolvers that also bear 6-inch barrels and are fitted with scrimshawed ivory stocks. These seem to have been used most for trick shooting exhibitions.

A nickel-plated .32 caliber Smith & Wesson Hand Ejector, with a 4-inch barrel, round butt, pearl stocks and excellent scroll engraving that appears factory original, graces the collection. With it are two other S&Ws. One is a .38-44 caliber New Model Number 3 target revolver, in superb condition. It was originally set up for use with a shoulder stock, but that desirable accessory is missing. The other is one of the very first of the .357 Magnums, the so called, "Registered Model." The .357 is blued, has a 6-inch barrel

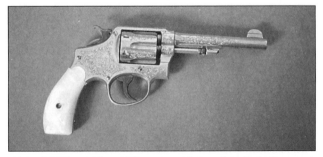

This S&W .32 Hand Ejector, with its nickel plating and pearl stocks has been tastefully engraved. It would be nice to know the uses to which Tom Mix put it, but no information about that is available at the museum.

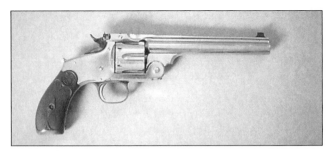

A rare Smith & Wesson New Model #3 target revolver chambered for the .38-44 cartridge. This item from the Tom Mix collection is set up for the attachment of a shoulder stock. Unfortunately, that highly desirable accessory is missing.

One of S&Ws early "Registered" .357 Magnums, this revolver is said to have been carried regularly by Tom Mix in a shoulder holster. For many years people have thought the stocks on it are ivory. Actually, they are wood, painted white.

and is thought to have been chosen for personal defense and often carried by Mix in a shoulder holster. On close examination, what appear to be carved ivory stocks on it are actually wood, painted white, with a red rectangular background painted behind Mix's name to make it stand out.

Tom Mix was known to have had a pair of SAA Colts in a fancy, hand-tooled, Bohlin rig that Lou Costello, of the comedy team, Abbott and Costello, owned at the time of his own death. What may have happened to them is anybody's guess, but they're probably a prized part of someone's private collection.

A Colt Bisley Model .45 with 4-5/8-inch barrel that he used in his last film, *The Miracle Rider*, which was released in 1936, is in the museum collection. Its finish is worn to gray metal and the gutta percha stocks are worn smooth from handling. It's a far cry from the more ornate six-guns he usually used on screen.

A mother-of-pearl stocked 7-1/2-inch SAA .45 and a .38-40 of the same barrel length, wearing

Not the fancy sort of sixgun normally associated with Tom Mix, this well worn .45 caliber Bisley Model was used by him in his last film, The Miracle Rider.

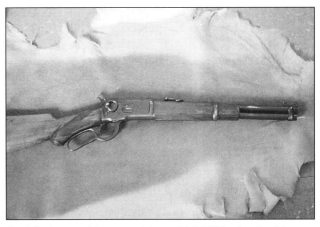

Its label says this smoothbore M-92 Winchester Trapper's Model, owned by Mix, is .44 caliber. However, the barrel is marked .38-40. It would be interesting to learn why the saddle ring was placed on the wrong side.

A custom Mannlicher Schoenauer rifle that Mix used for hunting is shown here with a Marlin lever-action .410 shotgun. Built on the Model 1893 rifle action, showmen liked them because they gave the audience the impression that the performer was demonstrating extraordinary marksmanship with a rifle, while they were actually making easy shots with a scattergun.

plastic staghorn-style stocks common to that era, are the only traditional cowboy-style sixshooters in the display. There's no indication of what significance they may have had in the actor's life.

A lever-action Marlin .410-gauge shotgun, that looks like a rifle to the casual observer, and several Model 92 Winchesters, one of which is a smoothbore (marked .38 WCF, but erroneously labeled in the display as being .44 caliber), appear to have been among the pieces he used for trick shooting exhibitions during personal appearances. Such firearms were often used in those days as much for the sake of safety, when shooting in crowded arenas and stadiums, as for the greater likelihood that the shooter would hit what appeared to the audience to be a difficult target.

During his lifetime, Mix was known to have given several of his personal guns to friends and associates, but when he died his attorney, Ivon Parker, received his personal effects, in accordance with the performer's will. Parker ignored the onslaught of requests for those items by collectors and fans. Everything was kept intact until his own death. But at that time, the lawyer's sons and nephews saw the collection in terms of dollar signs. When Mix's belongings were made available for sale, the people of Dewey, Oklahoma raised the necessary funds to purchase the lot and placed it in the museum that honors the showman's memory.

Today, the collection is owned and controlled by the Oklahoma Historical Society, to which we are indebted for permitting us to photograph the collection, and it continues to be housed and displayed in Dewey. In spite of there being little information regarding how Mix came to own and use most of the items on display, many are worthwhile for their own sake and the collection is well worth a look. If you happen to be in the neighborhood, drop in. You'll enjoy the experience.

CHAPTER 22

THE SAA COLT'S 20TH CENTURY RIVALS

Between 1900 and 1920, Colt produced about 146,000 Single Action Army revolvers. During the next two decades, only 19,000 were made and in the last five of those years output of that model trickled down to just 1,800 units. During the depression era of the 1930s as few as 100 were made in some years. Part of the reason for such a radical decline was that many people simply couldn't afford the price tag of about $36. Those who had the available cash often opted for something more modern, like Colt's Official Police revolver or the bigger New Service. The latter was a brawny, rugged handgun that could be had chambered for any of the big cartridges for which the SAA was then being made, but in a more modern, double-action design.

Following World War II, Colt quickly made the transition back to servicing the civilian market. Nearly the entire production output of the war years had gone to military contracts. The needs of law enforcement agencies were next in priority to be met. The civilian market had done without for nearly six years and consumers were hungry for the products Colt and other firearms manufacturers had to offer.

Taking careful note of the production figures for all their various handgun models in the years immediately preceding the war, Colt's management overhauled the product line. Gone were the M-1908 .25 Auto, the Model M .32 and .380 ACPs and the New Service. They were all very expensive to make, requiring a lot of hand fitting on the part of the assemblers. The Single Action Army revolver was especially so and it was an anachronism, dating

When WWII came to a close Colt dropped several popular handguns from their catalog. Some, such as the Model M, were cut because labor costs made them too expensive to produce. Others, like the SAA were considered obsolete designs.

back, at that time, more than 70 years. After all, Colt's executives thought, what shooter in his right mind would want to carry such an antique in the "Atomic Age"?

That decision probably made good sense in 1946, but in less than a decade things would change. The economic strife of the pre-war years had given way to a level of general prosperity that few could have foreseen in the period during and immediately following the war. People had

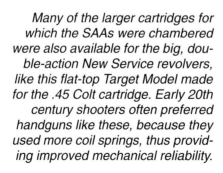

Many of the larger cartridges for which the SAAs were chambered were also available for the big, double-action New Service revolvers, like this flat-top Target Model made for the .45 Colt cartridge. Early 20th century shooters often preferred handguns like these, because they used more coil springs, thus providing improved mechanical reliability.

jobs and they had money. They also had more leisure time available to them than ever before. Hunters and target shooters could pursue their interests with greater frequency than ever before. What's more, they had television.

Invented in the 1920s, television had first been a curiosity, then a toy for the "idle rich." TV receivers were expensive, even after the war, but by 1950 everyone had to have one. Within another five years nearly everyone did. Much of what they saw on it, especially in the late afternoon and early evening hours, were the "B" Westerns of the 1930s and '40s; some of the stars, such as Roy Rogers and Gene Autry, had new half-hour series geared toward the younger members of the audience. By the mid-1950s, the "Adult Western" was a fixture in prime time and adult interest in the firearms used by the stars of these features was heightened.

Colt didn't really jump into reintroduction of the SAA, they were pushed. It actually started with the introduction by Sturm, Ruger & Co. of the .22 caliber Single Six revolver, in 1953. This was quickly followed by the Blackhawk, first chambered for the .357 Magnum. Ruger's single-action revolvers took advantage of the most modern manufacturing techniques, including investment casting of key parts, structural aluminum for others, and the use of music wire springs to increase functional reliability.

All the Blackhawks were equipped with fully adjustable rear sights and made with frames that are slightly larger than that of the old Colts, which gave them the strength to handle the most powerful of the modern Magnum cartridges. In the years to follow, Ruger would add chamberings in the

Ruger's .22 caliber Single Six revolver was rugged, reasonably accurate and relatively inexpensive. It appealed to many buyers who wanted a Western style revolver, but couldn't afford to pay the collector prices the original pre-war SAAs were beginning to command.

Blackhawk for the modern .44 and .41 Magnum rounds and for more traditional loads, like the .45 Colt and others. Tough and practical as the Ruger single-action revolvers were, their look and handling qualities were still so much like that of Colt's SAA that they held great appeal for many Western buffs. They were also very practical revolvers for the outdoorsman and sportsman in need of a rugged, reliable handgun in the field.

By 1956, Colt could stand the pressure no longer. The Single Action Army was reintroduced in that year, to the accompaniment of much fanfare. However, its price was about half again as much as that of the Ruger offering. While Colt's sales of the old thumb buster were gratifying, Ruger's never missed a beat. Many shooters considered the Blackhawk a compromise. They could pay a lower price for a sixgun made for a modern cartridge, yet still have their "cowboy" gun.

Colt returned the SAA to regular production a decade after dropping it, because popular demand, coupled with the market share enjoyed by Ruger's similar revolver, made it an economic necessity.

Ruger Blackhawk revolvers were first chambered for the .357 Magnum cartridge. For its time, this was the perfect balance between available power and cost efficiency in terms of ammunition. These handguns could be used for serious purposes, yet allowed for inexpensive practice when loaded with .38 Special ammunition.

The Blackhawk's larger frame made it possible to chamber it for more powerful cartridges than Colt's SAA could safely handle. The .44 Magnum was the first to follow the .357. Immediately after the .41 Magnum's introduction in S&W's Model 56 and 57 N-frame revolvers, Ruger began making Blackhawks like this one in .41 Magnum.

Not long after the reappearance of the SAA Colt, a California entrepreneur, Bill Wilson, using the corporate name of Hy Hunter, contracted with a West German manufacturer to make a clone of the Peacemaker that he called the Great Western revolver. So close a copy was it that parts were often interchangeable. However, quality varied considerably. Nevertheless, initial sales were excellent. One could have a much more Colt-like revolver than the Ruger, at about half the cost of the Hartford-made product.

Hollywood took careful note. The Colts that had been in the studio armories for decades had become valuable antiques, commanding significant collector premiums. How well the new copies could shoot was of no significance whatever, because in the movies and on television they were used exclusively with blanks.

It may surprise many fans to know that during the late 1950s, and for the next couple of decades, some of their favorite Western stars used Great Western revolvers to accomplish their cinematic exploits. Notable among these was James Arnes who played Matt Dillon in *Gunsmoke*. Even John Wayne carried a Great Western in some of his features. However, the well-worn revolver with the yellowed ivory stocks that was seen on his hip in so many of his movies of the 1960s and '70s really is a Colt of 1890s vintage.

A number of other single-action revolvers generally considered Western-style came to the market in the 1960s and 1970s. J.P. Sauer & Son was one of the more popular makers. In the 1970s, Interarms imported Hammerli's Virginian revolvers. While sixguns like these may have something of the traditional look, they are bigger and comparatively ungainly. Few owners really considered them reasonable substitutes for the real thing.

Since the 1980s some really good SAA clones have come into production. Most are made in Italy. The Jaeger revolvers marketed as the Dakota in the U.S. by EMF Corp, of Santa Anna, Calif., have been very popular and are reasonably good shooters. More recently, they've been marketing the Hartford Model revolvers, made for them by Armi San Marco. These are exact replicas of the 2nd Generation SAA Colt that are made with parts completely interchangeable with the originals.

Better known are the Uberti Cattleman and Armi San Marco's own line of SAAs. These com-

Uberti's Cattleman revolvers look, feel and operate so much like Colt's 1st Generation SAAs that many shooters prefer them for use on the range. The difference in price between the clone and a new 3rd Generation original is dramatic, but the difference in performance is usually negligible.

Demand for a Ruger single-action revolver, legal for use in the Traditional Class for Cowboy Action competition, led the firm to produce a fixed-sight version of the Blackhawk. Retaining all the improved strength and mechanical qualities of the adjustable sight revolver, the Vaquero looks more like it belongs in the 19th century than the 21st.

Jeremiah and Prairie Rose (John and Louise Downing), posed with their Ruger revolvers during a "Western Action" shoot, as such competitions are called in Australia. They appear prepared for a stroll through Dodge City, not Adelaide.

panies have gone to great pains to make quality reproductions of Colt's 1st Generation revolvers and those of their principal rivals of the 19th century. Priced significantly lower than a modern SAA Colt, these clones are of excellent quality and some will shoot groups that are the equal of anything ever shipped from Hartford.

On the other hand, they sometimes require some tweaking to get them to perform to their potential. Usually their lockwork is beautifully timed. Cylinder rotation almost always indexes perfectly. Triggers, however, are usually in need of smoothing and lightening in order to obtain optimum performance. Sometimes headspace needs to be adjusted to allow for use with the full range of cartridge makes appropriate to the caliber involved, particularly if the revolver has dual cylinders to accommodate such combinations as the .44 Special/.44-40 and the .45 Colt/.45 ACP.

The most frequent, though by no means universal, requirement in order to make the Armi San Marcos and Ubertis shoot to point of aim is for the front sight to be trimmed and/or bent to put them properly on target. This is often just as necessary with original Colts of all generations, so the Italian replicas shouldn't be faulted on that basis.

Even if minor faults require the professional intervention of a skilled gunsmith in order to make them perform to their potential, the difference in the cost between the Italian revolvers and a genuine Colt can make the effort very much worthwhile.

Back to Ruger. The standard Blackhawk revolvers, while perfectly suited to whatever reasonable purpose to which the handgunner may put them, have one drawback. They are relegated to the Modern Class in Cowboy Action competitions. The competitor participating in the Traditional Class must use a revolver with fixed sights. He may adjust point of impact by modifying the front sight or filing a wider channel in the rear sight, but sights that can be changed with the simple twist of a screwdriver simply don't qualify as traditional.

Missing out on a significant portion of any area of the firearms market doesn't seem to sit well at Ruger, so in 1993 they introduced the Vaquero. Mechanically identical with any of the current crop of Blackhawks, they have fixed sights and can be had in either brightly polished stainless steel, which looks similar to a nickel finish, or with the frame in case hardened colors and the rest blued. To make things even better for the traditionalist, they introduced a Bisley version of the Vaquero in 1997. The Vaqueros are chambered for the .357 Magnum, .44-40, .44 Magnum and .45 Colt cartridges.

With the rapid and widespread rise of the Cowboy Action Shooting events, there are, just as in the Old West, those shootists who prefer replicas of the Remington types and the recently introduced Schofields. Much of this trend is in keeping with the effort among participants to maintain, insofar as possible, the illusion of authenticity. There is nearly as much variety in armament seen at End of Trail as there was in Dodge City and Tombstone in the 1880s. This is as it should be. But, as long as the replica makers are about it, how about doing up some Merwin & Hulberts?

CHAPTER 23

STURM, RUGER'S SINGLE-ACTION .22 REVOLVERS

Nearly all Cowboy Action competition is done with center-fire calibers, but .22s of similar design offer relatively inexpensive practice. In more practical terms, Western-style firearms are just as useful as tools of the outdoorsman at the dawn of the 21st century as they were 100 years ago. Since their introduction, Ruger's single-action .22s, the Single Six and the Bearcat have been among the most popular.

When the Single Six was first introduced, in 1953, there were plenty of semi-automatic pistols and double-action revolvers chambered for the .22 long rifle, but single-action types were all but unknown. All the .22 handguns made by the better manufacturers, save Ruger's own Standard Model autoloader, were fairly expensive by the standards of the day. The new revolver seemed meant to address that share of the firearms market that preferred wheel guns and felt drawn nostalgically to the styles of America's cowboy era.

Not much smaller than the Colt SAA it was meant to emulate, the Ruger was well built and affordable. It appealed equally to those for whom a revolver is a tool of daily use, casual target shooters and the fans who wanted to own something like the sixguns their heroes of the screen, large and small, carried. What they got for their money was a reasonably accurate handgun that held up well under extensive use and could even withstand some moderate abuse, yet keep on working without fail.

Popular demand for a .22 WMR chambering was met in 1959 and followed a year later by the Single Six Convertible, sold with two cylinders, so use of either the small or large rimfire rounds could be changed at will. Choices of alloy frames for lighter weight and adjustable sights for greater versatility made buyers of the time and collectors of the future happy.

The Single Six underwent the same internal and external modifications as the Blackhawks when, in 1973, the New Models were brought out. Made with the transfer bar safety and two screws in the frame instead of three, the revolver was now as safe to carry fully loaded as any in existence.

I've long suspected that the Bearcat's suspension of production in that same year was very likely because, at the time, Ruger's engineers

Closely resembling Colt's SAA, this Old Model, 3-screw, flat-top, Ruger Single Six .22 is still with its original box and factory paperwork. These items make it more desirable to collectors.

Elegant in its simplicity, Ruger's Single Six is one of the most popular revolvers of its kind in the world. Inexpensive to shoot and utterly reliable, it can provide a lifetime of shooting fun. While still available with fixed sights, the Single Six is more commonly desired with adjustable sights. They make it easier to accommodate the use of different brands and types of ammunition.

were unable to come up with a means to do the same with that much smaller handgun. For reasons probably best left to lawyers, it had disappeared from the catalog by 1974, after a short run of the Super Bearcats had sold out.

One of the things I like best about the Bearcat is that it is almost exactly the same size as Colt's M-1849 Pocket Model revolver. A holster for one will accommodate the other without problems. Each is about as handy as the other in terms of practical use, except that the Ruger is, of course, a fixed-cartridge revolver, much faster to reload and get back into action.

Appealing as these handguns may be to the imaginations of those of us who thrilled to the exploits of Roy Rogers and Gene Autry at the Saturday matinees of a few decades ago they are, in the real world, among the most utilitarian handguns ever made. Most of us use our handguns for sport of one sort or another, usually in some sort of target application. But for the trapper, farmer or rancher, firearms are tools of the trade. For example, my wife's grandfather, Aden Lynn, grew fruit trees and raised pigs. When it came time to make the hams, bacon and sausage that would keep the family fed through the long winter months, a .22 Long Rifle round was used to humanely dispatch the animals.

Fox, badger, woodchuck and skunks were a frequently encountered nuisance on the farm. The .22 was often called upon to keep such predators and pests under control. While a rifle is certainly more accurate for such purposes, it is often impractical. Keeping a rifle on a tractor

can be troublesome and inconvenient. Getting it into action fast enough to be of use when a fox or coyote runs by is a matter of luck, at best.

It may seem an anachronism to city folk, but horses remain a favored mode of travel for those who work cattle and sheep, although some have chosen motorcycles over hay-burning horsepower. Having done so, I can attest to the fact that carrying a rifle in a saddle scabbard on horseback may look macho in a Western movie, and may actually be perfectly fine for traveling some distance by horseback, but doing so while working stock is uncomfortable and irritating to man and beast.

Traveling is mostly a matter of moving in a relatively straight line. Working stock requires a lot of twists and turns that can cause the rifle to rub and chafe your mount's side and your own leg. A .22 caliber revolver, carried at an angle for a cross-draw or high and tight behind the strong side hip is far more comfortable and convenient while riding either a horse or a machine.

Aside from its ruggedness and reliability, one of the factors that makes the revolver so good and, in general, a better alternative than a semi-auto pistol of like caliber, is its versatility. For many reasons, Ruger's New Bearcat .22 revolver is an excellent choice. Weighing in at just a pound and a half, with its fixed sights and 4-inch barrel, this diminutive sixgun offers a lot of performance in a tiny package at just half the weight of the full-size Ruger Single Six with the shortest barrel.

It's interesting that the shape and form of most of Ruger's single-action revolvers have their roots in those of 19th century Colts but, except for the missing sail-like rib beneath the barrel, the Bearcats more closely resemble the Remington-Rider revolvers.

First introduced in 1958, then, as noted above, discontinued in 1973, the Bearcat's

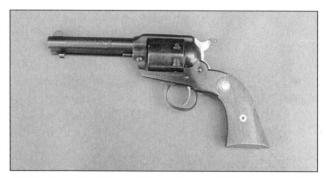

Unlike the other Ruger SA revolvers, which have profiles similar to the Colt Peacemaker, the Bearcat more closely resembles the 19th century Remington revolvers.

When Ruger reintroduced the .22 Long Rifle Bearcat in 1993, it was sold with an auxiliary .22 WMR cylinder. However, the current catalog doesn't list it as an option.

The front sight of the test revolver is a bit high, so group placement was below point of aim. A few minutes careful work with a file is all that's needed to regulate elevation.

return to the marketplace was announced in January, 1993. It wasn't until 1994 that the New Bearcat actually began to show up in dealers display cases, but demand has been so high since then that they remain nearly as scarce to the consumer as were the used and very collectible older ones.

During the first year that the New Bearcats were produced they were made with auxiliary cylinders chambered for the .22 WMR cartridge. Currently, only the .22 LR chambering is cataloged. I was unable to get an explanation, but confirmed that the WMR cylinders are no longer available.

Since their reintroduction, the New Bearcats have sold so well that they're out the door nearly as quickly as they come in. Finding a new one in a dealer's showcase is about as common as locating a used original Bearcat. Don't hold your breath. If you want one, your best bet is to have your dealer order it just for you, then wait your turn, because you probably won't be the only one waiting.

The original Bearcats were made with a brass trigger guard and alloy frame. Like the short-lived Super Bearcat, the New Bearcats have steel frames and trigger guards and have now been updated to include a transfer bar safety mechanism. By cocking the hammer, then pulling the trigger to the rear, as one would do during the firing sequence, the transfer bar can be seen to rise, so that the falling hammer may strike it, transferring the blow through it to the frame-mounted floating firing pin, which will then strike the cartridge rim for ignition. In any other circumstance the transfer bar blocks the hammer's forward movement and prevents it from contacting the firing pin. For that reason the New Bearcat revolvers may be safely carried with all six chambers loaded.

Some years ago I traded off my Super Bearcat and have regretted doing so ever since. When they announced the New Bearcat I asked Ruger to send one for test and evaluation. They kindly accommodated my request and in short order it was delivered to my local gunshop. Once the legal niceties were overcome it was quickly taken to the range for some preliminary shooting. Within an hour I'd gathered my gear and a modest selection of ammo and was on my way to put it through its paces.

Time was limited that afternoon, because a match was scheduled to begin at 5:00 p.m. That gave me less than an hour to get acquainted with the new handgun. I'd brought some Remington SubSonic and their standard velocity target loads, as well as some Winchester Power Point and Super-X. Shooting over an Uncle Bud's Bulls Bag rest from the 50-foot mark, all four ammunition variants shot groups of less than 1.5 inches. However, they all printed consistently low in relation to point of aim. Group size appeared promising, but it was obvious that it would be necessary to trim the height of the front sight in order to put groups where they belong. The Bearcat's light weight and ease of carry have much to recommend it, but that counts for little if the revolver doesn't shoot where it looks.

Looking more closely at the Bearcat, the blue has a flat dark tone, well executed. The grips are made of rosewood and fitted perfectly. Weight of pull of the trigger is a crisp 4 pounds. It's an attractive little revolver, available only with a 4-inch barrel, that fits nicely in all but the largest of hands. It is easily controlled and carries comfortably.

The recessed chamber of the Bearcat surrounds the cartridge head with a ring of steel to help contain escaping gases in the event of case failure. It's a rare occurrence, but this feature indicates quality of design and added consideration of safety.

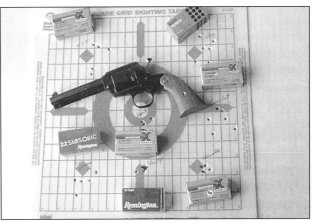

Small, light and easy to carry afield, the Ruger Bearcat is capable of remarkably good accuracy. All the groups shown here can be considered respectable for a handgun of this kind from a distance of 25 yards, but it did particularly well with Winchester's Silhouette (which has unfortunately been discontinued) and performed like a match-grade pistol with the Remington Target load.

The next range session was more enlightening. To the loads listed for test above, the following were added: Eley Ten-X, Remington Target, Winchester T-22 and Winchester Silhouette. Distance from the firing line was extended to 25 yards. All groups printed about 2 inches below point of aim, confirming the need to trim the front sight. By the same token, all printed inside of 2 inches. Remington Target ammo did best in the test revolver, with seven of 12 rounds making one ragged hole. The rest of the five in that group gave a total measure of just 15/16 of an inch in diameter. However, shooting off-hand with all the same ammo variants, from the same distance, produced groups roughly twice the size of those shot from a rest. Welcome to the real world.

Because it's so light, fast and easy to handle, the Bearcat is quick to put into action. However, if the target is small, one should take advantage of a rest if at all possible, in order to maximize the revolver's rather good accuracy. As well, if one is to use the pistol regularly, whichever sort of ammo shoots best in your particular revolver should be used to the exclusion of all others and the fixed sights modified to place shots precisely where they belong.

While the Single Six's weight and greater choice of available barrel lengths probably makes it the better choice for long-range shooting, and it is certainly more versatile with the option of using the .22 WMR cartridge, the Bearcat is the more comfortable and convenient revolver for carrying. Both shoot well. One's own individual needs will dictate which will serve best.

CHAPTER 24

THE BLACKHAWK: STURM, RUGER'S REVOLUTIONARY REVOLVER

One success had followed another at Sturm, Ruger & Co. Seldom in the history of arms making had fortune smiled so graciously on a new enterprise. Close after Bill Ruger's semi-automatic Standard Model .22, the company introduced the Single Six, a revolver that closely resembled the Colt Single Action Army in many respects, but its lockwork used high-quality coil springs that were virtually immune from breakage through metal fatigue.

Public acceptance of the new revolver was enthusiastic and between them, the two .22 caliber handguns kept the Southport, Connecticut, factory very busy satisfying the seemingly unending demand. This demand apparently got people at Ruger interested in testing the waters of the center-fire market. Would a center-fire based on the SAA design sell? Marketing theorists in the industry had differing opinions.

Colt had ceased production of the Single Action Army in 1941, to concentrate it's entire production to the war effort. Although a few of them were assembled from leftover parts on hand after WWII, as noted earlier, Colt's management was convinced that the market demands for the 19th century revolver were insufficient to justify retooling and restoring it to production. Before the war, sales had declined to a trickle. As Colt regrouped to serve the civilian market following the war, the idea that shooters would be interested in such an antique seemed absurd.

Even in the days of the Old West, the cowboy's handgun saw far more service working stock than it did living up to the fabled, feats that grew from the exploits of men like of Wild Bill Hickok, Billy the Kid and Wyatt Earp. The reality of putting down a horse with a broken leg or defending oneself against a longhorn steer with a vicious streak was, by far, more common than showdowns at high noon. Circumstances haven't changed much. Injured stock, predators

The Old Model (three-screw) .357 Magnum Blackhawk proved to be capable of handling high performance loads while standing up to hard use. Soon after its introduction Ruger began making it for other cartridges and now the shooter can find just about any caliber to suit his fancy.

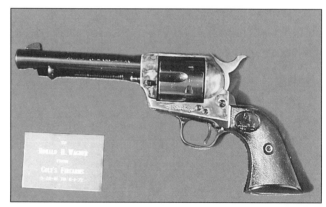

Assembled in the late 1940s, using pre-war parts that remained in inventory, this Pre-War/Post-War SAA was one of about 338 put together after WWII. Chambered for the .38 Special cartridge, it was presented to Colt Historian Ron Wagner on the occasion of his retirement, in 1972. Some of these revolvers remained in inventory as late as 1980.

and pest species will remain matters with which to be dealt as long as man continues an agrarian lifestyle. In spite of mechanized equipment and improved communications, the rancher and farmer often finds a potent handgun useful.

By the mid-1950s those old SAA Colts were beginning to command impressive amounts of money in the used market and collectors weren't the only ones buying them. Colt continued to resist the pressure to bring it back, but Ruger saw a gaping hole in the market and proceeded to fill it. Thus, the center-fire Ruger Blackhawk revolvers came to be.

First chambered in .357 Magnum and fitted with a 4-5/8-inch barrel, the Blackhawk was made with an investment cast frame of slightly larger dimensions than that of Colt's SAA. This made it markedly stronger and better able to handle a steady diet of the high-pressure loads for which it was made. The first revolvers were of the, so called, "flat top" variety. The adjustable rear sight, wire springs and extraordinary strength of the Blackhawks attracted more than just cowboy cultists. Here was a handgun of thoroughly modern construction, with up-to-date internal modifications, that quickly proved rugged enough to withstand the punishment likely to be put to it by an outdoorsman who would carry it in rough country on a daily basis, in all sorts of weather.

Colt could no longer stand the pressure. The SAA was returned to market with much fanfare, flourish and brisk sales, but that made no difference to Ruger's sales. They continued apace. The year following its introduction, the .44 Magnum chambering was offered for the Blackhawk, followed in 1965 by the .41 Magnum. It was seen in .30 Carbine in 1967 and by 1971 the .45 Colt had arrived.

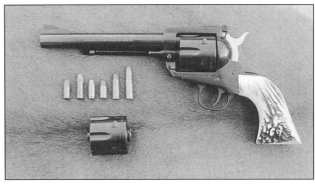
Interchangeable cylinders makes the single-action revolver especially versatile. This Blackhawk is made for the .32 H&R Magnum and .32-20 cartridges, but it will also shoot the .32 ACP, .32 S&W and .32 S&W Long. Although ignition is unreliable with them, it will also handle the .32 Short and Long rimfire rounds in a pinch.

Throughout this time, the one major mechanical relationship to the old Peacemaker that remained was the need to carry the holstered Ruger with only five rounds and the hammer down on the empty chamber. The reason was for the sake of safety because, like the Colt revolver it so closely resembled, a blow to the hammer could cause its safety notch to break and the revolver might be caused to fire accidentally. As earlier described, that ended in 1973 with the addition of a transfer bar mechanism to the Blackhawk's action. The transfer bar prevents the hammer from contacting the firing pin unless the trigger is held to the rear. For the first time in 100 years, a revolver of this kind could truly be considered a six-shooter, because it was now perfectly safe to carry it with a live round under the hammer.

In the years since, a number of special editions have been issued with chamberings, either primary or secondary, as diverse as .32 H&R Mag-

An early 2nd Generation revolver, this .38 Special SAA was made in 1956. Economic reality, as demonstrated by sales of Ruger's Blackhawk, forced Colt to resume production of the Model P.

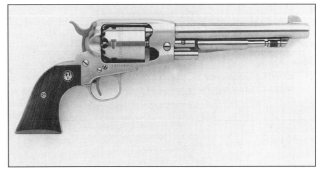
By using the Old Army revolver, even black powder shooters can compete with a variation of Ruger's Blackhawk. Made in blued carbon steel and stainless steel, it is now available in a fixed-sight version.

In 1986 Ruger began making the Bisley Model. This version of the Blackhawk has handling characteristics that are particularly liked by long-range shooters. Its wide trigger and low hammer spur help make rapid repeat shots easier to place accurately.

num, .32-20, 9mm, .38-40, 10mm, .44-40 and .45 ACP. With these and the standard offerings noted above, the Blackhawk could be found for a sufficient variety of cartridges to match the needs or preferences of virtually any user. Even those who wanted a black powder cap-and-ball revolver could be satisfied, because in 1972 Ruger began making the .44 caliber Old Army Model. This revolver is unique among the breed, because tolerances are deliberately adjusted so that one may safely dry fire this revolver without damaging the nipples, yet with a cap in place it will ignite its load reliably. It is probably the only percussion revolver ever made that allows this to be safely done.

In 1986, Ruger looked back into history and evaluated the Bisley Model. Colt's initial purpose in making this variation was to satisfy the needs of target shooters, who found the standard SAA accurate enough for their needs, but were frustrated by the plow-handled gripframe sliding in the hand under recoil, requiring readjustment for each successive shot. By making the gripframe longer and moving it forward and slightly under the rearmost portion of the revolver's frame, recoil forces were caused to move more directly to the rear, reducing muzzle rise and allowing the shooter greater control, particularly during fast, repetitive, one-handed shooting.

To further improve matters, the hammer spur was made wider and lower. This kept it from blocking the shooter's view of the sights during the hammer's fall, allowing proper follow-through. It also permitted the revolver to be more easily cocked with the thumb of the shooting hand, without shifting its position on the gripframe. The trigger, too, was made wider, giving the subjective impression of it having a

lighter weight of pull and adding further to the user's mastery of the handgun's controls.

Ruger adapted a version of the Bisley styling to the Blackhawk that closely follows that of the Colt insofar as the hammer and trigger designs are concerned, but the gripframe is more in keeping with Elmer Keith's Number 5 modification, as exemplified by The Texas Longhorn Arms revolver illustrated in Chapter 13. The toe of the Ruger's frontstrap is not as far forward and the heel curves slightly more to the rear. In practical terms, it is an excellent design and directs recoil forces straight into the palm of the hand. Recovery for fast repeat shots is vastly improved over that of a standard Blackhawk revolver, but there is a price to be paid. Many users find the heavier Magnum loads uncomfortable, sometimes even painful to shoot, because the palm can be subjected to a severe pounding.

While the Blackhawk and the bigger Super Blackhawk are very popular for long-range silhouette target work, many prefer the Ruger Bisley Model's shooting and handling characteristics for that purpose. If, on the other hand, your handgunning activities don't often require the need for getting the next shot off quickly, the standard Blackhawk design is easier on the hand and perfectly suited to most practical applications.

Most Blackhawk revolvers are reasonably accurate and will hold 25-yard groups of 2 to 3 inches without fussing about with load variants. With proper handload development or careful selection among factory offerings, some will

Most Ruger Blackhawk revolvers deliver good accuracy, as demonstrated by this group, using .32 S&W Long cartridges, loaded with wadcutter bullets. With good load development, or carefully selected factory loads, many will provide near match-grade performance.

When chambered for the .44 Magnum cartridge, the Blackhawk has the power to deal with the largest of feral pigs and to reach out to drop the 300-meter ram at Silhouette matches. It's regarded by many to be one of the best sporting handguns ever made.

The Vaquero offers the shooter all the strength and engineering improvements that modern technology can provide. At the same time, its fixed sights and frame finished in case hardened colors offer the traditionalist a similar look to the revolvers of the 19th century.

provide match-quality performance. At present I own three which, with their auxiliary cylinders, permit the use of no fewer than eight different cartridges. The one chambered for the .32 H&R Magnum with .32-20 Winchester auxiliary cylinder shoots .32 ACP, .32 S&W and .32 S&W Long, as well. All four rounds seem to shoot to about the same point of aim and all stay well within a 2-inch circle.

Careful experimentation with a variety of factory ammunition and/or handloads will often bring the Blackhawk into the realm of serious target accuracy. Among silhouette shooters, for example, the behemoth Super Blackhawk .44 Magnum is regarded as one of the best choices for dropping the steel ram. The slightly smaller standard Blackhawk is once again available in that chambering and will provide similar perfor-

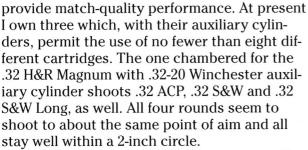

The Ruger Blackhawk is also available in stainless steel, which can easily withstand the worst that the elements may provide. Add a telescopic sight and it becomes an excellent tool for long-range target work or hunting.

mance on target, albeit with recoil levels so significantly increased that the shooter with large hands may find it uncomfortable to shoot, because the trigger guard may strike the middle finger quite hard. Preventing that annoyance was part of the reason for which the distinctive, flattened rear, Dragoon-style trigger guard of the Super Blackhawk was designed.

In 1994, the fixed-sight version of the Blackhawk, called the Vaquero, was introduced. Its purpose was to provide the working man with a desire to compete in the Cowboy Action Shooting matches with a revolver that would qualify for the traditional class and have a greater resemblance to the Colts of the 19th century. To add to its look of authenticity it even has a case hardened colored frame. From the very moment of its introduction the Vaquero has been in great demand. In 1997 Ruger added a fixed-sight Bisley styling to the Vaquero line.

The Vaquero is as good as any other Blackhawk variation in terms of function and accuracy potential. However, the lack of adjustable sights and its very different sight picture make it less practical for truly efficient long-range target work.

The outdoorsman or stockman in search of a utility revolver and the Cowboy Action contestant or target shooter in need of speed and accuracy is sure to find one of the several versions and chamberings of the Blackhawk a good choice for his handgunning needs.

CHAPTER 25

CIMARRON'S SHORT-BARRELED SAA .45

Collectors have always prized Colt's Sheriff's Model SAA revolvers, both the 1st and 2nd Generation variants have become rare and valuable; too valuable to shoot. The 3rd Generation pieces are more common and somewhat less costly, but they appear to get much the same treatment. Most owners treat them more as collectibles than as handguns meant for general use and the Colt factory certainly encourages that thinking. That's one of the reasons that the makers and marketers of replicas have enjoyed so much success. Their products have much the same look and exactly the same feel as the originals, but cost a fraction of the amount that the genuine article, old or new, will bring.

If a replica becomes worn or damaged, it's not as great a financial loss. For the single-action buff that's a major advantage. You can use an SAA clone to your heart's content, without worrying about what it will look like when you're done. As long as ordinary care is taken to keep it properly cleaned and lubricated it will work just as well the next day as it did the day before. For the shooter, how it works is nearly always more important than how it looks.

As we discussed in Chapter 12, it used to be that Sheriff's Models were, by definition, made without ejectors. Most were made with barrels of shorter than usual length, but there were some original ejectorless Colts made with barrels as long as 7-1/2 inches. Just to be different, or perhaps confusing, in the past decade or so, some have been made commercially with functional ejector systems and barrels as short as 3 inches while, traditionally, the shortest barrels with ejector housings were those of 4-5/8 inches in length.

It seems that the original designers considered the latter as the minimum operative length for a barrel fitted with an ejector rod, because that's how much it takes to clear a cartridge completely when removing it from the chamber.

Black Hills .45 Colt ammunition was exceptionally accurate. One of its most distinctive attributes is uniformity of performance from round to round and from one lot to another.

However, many users seem to feel that even if the ejector rod won't completely remove it from the cylinder, having sufficient length to bump the cartridge case part way out, allowing the shooter to grasp it for complete removal, is preferable to having to use a pencil, or some other improvised tool to push the fired case out past the loading gate and even more preferable than completely removing the cylinder from the revolver to perform that chore.

The 3-1/2-inch barrel length of the test revolver allows it to be carried more conveniently and be put into action a bit more quickly than a gun of standard length. Carried in a holster behind the strong-side hip, or for cross-draw, in front of the weak side hip, it rides comfortably. One has the handiness of a kit-gun and the power of a .45 close at hand.

There's nothing new about short-barreled SAAs with ejector rods. My friend, Peter Stebbins, carried a 2nd Generation Colt with a 3-inch barrel and barely functional ejector, chambered for the .38 Special cartridge, for nearly 25 years. An auxiliary cylinder for the .357 Magnum cartridge allowed him to maximize the revolver's potential. In 1955 the gun was shipped from the factory with a 5-1/2-inch barrel, but some time in the early 1960s it was expertly reconfigured to its present form. No one could ever prove it, but it appeared to be a factory conversion. Even the two-line address on the top of the barrel appeared correct. The rollmark there is identical to the one found on a typical Detective Special of the same period.

Into this mix has come Cimarron Arms, one of several distributors of Aldo Uberti's excellent replicas. Most of the other distributors market the more common and straightforward products that come from Uberti's factory in Gardone, Italy, but Cimarron adds distinctive little touches of their own. For example, a couple of years ago they came up with a gripframe similar to that of the Model 1877 Colt double-action revolvers and applied it to Uberti's SAA Cattleman. Dubbing it the "Thunderer," its humpbacked birdshead gripframe is distinctive and has proved very popular. They're available with barrel lengths of either 3-1/2 or 4 inches.

That's one of the nice things about replicas; as Cimarron implies in their advertisements, now we can make guns the way they should have been rather than just settling for what was. But having personally handled the Thunderer, I've concluded that I'm too much of a purist to

accept such a change. The standard gripframe suits my personal sensibilities much better. However, the new and innovative profile has proved very popular. Differences of opinion are what makes horse racing so interesting. As author Robert A. Heinlein observed, "...Certainly one horse can run faster than another, but which one?"

Having decided that I like the more traditional gripframe better, I spoke with Mike Harvey, President of Cimarron Firearms Company, and he sent me one to try for myself. The revolver requested was to be .45 caliber, have a standard blue finish, 3-1/2-inch barrel with ejector and be fitted with both .45 Colt and auxiliary .45 ACP cylinders. None with that finish was available at the time, so Mike shipped a revolver from stock on hand with a charcoal blue barrel, cylinder and gripframe and added a .45 ACP cylinder of standard blue to the package from his spare parts inventory. His cover letter informed me that in the process of fitting the cylinder he'd dropped the revolver and it landed on the front sight, which flattened it slightly and caused a slight bend to the right. No matter; that didn't affect its mechanical performance, and once I figured out where it was shooting it would be a simple matter to trim the sight with a file to compensate.

Typical of Uberti's products, the fit and finish of the handgun is excellent. The timing of the revolver's lockwork is perfect. A one-piece walnut stock is fitted to it and it has a double-bordered checkering job that appears to be 20 lines to the inch. The case-hardened colors of the frame don't have as much blue and green as one would find on a Colt, but they're very attractive

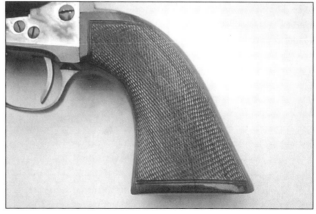

One of the nicest features of the test revolver is the fine checkering on its nicely figured walnut stocks. Fit and finish are excellent.

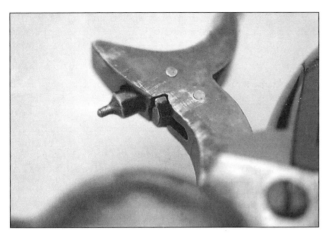

A safety mechanism designed to prevent the firing pin from accidentally contacting the cartridge is built into the revolver's hammer. Finished with case-hardened colors, this adds an attractive accent to its appearance.

The Uberti Cimarron revolver provided for our tests was made with the 19th century black powder-style frame. It uses a set screw to keep the cylinder pin in place. Those who choose a revolver with interchangeable cylinders may prefer having one with the later-type transverse latching mechanism.

just as they are. On this specimen, even the hammer is case hardened.

While charcoal bluing gives the revolver a deep, rich, fire blue color, the heat oxidation process used to achieve this color doesn't go deep into the pores of the steel. The finish is fragile and wears quickly. It's also easily damaged by such compounds as lacquer thinner and acetone; chemicals that don't usually affect firearms finished with the more common bluing processes. Strange as it may seem to those of us used to the normal way of doing things, many shooters like the charcoal blue, because as it wears it takes on a gray tone that gives the revolver an antique's patina.

The specimen provided has a remarkably light trigger. Without any modifications its weight of pull is just 2.8 pounds and is as crisp as a fresh saltine cracker. I don't know it for a fact, but I suspect it was made so in Cimarron's workshop. Other Uberti-made single-actions that I've worked with have typically come from the factory with triggers of 4 to 6 pounds pull.

As I've done with such revolvers before, this one was examined to see how close its dimensions come to an original by placing a 2nd Generation .45 ACP SAA cylinder in it. It indexed perfectly and locked up as well as if it had been made specifically for the Uberti, rather than the 30-year-old Colt revolver from which it had been removed.

The test revolver has what is referred to as a "black powder frame." This simply means that in order to remove the cylinder one must first remove the retaining screw that holds the cylinder pin in place. Among the original Colts, with the advent of smokeless powder, came the

introduction of a transverse latching mechanism that could simply be pushed from left to right to permit removal of the cylinder pin. It's perfectly safe to use smokeless powder ammunition in these modern revolvers. Because the barrel is so short, the ejector rod must be moved about 1/2 inch to the rear, which moves it slightly to one side, to allow the cylinder pin to clear it. Otherwise, it will bump into the head of the rod. Those who expect to exchange cylinders frequently would be better served with a revolver with a smokeless powder style frame.

Between .45 ACP and .45 Colt chamberings in my present inventory there are seven handguns capable of taking one round or the other, several can be used to shoot either cartridge. For that reason I always have a good supply of both

In order to remove the cylinder pin the ejector rod has to be partially retracted. Otherwise, the pin bumps into the head of the rod.

The first groups fired from the Uberti Cimarron revolver were much too large to be satisfactory. Problems with headspace and rotational balance of the cylinder proved to be the cause.

expect the piece to be suited for ISU competition, but this was unacceptably poor accuracy.

Another problem occurred as changes were made from load to load. The Black Hills cartridges that went through it first had chambered and functioned normally, as did the Remingtons. But the Winchesters and Federals dragged against the rear face of the frame. Headspace on the revolver was obviously minimal. These are all factory loads made to SAAMI tolerances, but there are always minor differences in dimension, especially in case length and the thickness of the brass.

Changing over to the .45 ACP cylinder, there was no appreciable improvement in group size, but headspace problems worsened. Again, the Black Hills ammo, as well as the 4W offerings, went through the revolver with little or no drag, but Winchester hardball slowed the cylinder down. A cylinder-full of Winchester's 185-grain Match FMC ammo, a round that shoots very nicely in all my .45 ACP revolvers and semi-autos, bound the cylinder so tightly that it would not rotate. They could not be fired. In order to unload the revolver, the cylinder had to be removed.

These problems are easily corrected, but a gunsmith with specific knowledge of single-action revolvers should be selected in order to do so. It's a matter of trimming the length of the cylinder bushing just the right amount. If it's overdone, there can be problems with the cartridge case setting back when it's fired; possibly even rupturing near the head.

Tests continued with the .45 Colt cylinder in place. Bringing the target back to the 10-yard line, some point shooting was done. The results were relatively good. Handgun targets in most Cowboy Action shoots are set pretty close, and the Cimarron's short barrel and slick action could prove a real advantage for that sort of shooting. Keeping one's shots well centered on the man-size cartoon-style targets often used in such matches is no trouble at all.

To confirm my assessments of the headspace and accuracy problems, the .45 ACP cylinder from Colt was installed. All brands loaded and cycled through the revolver properly and accuracy was improved greatly. Both Cimarron cylinders were taken to a gunsmith, who examined and measured them. He found the cylinder bushings to be about .002 inches too long and to have irregular faces. By trimming them to proper length, he also removed the irregularities. Following corrective adjust-

rounds on hand. Ammunition used in the tests of the Cimarron revolver with its abbreviated barrel included .45 ACPs in 230-grain LRN and 185-grain JHPs from Black Hills, 230-grain JHPs from 4W, and Winchester's 230-grain FMJ Ball as well as their 185-grain FMJ SWC. Ammo for the .45 Colt came from Black Hills in 255-grain SWC, Federal 225-grain SWC HP, Remington's 250-grain LRN and Winchester's 255-grain LRN.

Shooting began with the .45 Colt cylinder in place. As expected, the revolver's front sight was too high. Groups were centered about 12 inches low and 3 inches to the left. Those familiar with these guns usually expect to have to do some filing to bring elevation to point of aim. The slight bend that resulted from its being dropped would all but disappear with shortening the blade, and bring groups back to proper windage.

Group size was a disappointment. None of the loads used shot tighter than 6-inch groups over the sandbags from 25 yards. Several groups were as widely dispersed as 8 inches. I didn't

By trimming the cylinder bushings, headspace was adjusted to proper dimensions and the chambers were made to line up straight with the bore. The result was a dramatic improvement in the revolver's accuracy.

ments, the Black Hills 230-grain LRN load was again tried. The cartridges fit properly and groups fired offhand with that load measured less than 3.5 inches from the 15-yard line.

Another factor often affecting accuracy is the matter of bore diameter. As with the originals of the 1st Generation, many of the Italian-made revolvers have bores measuring .454 inches. That was the case with the test revolver. Most modern .45s have .451 or .452 inch bores and ammunition makers size their bullets to be compatible with that dimension, so they are under size for use in our test revolver. Lead loads tend to upset enough going down the barrel to make up for this, but larger diameter bullets shoot better. Hand-loads made up with Keith-style semi-wadcutter bullets, sized .454 inch, were tried in the Cimarron's .45 Colt cylinder. The difference in group size was dramatic. Twelve rounds from 25 yards went into 4 inches, but seven of them formed a cluster just an inch and a half in diameter. From 15 yards, another 12-round group fired over the sandbags measured a mere 1.75 inch. With projectiles of proper size the little sixgun shows definite promise.

One of the more impressive things about the test revolver was extraction of the fired cases. Most of the time they simply dropped out as the cylinder was rotated. When they failed to do so, a light bump with the extractor rod was all that was required to make them drop free. Only once out of about 150 rounds fired did a .45 Colt case need to be assisted with a flick of the finger.

As mentioned, the buyer of one of these revolvers should expect to have to do some filing on the front sight in order to make it shoot to point of aim. It's also possible, as we saw in this instance, that some minor adjustments will have to be attended to by a qualified gunsmith in order to adjust headspace and assure trouble free mechanical function. However, to be fair, it's worth noting that having used several Uberti-made SAA revolvers in the past, this is the only one that's ever demonstrated a need to adjust headspace.

Considering the cost of a genuine Colt SAA of any vintage, the savings would still be prodigious. The Cimarron/Uberti replica revolver is a workhorse, not a thoroughbred. On the other hand, by loading it with a compatible bullet, it started performing more like a show horse. If you don't mind a few veterinary bills, if needed, to put it in good health, this snubnose Cimarron can be just what you need to get the herd to the railhead.

The ejector rod on the Uberti Cimarron is just long enough to bump the fired cartridge case out of the chamber. In most instances it wasn't necessary to use it because chambers are polished so smooth that cases simply dropped out without assistance.

CHAPTER 26

UBERTI'S BISLEY .45

For reasons I find unfathomable, many single-action buffs don't like Bisleys. The objection I've heard most is that they "look funny;" not like a "real" SAA Colt.

I've always liked them. The old ones, made by Colt from 1894 to 1912, were based on the Single Action Army revolvers, but modified to better meet the needs of shooters interested in getting as much accuracy as possible from their sixguns.

We've already reviewed some of the physical characteristics that make it different and desirable, but let's repeat a few and go over some others that are worthy of note. For example, the Colt Bisley mainspring differs from that of the standard SAA. It is longer and engages the hammer with a stirrup linked to it and a dual hook at the tip of the mainspring, rather than a roller at the back of the hammer and a groove in the mainspring, as the standard SAA does. This

improves the hammer's mechanical advantage and smoothes its cocking action considerably. Colt found this feature worked so well that they continued using a similar hammer linkage on

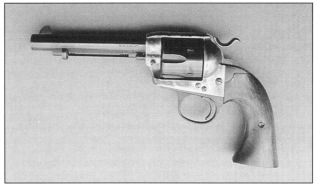

Uberti's new Bisley Model revolver is a close copy of the original Colt styling. However, there are some subtle differences in the size of its gripframe and the shape of its mainspring.

All the ammunition variants tried in the Uberti Bisley shot well, but Black Hills .45 Schofield loads, shown here, provided unusually mild recoil, with very nice accuracy.

The Uberti Bisley's hammer spur is set low, to make thumb cocking easier to accomplish without shifting one's hand on the handle. The safety mechanism built into it prevents contact of the firing pin with a cartridge unless the trigger is held to the rear.

the mainsprings of their later double-action revolvers throughout most of the 20th century.

The gripframe is longer and underslung, so that recoil forces move more directly to the rear,

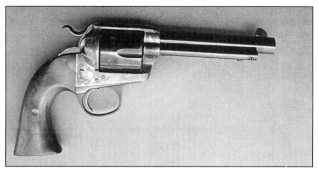

The saw-handle shaped gripframe may look odd to some, but it changes the revolver's shooting characteristics significantly, making it better for deliberate placement of fast repeat shots.

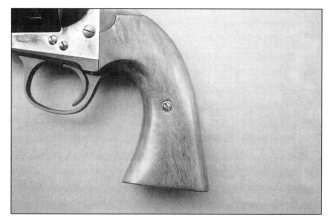

Its dimensions are slightly smaller than those of an original Colt, but the gripframe of the Uberti Bisley is so close that it still feels right in the hand.

into the shooter's palm. This lessens the tendency of the revolver's handle to slide in the hand under recoil, which would cause the user of the ordinary SAA to more frequently shift it back into proper position as shooting continued.

In order to accomplish these changes the frame of the Bisley Model was made 1/4-inch deeper at the rear, hiding the backstrap screws inside, so that the stocks have to be removed to loosen or tighten them. The enlargements to the frame and grip assembly were also necessary to accommodate the changes to the hammer and mainspring.

While they may have been marginally slower to shuck from a holster and fire the first shot, the Bisley Models did what they were designed to do. That is, make it easier for the user to shoot more deliberately aimed rounds in succession, with greater precision.

The originals are rare and expensive, so it was with much anticipation that lovers of the Bisely looked to Uberti. The Italian gunmaker had been promising for several years to bring back the Bisley Model. They finally did so in 1997. I wasted no time getting one. It's chambered for the .45 Colt cartridge and fitted with a 5-1/2-inch barrel. It's also available in .44-40 and .38-40 with all three standard barrel lengths.

Fit and finish of the revolver is, as usual with Uberti's reproductions, very good. The timing of its lockwork is very precise. Weight of trigger pull is a crisp 5.5 pounds. Drawing the hammer to the full cock position feels lighter than it usually does with original Bisleys and the reason for that was quickly revealed. With the straight-grained walnut stocks removed, the mainspring is shown to be a little longer and has a recurved

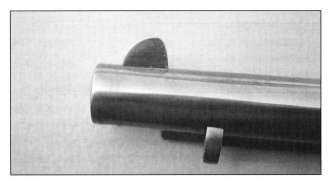

The front sight of this Bisley is the right height for placing groups to point of aim at 25 yards. The sights on most of the Uberti single-action revolvers the author has used have had to be trimmed in order to do so.

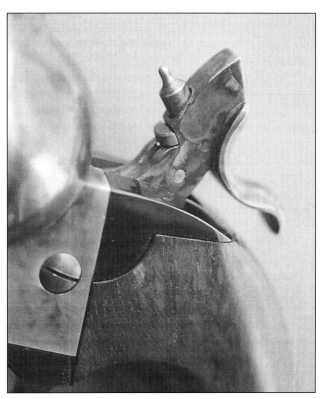

A passive safety mechanism is built into the Uberti Bisley's hammer. Some manner of blocking device is required for legal importation into the U.S.

shape rather than the usual type found on the Colt revolvers of old. This modification substantially reduces the amount of pressure required to depress it.

I've come to expect Uberti single-actions to shoot very low when sighted with the usual 6 o'clock hold. Some have printed groups as much as 18 inches below the bull from a distance of 25 yards. Most require substantial application of a file to the front sight in order to properly regulate elevation. On the day that I first tried the new Bisley revolver I thought, initially, that this one must be shooting exceptionally low. Instead of seeing the first rounds through it cluster at the bottom of the target, low in the 5-ring, it seemed to be shooting farther down, off the paper.

When the mechanical target carrier returned the paper to the firing line, what I thought had been a blank target turned out to have 5 holes neatly drilled into less than 2 inches diameter at the 8 o'clock position of the nine ring. The revolver was actually shooting to point of aim for elevation. Windage for that group was about 2 inches to the left of center.

The ammunition used for that test was Black Hills standard 255-grain SWC load, a round that had proved particularly accurate in other revolvers chambered for the same cartridge. Additional brands and styles tried in the revolver included: Black Hills 250-grain RNFP Cowboy Action load and their 230-grain RNFP Schofield; Hornady's 255-grain LFP, Remington's 225-grain LSWC and 250-grain RNFP; 3-D's 255-grain LRN Cowboy Action load; Winchester's 255-grain LRN and their Cowboy load using a 250-grain lead round-nose flat-point bullet.

The Uberti Bisley Model handles beautifully. But, it's worth noting that until one gets used to

them, Bisleys have a tendency to point low. However, once the user gains some familiarity with the revolver, compensating for that becomes natural and their other characteristics, as discussed above, are quickly appreciated.

As noted before, it's also become my practice, to check the parts of original revolvers against those of reproductions to see how closely they

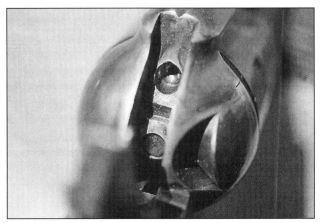

An indentation milled into the frame of the Uberti revolver serves to accommodate the safety mechanism built into the hammer. This keeps the firing pin from striking the primer of a loaded cartridge unless the revolver is deliberately fired.

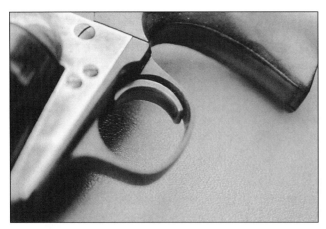

The wide Bisley trigger distributes the weight of pull over a greater area, so that it seems lighter than it really is.

The Bisley hammer rolls back into the gripframe, so that it can engage the mainspring with greater mechanical advantage. This makes the revolver easier to cock during rapid shooting events.

match. In this instance the backstrap, trigger guard and frame of a vintage Colt were compared to the corresponding Uberti parts. The results were interesting. Like the originals, this revolver's frame is 1/4 inch deeper. The gripframe is very close, but slightly more narrow from front to back. Its length is slightly shorter. Thus, original Colt stocks are too big for the replica and the Uberti's are too small to be used as replacements for an original. However, the disparity is so slight that, in terms of basic handling characteristics, there is no appreciable difference.

The 1st generation .38-40 Bisley Model Colt with 4-5/8-inch barrel that I owned three decades ago got a lot of use while I had it. Thousands of rounds of handloads made up with 8 grains of Unique behind a 180-grain bullet cast from a Lyman #40143 mold went through that old revolver before I foolishly decided to trade it off, just because it had been re-blued. The lack of original blue and case hardened colors offended my sensibilities as a collector. As a shooter, I've regretted its loss ever since because it was one of the most accurate handguns I've owned. Several others have come and gone in the years since, but none had the fine edge of precision that one had. The Uberti-made Bisley revolver comes very close.

I'm sure the compatibility of the styling of these revolvers with my own shooting techniques has something to do with the fine results I had with it. That aside, on its own merits this is one of the most accurate revolvers of its kind that I've encountered. One of its characteristics with which I was most impressed is that it did well with each of the ammunition variants with which it was tested. The largest of the groups was less than 3 inches in diameter. Most were

much less. The only individuality they exhibited was in the position of the groups on target. As is to be expected, the various brands caused the projectiles to print at slightly differing points on the paper, but all were tightly clustered together.

It should be pointed out that, while I would expect another Uberti Bisley Model revolver of like caliber and barrel length to perform in the same fashion as the test revolver, a change in barrel length and/or caliber might require modification of the front sight or, require handloads specifically tailored for it in order to shoot its best.

If one were to view the subject strictly from the perspective that Hollywood has portrayed over the past 90 years or so, it might easily be believed that Single Action Army Colt revolvers of the standard configuration were used in the Old West, to the exclusion of nearly all other handguns. As we've already seen, history and common sense tell us otherwise. Likewise, the flamboyant costumes worn by the heroes in most of the "Oaters" of the period from the 1930s until the 1970s would have made a real working cowboy of the 1880s double over with laughter.

Authenticity of dress and equipment have become a matter of pride among the rapidly growing legions of Cowboy Action shooters and many have chosen to engage in this fun sport with firearms that are authentic to the period, but quite different from those of the usual Hollywood mold. The Uberti reproduction of the Bisley Model revolver offers such authenticity while being just different enough to allow for the individuality that many like to display. More importantly, it does so with a smooth action and very good accuracy. Who could ask for more?

CHAPTER 27

EMF'S .38-40 HARTFORD BISLEY

When I encountered one of EMF's Bisley Model revolvers with a 4-5/8-inch barrel and chambered for the .38-40 cartridge I saw it as an opportunity to finally replace that Colt I'd so regretted trading away so many years ago. Maybe this one would prove a worthy successor.

One of the problems that is unique to the .38-40 relates to its companion round, the old .41 Long Colt. It can be difficult finding a 1st Generation SAA Colt of either chambering with the right barrel dimensions. That's because Colt redesigned the .41 LC round in 1896, changing it from a heel-type bullet to a hollow base style. The new version of the cartridge used a soft lead bullet of .386 inches that was designed to expand under the gas pressure generated by firing and grab the barrel's rifling to impart spin to the projectile. The design is much the same as that of the Miniè ball, used in mid-19th century military muskets.

The bullets actually worked reasonably well, because the bores of the barrel stock used for handguns made from then on were changed to measure between .401 and .403, the same dimensions as for the .38-40. The .41 LC revolvers made before the change had bores of between .408 and .410. However, many guns of both calibers were made up using the oversize barrels. The problem was that Colt, with its "waste not - want not" policy, continued to use up the old barrel stock, mixed in with the new, until supplies of the old were depleted.

Revolvers chambered for either caliber made with those oversize barrels cannot be made to shoot straight without seriously compromising their collector value. The only hope is to get a replacement barrel correct for the period, and of proper bore dimensions, or to trade the piece off to a collector who won't shoot it and doesn't care, then try to find another sixgun with the correct bore size.

Some readers may question why anyone would choose a firearm made for the .38-40 for shooting, instead of the .44-40. The latter is much more frequently chambered in both original and clone firearms, both rifle and handgun. At the same time, .44-40 ammunition is far easier to find.

To begin, modern replica .44-40 firearms are often made with barrels of .429 groove diameter. Factory-loaded ammunition has, at least until recently, usually made with JSP bullets of .425 inches or lead bullets sized to .427. This is to accommodate the smaller bores of original Marlin, Remington and Winchester rifles. Modern clones must be handloaded with appropriate larger-size bullets in order to get the best accuracy from them. A lot of searching about for the right bullest isn't needed when you have a .38-40 with a proper barrel.

At present, factory offerings for the .38-40 cartridge are limited to Winchester's JSP load and Black Hills LRNFP cast bullet cowboy ammo. The author tested some old Remington factory JSP's, too.

The EMF Hartford Model Bisley's outward dimensions are so close to those of an original Colt that you have to measure them to determine the differences. They're so minor that you can't tell by feel.

Those .38-40 handguns (and rifles) with proper bore dimensions and compatible cylinders (some of those are grossly undersize at the mouth, but that can easily be corrected) can be real tack drivers. With nearly 35 years of experience shooting a wide variety of firearms chambered for this round I've concluded that, of all the Old West cartridges, it has the best accuracy potential. I've owned a few handguns of that chambering that could put a couple of cylinders full of rounds into one ragged hole from a distance of 25 yards and a couple of rifles that could do the same with a magazine-full from a distance of 50 yards.

Original Colts of that vintage have become prohibitively expensive collectors items for most of us; particularly those who want a nice one to shoot. When EMF announced their Hartford Model Bisley revolver, made for them in Italy by Armi San Marco, I was anxious give it a try.

One of the first things I did with the new revolver was to slug the bore, using a cast lead bullet sized .403. The projectile measured exactly .401 when it came out of the barrel. The chamber mouths were determined to be .0005 larger. These dimensions were what I'd hoped to find. The gap between barrel and cylinder wouldn't quite pass a .004-inch feeler gauge. All these factors together made the probability of the revolver producing a reasonable level of accuracy look good, but that slight cylinder gap would require that it be cleaned regularly to prevent any buildup of powder and lead fouling that might compromise the cylinder's rotation.

One of EMF's strongest selling points for the Hartford Model single-action revolvers is that their parts allegedly interchange with those of original First and Second Generation SAA Colts. This was found to be true of most of the internal parts, but the gripframe of the EMF Bisley is slightly smaller and the curvature of the hammer is not quite as acute at the rear. The shape and character of the hammer's knurling is nothing like that of an original, nor is the shape of the firing pin. The pin of a First Generation revolver is too big to fit through the corresponding hole in the recoil plate. Nevertheless, the revolver feels good in the hand and the external discrepancies between it and a genuine Colt are so minor as to make no perceptible difference in its handling qualities.

The greatest disappointment was that the cylinder of a Colt will not interchange with that of this EMF revolver. I'd hoped that my 1st Generation .41 Long Colt cylinder would fit and that an extra 2nd Generation cylinder on hand, chambered in .357 Magnum, might be reamed to allow the use of .40 S&W ammo, making the revolver more versatile. But this was not to be.

Timing of the EMF Hartford Bisley's lockwork is very precise. Cocking the hammer is smooth and almost no play remains when it locks all the way back to the full cock position. Its trigger release is crisp and very light, with the sear letting go with, according to my RCBS trigger gauge, just 3 pounds, 2 ounces of pressure.

A manual safety mechanism of some sort is required to import these Italian made replicas. This was done as unobtrusively as possible, by making the cylinder pin slightly longer than usual and cutting an extra step into it. When seated as deeply as it will go, the near end of the pin reaches beyond the hole cut for it in the back of the frame and blocks forward movement of the hammer sufficiently to prevent the firing pin from contacting a loaded cartridge. Nevertheless, the revolver should still be carried with the hammer down over an empty chamber, as is standard safety procedure with all Colt-type single-action revolvers.

Fit and finish of EMF's Bisley are very good and the case-hardened colors of the frame are dark and attractive.

The EMF Bisley is richly finished in deep black, except for the frame and hammer which are color case-hardened. The colors are dark and attractive. They don't look like Colt's, but are much better than those found on most single-action clones we've examined. The grips are a brown hardwood that may be European walnut, but look to me like walnut-stained birch. It's difficult to tell, but they are well fitted to the gripframe and nicely rounded so that they feel comfortable in the hand.

There are those who think the Bisley looks strange and, for that and other reasons, prefer SAA-type revolvers to be of standard configuration. They are perfectly welcome to their opinions, but the Bisleys have some virtues all their own and are well worth considering. The first of them were made with flat topstraps and adjustable sights, designed specifically for use as target revolvers. The other modifications that distinguish them from the traditional SAAs make them much better suited for that purpose. We've already discussed those at length, so there's no need for further repetition. Suffice it to say that the individual more interested in good shooting than speed from the holster will often find the Bisley's styling to be the better choice.

At present, factory loaded offerings in .38-40 from the major ammo makers are limited to Black Hills LFP Cowboy Action load and Winchester's JSP. Also on hand was a small, long-hoarded, supply of Remington's factory loaded JSP; a loading discontinued by the firm more than a decade ago. There are, at this time, four other pieces in my collection chambered for this cartridge that get frequent use, so a good supply of handloads with which to feed them is always kept on hand. These are made up with Lyman's 180-grain LRNFP #40143 (it's an old mold - the current designation is 401043) and

their discontinued 200-grain #401452 semi-wadcutter; both with 8-grain charges of Alliant's Unique powder. These five loads were the first used to evaluate the EMF Bisley's accuracy.

While on the subject of handloads for the .38-40, it is worth noting that firearms for this cartridge have an unusual characteristic. Without exception, the chamber of every firearm of this caliber that I've ever encountered has blown the shoulder and base of the neck of the fired cartridge forward. The change is very pronounced and no two guns ever seem to do so quite the same way. While it is possible to neck size cases for use in just one rifle, thereby minimizing work stress to the brass and increasing case life, handloads made in that manner won't work in any other guns of like caliber. Often, an attempt to do so for a particular handgun becomes frustrating, because individual chambers of the cylinder are often too different. Visually, they may not seem so, but a caliper or micrometer will show some minor differences. For practical purposes it's best to full-length size all .38-40 cases.

Case failure, naturally enough, usually occurs at the neck and shoulder and, most often, the Remington brass, which is thicker and more brittle, fails more quickly than Winchester's. With any brand, you may be able to get an extra two or three reloads by making annealing a part of your case preparation routine.

Also worthy of note is that the semi-wadcutter shape of the #401452 bullet will not feed from the carrier into the chamber of Marlin or Winchester lever-action rifles. Cartridges assembled with it must be loaded by hand, one at a time, into those guns. It will work through the action of Remington's M-14-1/2 pump rifle, because its feed mechanism presents the car-

The author's handloads, as described in the text, and (L to R) Winchester, Black Hills and Remington factory loads. The fired case illustrates the way .38-40 cartridges routinely expand at the shoulder and neck. This makes for relatively short case life but the cartridge's accuracy makes up for that shortcoming.

As demonstrated here, the cast semi-wadcutter bullets shoot very nicely from the EMF Bisley, but they aren't suited for use in lever-action rifles.

All three factory loads shot reasonably good groups, but the EMF Bisley shows a slight preference for Black Hills cast bullets.

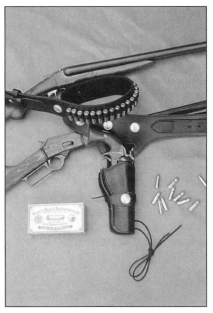

Here we are, all set up to go Cowboy Action Shooting, with lever-action rifle, double-barreled shotgun and a box of Black Hills ammunition for EMF's Hartford Model Bisley revolver in .38-40. The Buscadero rig is the Laredo Model, from Kirkpatrick Leather Co.

tridge to the chamber straight on, rather than at an angle, as do the two other maker's guns. If you are lucky enough to find a mold for that bullet, consider it to be solely for use in handguns, unless you happen to have one of those scarce Remingtons.

Setting up at the club's indoor range, from a distance of 25 yards, our tests were conducted over an Uncle Bud's Bulls Bag sandbag rest. Fluorescent lighting provided good, consistent visibility and the temperature was mild.

Most Italian-made SAA clones have front sights that are too high, causing the revolvers to place groups well below point of aim on target. The .38-40 EMF Bisley wasn't too far off. It printed five to six inches under the bull's-eye, depending on the load used. Some modest filing of the front sight will be required in order to compensate, but that was expected.

The groups produced by the revolver were surprisingly good. Both brands of JSPs and the factory lead RNFPs produced groups measuring 2 to 4 inches in diameter. The cast bullet handloads were dramatically different. With both styles, groups shrank to 1-1/2 to 2 inches. It was obvious that the revolver preferred the cast lead bullets from the Lyman molds. Some further experimentation and load development was clearly in order. We finally settled upon a charge of 5 grains of Hodgdon's Clays powder, ignited with a standard Winchester large pistol primer. Both bullet styles provided clusters on target worthy of a match-grade pistol using

that powder charge. A few 12-round groups produced one ragged hole in the paper.

It seemed only right for a sixgun that performs as nicely as this to have a fancy belt and holster rig all its own to go with it. As I looked over the ones I already had, it occurred to me that, their varied styles notwithstanding, all four of them had one thing in common. All were made of brown leather. The EMF Bisley would be dressed in basic black.

After looking through several catalogs I chose the "Laredo" style from Kirkpatrick Leather Co. It's beautifully crafted, with seven silver conchos to highlight the rich black leather, and equipped with 24 cartridge loops. Both belt and holster are fully lined with suede. Joining the Laredo rig with the EMF Hartford Bisley is like a marriage made in the Wild West. They compliment each other as surely as snow-capped mountains do a sunset.

I'm not going to beat myself up any more over that long lost Bisley Model Colt. The EMF Hartford Bisley shoots very nicely. Maybe not quite as well as my old Colt, but it's just possible that my memory of its accuracy is better than the reality. The EMF Bisley may not be a collectible and will probably never become especially valuable. But, as a practical matter, it's a fine little shooting machine. That makes it fun to use and is reason enough to give it a permanent home.

CHAPTER 28

SOME OTHER SINGLE-ACTION CARTRIDGES

So much good work has been done by such experts as the late Elmer Keith, and by Dave Scovill, John Taffin, Mike Venturino and others, regarding handloading for the old sixguns that anything I might include here would be redundant. But, some brief commentary about the cartridges for which the SAAs were chambered is in order.

If your primary source of information about the guns of the Old West comes from viewing the old Republic, Lone Star, Columbia and Monogram Studios Grade "B" Westerns of the 1930s and '40s and the "Adult Westerns" of the 1950s and '60s you're sure to have heard the term, "Colt .45," often (and, if you're over 50 years of age, you probably don't automatically associate the term with an alcoholic beverage, either). You've also probably heard the line from Gene Autry's old signature song, *I'm Back in the Saddle Again*, singing about "...packin' my old .44."

Those are the two calibers most often associated with Colt's Single Action Army revolvers. For that reason, it comes as no surprise that a lot of people are pretty much convinced that the .45 Colt and .44-40 were the only cartridges that a cowboy, cavalryman or "Injun Scout" ever used.

In most literary and cinematic references to the Single Action Army Colts one could conclude that production of the revolver was limited to .45 Colt and .44-40 cartridges. These were, of course the most popular offerings, but many more were available.

Auxiliary cylinders for the .45 ACP cartridge are popular accessories. Ammunition of that caliber is relatively inexpensive and somewhat more versatile than most available .45 Colt loads. Few semi-auto pistols can reliably handle the variety of .45 ACP bullet designs shown here. An SAA can do so with aplomb.

Horsefeathers!

Before we go into the subject any further, let's review a couple of matters. First, those of you who wish to take issue with me for calling that big old cartridge the .45 Long Colt and maintain that its proper name is simply, ".45 Colt," have no sense of history. It's been called the former a lot longer than the latter. Take a glance at the section of Colt's catalog that deals with the Single Action Army revolver and see what they call it.

With that said, let's have a look at why it's called "Long." In the 1870's Smith & Wesson wanted a piece of the big government contract pie for themselves. Colt was supplying handguns to the military. The U.S. Army Ordnance Board gave their Model Number 3 single-action revolvers with the Schofield improvements an opportunity to strut its stuff. However, there was a problem. The cylinders of the S&Ws, with their simultaneously ejecting break-top actions were too short to take the standard round made for the military SAA Colt. A new cartridge, with a bullet 20 grains lighter, a powder charge reduced from 40 grains to 28 grains and a case made 0.165 inch shorter, was developed so that it could be used in either revolver. It was named, rather unimaginatively, the .45 Government cartridge. Civilian versions were labeled variously as the .45 Schofield and .45 S&W. For a long time it was thought that it had never actually been known as the .45 Short Colt, but some old cartridges have actually turned up bearing headstamps with that nomenclature. So, to all you young whippersnappers who want to take me to task, I say, "So, there"!

To be sure, the .45 Colt was far and away the most popular of the chamberings for the old Peacemaker, but the reason for that was its application in fulfillment of military contracts. Civilian sales seem to have favored the .44-40. Much of the popularity of that round had to do with it also being chambered in rifles made by Marlin, Winchester and others. That couldn't be done with the .45 Colt, because the cartridge case, as originally designed, didn't have enough rim for a rifle's extractor to engage reliably. Modern versions of it do.

Having both rifle and handgun chambered alike was of more interest to lawmen and outlaws than ordinary citizens. Then, as now, most hunters and stockmen preferred a rifle with more range and power; reserving the handgun for small game and varmints at close range or to deliver the coup de gras to downed large game. The .44-40 stood quite nicely on its own as a

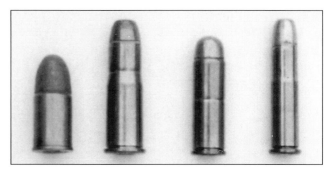

Lesser known to most shooters, but nevertheless quite popular in their day, the Single Action Army Colt was regularly chambered for such cartridges as the .455 Eley, .38-40, .41 Long Colt and .32-20.

handgun cartridge in the minds of those who carried them primarily as defensive arms.

Without question, the .45 Colt and .44-40 are the best known of the Old West cartridges. The Model 1873 Winchester was chambered to use the .22 Short and Long rimfire, the .32-20, .38-40 and .44-40. The Model of 1892 was made for the same center-fire rounds as the '73 and for the .25-20 as well. There have been claims that the SAA was chambered for 36 different rounds. Not so. However, it was chambered for at least 24 separate and distinct cartridges and marked with the names of several more that were actually interchangeable. For example, those marked .38-44 were not the hot-loaded .38 Specials of the early 20th century. They were extra long .38 Colt cases designed to be loaded in a similar fashion to the modern .38 wadcutter. The purpose was to shorten the jump from cartridge case to forcing cone, to minimize distortion of the bullet as it enters the barrel.

The .38-40 was next in popularity to the .44-40. It's a very similar round, in terms of case dimensions, and no one has quite figured out why it was made in the first place. I'm glad they did, because it's a very accurate cartridge. In a good sixgun or rifle, made with proper chamber mouth and bore dimensions, it will shoot better than the .45 or the .44-40 six ways from Sunday. The funny thing about it is that it's actually not .38 caliber at all. Correct bullet diameter is .401 to .403. This really makes it a .40-40. Now can't you just imagine the confusion that would have resulted if that's what they'd actually called it?

Its curious origins notwithstanding, there were many lawmen and gunfighters who favored the .38-40 because, according to them, its 180-grain bullet "hit harder." Ballistics tables be hanged, that opinion had a solid measure of validity. A bullet from that cartridge tended to penetrate well, but stay in the body of a person or a large animal when hit, rather than shoot all the way through the way a .45 Colt or .44-40 often did. For that reason, all its energy was expended where it belonged. It's interesting to note that the round is the ballistic twin of the .40 S&W, introduced in 1990.

Next in popularity among standard chamberings of the SAA was the .32-20 cartridge. Farmers and ranchers favored it, because it has a relatively flat trajectory. That gave it a distinct advantage when it came to ridding the family homestead of four-legged varmints and snakes.

Not many peace officers used it, but there were a few that considered it to be just dandy bad-guy medicine. You'll recall my mention in Chapter 13 of the elderly retired sheriff who had carried a 5-1/2-inch Bisley Model, chambered for the .32-20, throughout his 50-year career as a lawman. You can be sure he never considered himself to be under-gunned.

The .41 Long Colt (yes, there was a .41 Short Colt, made for a number of single-shot derringers and small pocket revolvers) was considered a very good cartridge in its early years. It ranked fifth in popularity, among the cartridges for which the SAA was produced, but it started out being chambered in Colt's first-ever double-action revolver, the Model 1877. In that chambering, the revolver was called the "Thunderer." As a matter of interest, the revolvers of that model designation made for the .38 Long Colt cartridge (another one for which there was a short version) were called "Lightnings."

As originally loaded, the .41 Long Colt featured an outside-lubricated heel-type bullet of .408" to .410" diameter, using a 200-grain bullet that left the barrel moving out at about 730 fps.

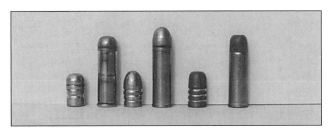

Fifth in popularity among SAA chamberings during the 1st Generation of production, the .41 Long Colt cartridge has a reputation for poor accuracy. It's actually capable of very good accuracy, but bullet size must be matched to bore size in order to achieve it. In some instances there may be as much as .009 inch difference between the two dimensions.

The pre-war Single Action Army Colt was offered in such calibers as the .45 ACP, .38 Special, .357 Magnum, .32 S&W Long, .32 S&W, .32 Rimfire and the lowly .22 Rimfire. Original revolvers in these calibers are extremely rare and command premium prices among collectors. Of course, the .38s and .357s are quite common among the post-war SAAs.

Not what one might call a hot load, it still had a fine reputation in its day as a fight-stopper.

As the 19th century came to an end and a bright new 20th dawned, many changes were occurring in the world of firearms and shooting. For example, as much as the British and their colonial brethren liked their home-grown Webleys and Enfields, the Colt SAA was also much admired. For that reason, many of them were ordered for such rounds as the .45 caliber Boxer, Webley and Eley family of cartridges, to serve civilian marksmen and the military forces of the Commonwealth nations.

With the new century, American tastes began to change, too. The SAA was chambered for cartridges such as the .38 Special, .44 Special and, later, the .357 Magnum. A few were even made to shoot the .45 ACP; a common auxiliary cylinder option today. Some of the pipsqueak rounds got into the act, too. In the 1880s, a few SAAs left over in inventory made for the .44 Rimfire were converted to shoot the .22 Rimfire.

The .32 S&W and the .38 Colt, rounds that are relatively quiet and generate almost no recoil from a revolver the size of the SAA, were also made in small numbers. There were as well, some rare special orders for foreign governments, like the .44 German and special-request chamberings like that of revolver #357633 for the .30 Carbine round.

In the early 1940s John Parsons, one of the pioneer arms historians, researched Colt's records and assembled a list of all the Single Action Army and Bisley Models, including both the standard and the target configurations according to the cartridges for which they were chambered. The figures he derived from those records have, ever since, been used to determine the relative scarcity and values of those 1st Generation SAA Colt revolvers.

However, the human factor was not computed into those figures, so they must be used judiciously. For example, the clerks working in the shipping department and recording the specifications of the guns being sent to dealers and individual customers were doing their job by hand, transcribing the descriptions of each firearm into a big hard-bound ledger. Probably few, if any, were shooters or collectors. The only interest some of them had in guns was the fact that their paychecks came from a company that made them. If, for example, a revolver's barrel was marked .44 Special, it was as likely as not to be recorded as simply, "Caliber .44." Those chambered for the .44-40 might suffer the same fate. Much depended upon the individual clerk and how meticulous he might have been at any given time. Frankly, it would be no surprise if some of them wouldn't have known the difference. Parsons seems to have made the assumption that, unless otherwise specified, "Caliber .44" always meant .44-40.

More than 50 years after he completed his work, the fruits of Parsons' labor remain the standard by which matters of relative SAA rarity are judged. In most instances, his figures are probably not too far off the mark. But, don't be surprised if you find, as I have, indications that they are not entirely accurate.

If Colt had resumed making the SAA immediately following the end of WWII, it's very likely that production figures for some of these cartridges might have been very different. However, they waited 11 more years to do so and preferences among the shooting public changed during that time. We can only speculate about what might have been. What is clear, is that when you see one of those old cinematic morality plays, it's probably an even money bet that the Peacemakers on the hips of the performers won't fit the dummy .44-40s or .45 Colt cartridges in their gunbelts.

CHAPTER 29

SINGLE-ACTION ART AND ARTISTRY

Nearly every creature on the face of the earth is equipped with some sort of natural weapons system. There are those that rely on brute strength; others use fangs, claws, hooves, poison, horns, cunning, camouflage and deceit. Some use combinations of several of those attributes.

Man is limited in his capacity to use his body as a weapon, the oriental martial arts notwithstanding. What is unique about him is that, for all his comparative physical weakness, he dominates all other creatures. The combination of his brain, opposing thumbs and the capacity to work in concert with others allows him to make and effectively use whatever weapon his needs may dictate.

Ever since the first of our Neanderthal or, perhaps, Cro-Magnon ancestors first tied a bird feather to his spear or painted berry juice stripes on his bow, stepped back and said in whatever language his tribe used, "My, that looks nice"; man has decorated his weapons. The form and fashion of that decoration has differed according to the time and place of its crafting and may now be represented by anything from the addition of highly figured woods or some exotic material, to intricate carving and inlays in wood and metal.

During the last century and a half, the art of the engraver has been dominated by European practitioners. Most have been British, German, Austrian or Italian. Many Americans who practiced these skills during the same period were immigrants who learned their craft in the countries of their origin. Engravers such as Nimschke, Kornbrath, the Ulrich family, Helfricht and Glahn

In recognition of the great masters in their employ over the previous 150 years, Colt offered the Sampler Commemoratives in 1986. The styles of Kenshaw, Nimschke, Helfricht and the modern practitioners are representative.

Each of these revolvers is a rarity. Their engraving is accented by plating in nickel, silver and gold. The stocks are of carved ivory and rare, delicate, mother-of-pearl.

135

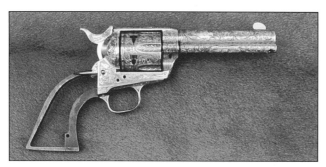

Ken Hurst's work on this unfinished SAA revolver exemplifies the freedom of expression typified by modern American engraving. The hidden eagle is one of his favorite themes.

had distinctively European styles, in keeping with their heritage and training. As little as 40 or 50 years ago, the works of Cole Agee, Angelo Bee and Edward H. Bohlin that graced the hips of many cinematic cowboy heroes continued to exhibit evidence of an Old World flavor.

The past few decades have seen the advent of practitioners of new styles and techniques. Among them, such modern masters as Ken Hurst, Leonard Francolini, Martin Rabeno, Howard Dove and a host of others who have gained an international reputation among the literati. The difference is that the new breed of engraver exhibits an originality of concept and execution of his work that is all but unknown among the old masters.

In 19th century Europe, the master taught the journeyman who taught the apprentice. The key to success was imitation. This is one of the reasons that the various "schools" of this art form are usually known by the names or the nationalities of their practitioners.

Many modern American engravers are, for the most part, self-taught and what little instruction they receive is in the form of coaching among each other, rather than formal schooling. The result is a sense of freedom that develops into new, innovative techniques and design concepts that were unknown even a few decades ago and would have been considered heresy a century ago.

Like beer, olives and brussels sprouts, appreciation of art is largely a matter of taste. The works of one meistergraver are not necessarily better than those of another, no matter which school or period is represented. They are simply different and the differences just make the subject more interesting. Each artist has his own fans and followers.

Few of us can afford to own great works of art. That doesn't make a lot of difference. Those who can afford the artworks are usually generous

enough to share them with others through public displays of one kind or another or the willingness to let others enjoy them through photographs.

No firearm in history has more often been the subject of embellishment than Colt's Model P, the Single Action Army revolver. Its graceful curves and its association with the romance of the Old West, albeit much distorted by Hollywood's exaggerated descriptions of events and characters, make it a natural choice. But any fine firearm may provide a canvas for the artists craft.

Daniel Baird Wesson, co-founder of Smith & Wesson, sincerely believed that his firm produced the finest and most modern handguns of the age. That belief might be argued, but any conclusion would be a matter of opinion. Certainly a good case could be made for his side. In any event, he reasoned that because he made the best, he should have the best of the best. With that premise in mind, he had his artisans engrave and inlay in gold the top-of-the-line product in his catalog at the time. The result is what surely is the finest of its kind in the world, a .32 Rimfire caliber Old Army Model No. 2 revolver.

Leonard Francolini's work demonstrates the tight scrollwork typical of 19th century English engraving. He combines with delicate gold inlays to create an elegant final piece in the SA-prefix series.

The oakleaf and acorn pattern is a popular engraver's motif. This Second Generation Sheriff's Model was done by Howard Dove. The plating is silver and the grips are ivory.

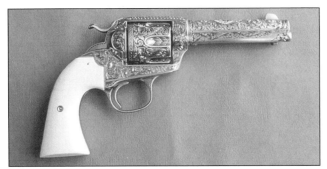

Ben Shostle's work on this Bisley Model revolver might be called bold by some critics and heavy-handed by others. It demonstrates the author's premise that the engraver's art is very much a matter of individual taste.

What may be called art is so much a matter of personal taste that a firearm does not have to be engraved to qualify. The craftsmanship that goes into making a fine, custom-grade firearm, with perfectly executed checkering, fitting wood or other stock material to metal and smoothing the action to work almost effortlessly is considered by many the greatest of the firearms related arts.

Nor does a gun actually have to be practical or even functional to be regarded as a work of art. Miniatures are a rare and interesting aspect of the subject. The basic concept is to construct it so that all parts are in the same relationship as in the original and work in exactly the same manner, but made so small as to be incapable of firing a cartridge, because no ammunition is made small enough to fit the chambers. However, if it could be constructed, the gun would work. One advantage to this sub-specialty is that few, if any, jurisdictions around the world place much restriction on their ownership.

Most owners of engraved firearms never shoot them. They tend to consider the idea tan-

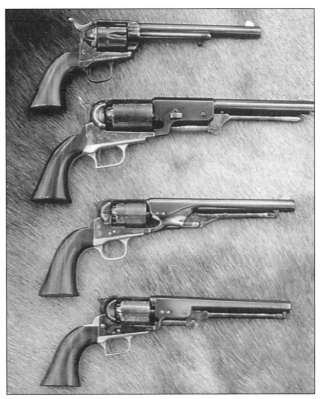

The miniature is an aspect of the gun as art that is seldom explored. These were so precisely done that the observer has to be told that those in this photo are not full-size.

tamount to painting a mustache on the Mona Lisa. In times past, no such attitude prevailed. In the last century and the first decades of this one, such firearms saw regular use. Their owners usually took care to treat them well, but generally felt that they shot better than the plain versions of whatever they chose to carry.

Much of that attitude has to do with pride of ownership. Few car buffs, for example, are inclined to hide their prized autos. Quite the opposite; they enjoy driving them and take

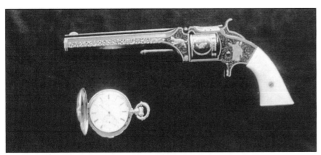

One of the most desirable firearms in the world, this was Daniel Baird Wesson's personal revolver. It's an Old Army Model No. 2 that was engraved by artisans in his own factory. The watch is one of four he purchased while on vacation in Switzerland. This one was kept for himself. The other three were gifts to family members.

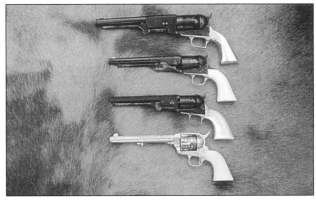

A more fancy set of miniatures, these revolvers are near perfect duplicates of the originals.

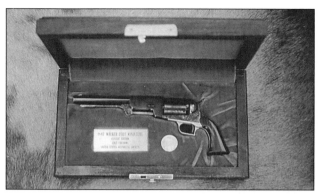

The penny with this cased miniature Colt Walker demonstrates just how diminutive the revolver really is.

every opportunity to do so. They also take appropriate measures to safeguard them from abuse. This has been my own attitude. Whenever my engraved guns are fired, they are cleaned immediately following the range session. They are rarely carried, but when it happens they ride in quality leather as handsomely crafted as the revolver. Such careful use hasn't harmed them at all and the results on target indicate that there may be something to the idea that engraved guns do shoot better.

Among the most often seen examples of engraved firearms are in the hands of the heroes of Hollywood's cinematic Westerns. The practice of placing fancy six-shooters in the holsters of motion picture cowboys goes back to the earliest days of the silent film. William S. Hart was the John Wayne of his day and the factory-done Valentine heart motif of the matched Colt SAAs in his hands belied the nature of the tough, hard-case characters he portrayed.

Even before motion pictures became widely popular, members of the cast of the Wild West Shows of Buffalo Bill, Pawnee Bill and the Miller Brothers 101 Ranch often carried fancy hardware. One of the finest examples of these is that of Texas Cooper, whose story is told elsewhere in this volume.

The simplest and least costly method of decorating a handgun is the addition of custom stocks of fancy wood, staghorn, ivory or other exotic material. A little light engraving, such as one's name or a simple legend on the butt or backstrap adds a personal touch. The 5.5-inch Second Generation SAA .45 in my collection has worn a handsome set of Sambar stag stocks for the 30 years that I've owned it. The backstrap bears the brief rhyme common to many 19th century rifles and revolvers: "Be not afraid of any man - No matter what his size - When danger threatens call on me - And I will equalize.

Many 18th and 19th century swords bore the admonition: "Draw me not without cause. Sheath me not without honor." A Bowie knife I once had that originated in Mexico, reassured its owner with the promise, "Duerme Con Tranquilidad, Que Yo Velaré Tu Sueño." — "Sleep in peace, for I will guard your dream." In centuries past, it was common to apply similar commentary to swords and knives. The practice often carried over, to be applied to firearms.

The simple block engraving on my Colt was done for minimal cost, by machine, at a trophy shop. A word of caution: The quality of such work can vary a great deal and good equipment is necessary for it to be done properly. But such simple embellishment can add substantially to a firearm's value to its owner and to the interest of others.

One aspect of the gun as art to be carefully considered is the investment factor. Generally speaking, the value of a typical engraved firearm can be reckoned by the following formula: Retail price + engraving cost + 30 percent = total retail value. However, this does not take into consideration the premium that may be added to a piece if it has been documented to have been factory original or done by a particularly well-known engraver whose work is in great demand. For example, a piece that can be verified as having been done by the likes of Cuno

Paul Mobley died shortly after retirement from his career with the Secret Service and just as he was earning recognition for his artistic talents. Still in the white, his rendition of Helfricht's style offers the observer a taste of what might have been.

Simply adding a set of custom stocks can turn an ordinary SAA revolver into a distinctive possession, but having your name or a clever saying engraved on the backstrap can add significant appeal.

Helfricht, A.A. White or Marty Rabeno will fetch a higher price than one done by an unknown artist or, for that matter, an undocumented piece from a famous one.

One of the more interesting techniques is theme engraving and inlay. Usually, this takes the form of commemorating some person's life or an historical event. Examples include the commercial commemoratives that have become so common since the 1960s. Presentation pieces that are made to honor the accomplishments of an individual, such as Marty Huber, Colt's Historian Emeritus, include such adornments as gold and other precious metal inlays representing the seal with which he embossed the factory letters verifying a gun's origins; the quill and scroll that refer to the scholarship and research required to investigate it and the book that represents the shipping ledgers that are the source materials from which the information comes.

Another interesting motif that uses a similar technique is exemplified by the "Texas Law" revolver that was done by Howard Dove. Beginning with a Sheriff's Model SAA revolver (naturally), the inlays tell the story of a lawman chasing down a cattle rustler and bringing him to the courts of justice and, ultimately, to the end of a hangman's rope.

Custom craftsmanship, such as that of Jerry Klufas, described in the chapter on Sheriff's Models, qualifies as art just as surely as does the work of the engraver. Adding appropriate accouterments and placing the grouping in an attractive casing makes it all the more appealing.

Sometimes engraving can be used for humor. It may take the subtle but crude form of the almost cliché cattle brand motif that includes the numeral "2", followed by another on its back, which would be read as "Lazy 2," then the

letter, "P." But, humor in engraving may also be more elaborate. Several years ago Smith & Wesson Historian, Roy Jinks, and his close friend, Larry Wilson, traveled together to a major gun show. While they were there, Jinks purchased a large collection. Later, while the two sorted

Previously reserved for commemorative firearms, the theme-style is now being applied to one-of-a-kind pieces. This Sheriff's Model, by Dove, tells the story in gold inlay of an outlaw brought to justice by a Texas Lawman.

The excitement associated with the history of the state of Texas looms large on this relatively small revolver.

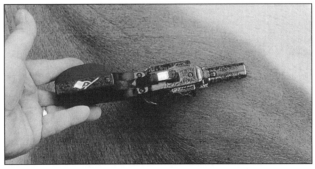

Exquisite scrollwork, delicate crosshatching and precision inlay work combine to help tell the story.

Each of the inlays on this revolver compliments the others to excite the imagination. One can almost see the action unfold, as though it were a movie.

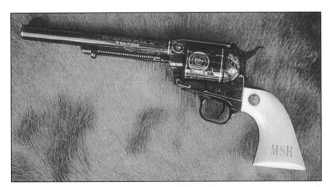

Marty Huber, Colt's Historian Emeritus, was presented this 7-1/2-inch SAA to commemorate his 50th Anniversary with the firm. The inlays represent many aspects of his career.

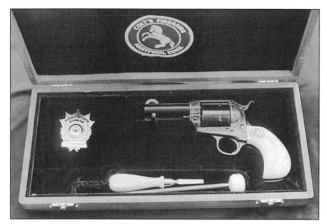

The late master craftsman, Jerry Klufas, made this custom Sheriff's Model, described in detail in Chapter 12. His modifications are as practical as they are well executed and most assuredly qualify as an art form.

Jealous as he was of his patents, and forceful regarding infringements, Sam Colt would probably have enjoyed this revolver and the spirit in which it was crafted.

through the items from it, Jinks came upon a Missouri Sesquicentennial commemorative .45 caliber Single Action Army Colt. Handing the gun to Wilson, he said, "Here, you take this. You're partly responsible for this kind of junk."

Wilson accepted it, but rather than add it to his own collection, he decided to do something quite different. He took it to master engraver, A.A. White, and between them it was changed in a very special way.

The original one line address on top of the barrel was changed to three lines and now reads:

MADE FOR
COLT'S PT. F.A. MFG. CO. HARTFORD, CT, U.S.A
BY SMITH & WESSON, SPRINGFIELD MASS.

The lower right side of the frame is now marked as modern S&W handguns are, with the following:

MADE IN U.S.A.
MARCAS REGISTRADAS
SMITH & WESSON
SPRINGFIELD, MASS.

On the lower left side of the frame the familiar S&W logo has been inlaid in gold, while on the left recoil shield there is a gold inlaid bust of Horace

Of course, no modern S&W revolver is complete without the trademark statement.

Smith. The revolver's stocks are made of ivory and the left panel bears the likeness of D.B. Wesson, also in gold. On the cover of the fitted presentation case made to hold the handgun, is an onion dome like the one that was on the roof of the Colt factory for more than five generations. However, at the top of it, where one expects to see a rampant Colt there is, instead, the S&W logo.

Horace Smith was a stern man and almost certainly would not have approved. But D.B. Wesson would surely have enjoyed the gag. For that matter, Sam Colt would probably have had a good laugh over it, too. Although we may speculate as to the reaction of these gentlemen, the revolver's true meaning lies in its representation of the deep friendship between two pillars of the gun collecting fraternity. However, the joke doesn't end there. A few years later Jinks had a S&W revolver done over in similar fashion by A.A. White for Wilson's son. That one was made to look like a Colt Python.

Because there are a limited number of examples of the work of some of the better known

Horace Smith's portrait on the recoil shield, D.B. Wesson's on the left ivory stock panel and S&W's logo in place of the Rampant Colt on the frame would certainly elicit suspicion as to this revolver's true origins, if one knew nothing of firearms.

engravers of years past available to the collector, and they command prices far outside the reach of most budgets, customers will sometimes request that a contemporary engraver copy the style of one of the old masters. The works of Nimschke, Helfricht and Kornbrath are among the most frequently emulated. Denise Therion's rendition of Nimschke's style is a noteworthy example. Ben Lane's version of Helfricht's technique rivals that of an original.

One of the most universally recognized firearms in the world is the engraved, ivory stocked

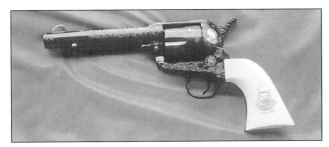

Humor in gun related art is seldom seen, but this SAA revolver's Smith & Wesson theme is certain to provide a chuckle.

SAA that belonged to that flamboyant military genius of WWII, General George S. Patton. The revolver was on display at the U.S. Military Academy, at West Point, N.Y., for many years, but is now held at Fort Knox, Kentucky. A national treasure, it will never be available in the marketplace so, a few years ago, a non-firing replica of it was offered to the public. One collector, however, was not to be satisfied by such a contrivance. He contracted Horacio Acevedo to duplicate it. Only the omission of the lanyard ring sets the copy apart from the original. This was done deliberately, lest someone suspect it of being the real thing and create a legal issue of the matter.

Mindful in recent decades of significant milestones in SAA production, Colt's have taken care to single such pieces out for posterity. The last of the New Frontier revolvers they made, for exam-

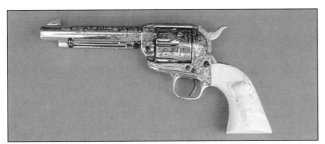

Nimschke's influence on this SAA .45 engraved by Denise Therion is clear.

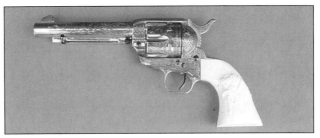

Ben Lane offers his version of Cuno Helfricht's style on this SAA revolver.

ple, was fitted with a 4 5/8-inch barrel, engraved by Dennis Kies and finished with nickel plating. It was purchased by Custom Shop Superintendent, Al De John, for his personal collection. The last one with the SA prefix, revolver number SA99999, was exquisitely engraved, gold inlaid over a full blue finish, stocked with ivory and presented to De John on the occasion of his retirement from the company.

The form, function and style of decoration one may apply to an SAA revolver is limited only by the imagination of the artist. One doesn't have to own a piece of art to appreciate it. But, when it comes to firearms, it's really not that difficult to do. Any gun with reasonable intrinsic value may qualify for embellishment. It is, simply, a matter of deciding how one wishes it to be enhanced, and negotiating with an artist with appropriate skills to have it done. The result is always something unique that can be enjoyed for generations.

Acevedo's copy of the Patton revolver lacks the lanyard ring of the original, so that the two will never be confused.

The last New Frontier revolver was engraved by Dennis Kies and purchased by Colt Custom Shop Superintendent, Al De John for his own collection.

CHAPTER 30

SOME UNUSUAL AND DISTINCTIVE COLT SINGLE ACTIONS

Originality of finish, caliber, barrel length, stocks and other features are normally of primary concern to the serious collector of firearms. In most instances, the item's value is based upon its condition relative to the day it first left the factory. From an aesthetic point of view this is as it should be, but from the perspective of history, a piece that remains as new is without merit except in terms of manufacturing detail. It can tell us a great deal about how similar firearms were polished, blued, casehardened or plated. That information can, in turn, help to verify the originality of the finish found on like guns of the same period. However, such firearms have been used to fight no wars, protected no families, assisted in or prevented no crimes or brought criminals to justice. In other words, they have no personality.

Fully restored to its original condition, this rare .22 caliber SAA revolver is finished in full, "civilian," blue.

Of course, if a gun can be documented to have been owned by the likes of Jesse James, Bat Masterson, Theodore Roosevelt, Gene Autry, or some other well-known person, its value ceases to have much relationship to its condition and everything to do with its association.

There is another category that's little recognized, but very much worth a closer look: those guns that are odd, unusual, customized or decorated in some manner that's particularly distinctive. A Single Action Army revolver with a John Newman slip-hammer or an Elmer Keith Number 5 gripframe could easily go unappreciated and those distinctive features regarded as damaging to the revolver's value among those who may be unaware of their significance. Yet, a collector who knows precisely what it is will very likely regard such a piece as more valuable than a new-in-the-box, unfired revolver of the same period. We've described a few such SAAs in previous chapters. Here, we'll have a look at some others deserving of interest for reasons all their own.

In Chapter 20, the history of the development of the .22 caliber Colt Frontier Scout revolvers was discussed. Mention was made that some 1st Generation SAAs, most of them originally chambered for the .44 Rimfire cartridge, left over from lack of sales interest from an early production run, had been converted to shoot .22 Rimfire ammunition. There are 107 such revolvers of standard configuration recorded by Parsons and he lists 93 more of that caliber made with flat-top frames.

During the past 40 years, I've personally seen only three original Colt SAA .22s. Two of the three were flat-tops, and both of those have been refinished. The one illustrated here was factory refinished in a high polish full civilian blue (which was standard) and retains nearly 100% of its refurbished condition. In handling the piece it quickly becomes clear that one of the reasons that so few revolvers of this model were chambered for the ubiquitous little cartridge is that these handguns are relatively heavy and burdensome to carry.

While their weight on the hip is of no great concern to the target shooter, during the course

The original .22 caliber Peacemakers were too heavy to be very practical afield or on the target range.

Krull carefully fitted target sights of his own design to the revolvers he modified.

of a match it would certainly prove stressful, causing fatigue and muscle tremors. The revolvers themselves might be very accurate, but the user's ability to squeeze that precision from them could quickly deteriorate as the match progressed. Therefore, as appealing as the idea may be, it simply isn't all that practical.

Well, maybe...

Alonzo Krull, who made his career as a postal worker, created a new job for himself after retirement in the 1950s by converting old junker Colt SAA revolvers and Colt's Lightning Model rifles to .22 caliber. Most conversions of SAAs to .22, when they were done at all, were accomplished by sleeving the barrels and cylinders, using aluminum alloy inserts to keep the revolver's weight close to what it was in its centerfire chambering. Krull had a better idea.

The cylinders of his .22 SAAs were machined of solid steel, just as were the originals, but the barrels, which were also made entirely of steel, were modified to reduce their weight and make the revolver more manageable. This was done by machining the barrel to about half its normal diameter, but a full length raised integral rib was left on top, to allow for a highly visible sighting plane and installation of the pinned front sight. Krull also provided an angled side rib to which the ejector rod housing was attached, so that it could be mounted in the conventional manner, and alinged properly with the corresponding recess in the revolver's frame.

Alonzo Krull's .22 conversions are better balanced than the original Colts of this chambering. This one was fitted with an auxiliary cylinder chambered for the .22 WMR cartridge.

The rear sights were his own design. Adjustable for windage and elevation, the tang was dovetailed into a radiused space machined into the topstrap of the frame for that purpose. The sight was then mounted permanently in place. It neatly matched the shape of the topstrap's curves, so that the parts blended together to present a natural appearance, rather than the look of something contrived.

While still a bit heavier than a centerfire SAA revolver, Krull's modifications put most of the extra weight close to the hand, so that the revolver balances comfortably. No modern small-bore pistol competitor would trade in his high-grade target autoloader in favor of one of Krull's single-action masterpieces for serious target competition. Still, his .22 SAAs are very accurate and made nice field guns in their day.

Krull is said to have made about 400 of his small-bore revolvers. They exhibit expert craftsmanship and command very nearly the price of a 2nd Generation revolver of like finish and condition. They are excellent examples of the reason that some non-original revolvers can still be desirable collectibles.

U.S. marked, cavalry issue, martial SAAs are among the most sought after revolvers of their kind. Most saw hard use and have little remaining original finish. One such as the piece we are about to discuss, which retains about 90% of its original blue and even more of its case hardened colors, will command serious money from the would-be purchaser. This one, however, is especially interesting.

I met its owner in the early 1980s, when the gentleman was, himself, nearly 80 years of age. As this is written, he remains healthy and vigorous and continues as an enthusiastic and discerning firearms collector. The revolver was a relatively recent acquisition at the time of our introduction and is an illustration of the patience sometimes required to get what one truly wants. He had known of its presence in the collection of the previous owner for more than 50 years and had sought to add it to his own for the entire time.

Original Cavalry Model SAA revolvers in this condition are very hard to obtain. It took the current owner 50 years to add it to his collection.

Over and above its remarkably fine condition, the revolver has a unique feature. Instead of a cylinder pin set screw of conventional design, in its place is one with a key-shaped head that has a hole drilled through its center, that can be turned in and out with the fingers. It appears that the idea was to make it possible to remove the cylinder from the revolver for cleaning, without the need for a screwdriver. Moreover, by attaching a cord or a piece of wire through the hole in the set-screw and securing the other

The practicality of installing a set-screw of this kind is obvious, but the exact origins of the idea are lost in the mists of time.

end to the trigger guard, that small part can be kept from being lost.

There is nothing in Colt's records to indicate that this was done at the factory. The revolver was shipped in 1890 to the Springfield Armory. The modified set-screw is case colored and matches those of the revolver nicely. The consensus of opinion among all the knowledgeable collectors to whom these photos have been shown is that this is either a one-of-a-kind experimental item done up at Springfield Armory, or some later owner's clever idea. Some of the leading experts in the field have been consulted and none has ever seen or heard of such a thing before.

Whatever the truth of the origin of this unusual feature may be, we will never know. However, it's certainly a clever idea and adds an air of mystery to a very fine piece.

Factory records of 1st Generation production show only one SAA revolver having been completely finished at the factory with gold plating. It was shipped in 1920 on special order for one L.M. Moore, whose name is engraved on the backstrap.

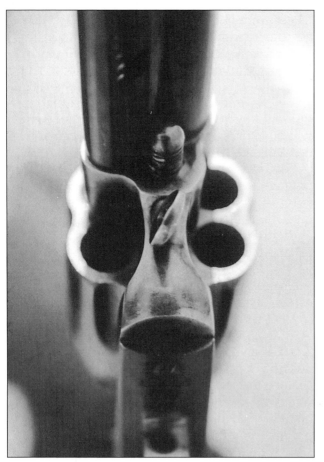

The key-shaped head of the cylinder pin's set-screw makes it possible to remove and replace the part without resorting to a screwdriver.

If one were to attach a wire or small chain through the hole in the set-screw, and connect the other end to the trigger guard, it would be difficult to lose this small, but essential part in the field.

Originally finished entirely with gold plating, at first glance this revolver appears to have been nickel plated, but that was just the undercoating.

Traces of gold plating remain in the engraving of the original owner's name on the backstrap of this one-of-a-kind 1st Generation revolver.

At first glance, it looks as though it were a nickel plated revolver in near new condition, but traces of the original finish remain in protected areas around the trigger guard, within the engraving on the backstrap, the base of the recoil shield, of the hammer and on the screws.

The nickel under-plating is in such fine condition that if that had been the final finish the sixgun would be classed as near 100% mint. But the gold is so far gone that it rates less than 10% original finish. This presents a quandary for the collector. Here we have a one-of-a-kind rarity, in near mint condition, with almost no original finish remaining; an oxymoron if ever there was one.

While still not what one would consider common, gold finish has been applied to several 2nd and 3rd Generation SAAs (not counting commemoratives, among which it was fairly common) both at the factory and on custom engraved pieces. What this revolver illustrates quite clearly is that unless the piece is to be used solely for display; never handled, never carried and certainly never fired, gold plating is a big mistake. The simple act of wiping fingerprints away with a lightly oiled rag will eventually remove the soft metal plating from the gun.

Among the big cow outfits, mining operations and railroads of the Old West, there was an expression often heard among loyal employees; " I ride for the brand!" When the employer was subjected to predation by outlaws or hostile Indians such workers were expected to defend the boss's property. Often these men acted almost as a private army.

While the Colts, Remingtons, Smith & Wessons, Marlins and Winchesters that are so much associated with that time and place were highly prized, the major employers understood fully that many of those in their hire were unlikely to be able to afford the cost of such arms from their own wages. An SAA and a Model 1873 Winchester of matching caliber, along with a single box of ammunition with which to feed them, would cost a cowboy more than a month's pay. Some had nothing better to spend their hard earned dollars on, but others were more interested in spending their money in saloons and brothels or had family obligations that made such an expense too great a burden.

The big companies often purchased the arms and ammunition needed to supply their employees and marked them so that their corporate ownership was undisputed. Today, firearms marked with such well known names of yesteryear as Wells Fargo, Railway Express, XIT or 101 Ranch, among many others, are prized as much as historical artifacts as for their value as antique arms.

An SAA .44-40, with 4-5/8-inch barrel that appears to have such an association is marked on the left side of the frame with the numeral 3 and a stylized "brand" combining the letters U and P. Some have suggested that it might have been owned at one time by the Union Pacific Railroad. This hasn't been verified.

Colt's records indicate that it was originally shipped to a hardware store in Texas in 1903, but it might have gone anywhere from there.

Whether the true history of such a piece is ever discovered or not, may be less important than the knowledge that at some time it was

Marked with the stylized combined letters U and P and the numeral 3 on the lower frame, this SAA revolver was almost certainly the property of a company, rather than an individual.

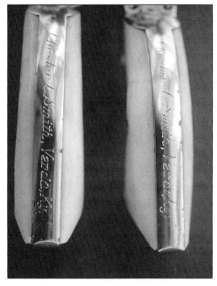

The name and home town of the original owner of these pre-war SAA .357 Magnums was engraved on the backstraps of the revolvers.

Some have speculated that the markings designated this revolver as the property of the Union Pacific Railroad. It might also have belonged to Universal Pictures, in Hollywood. There's simply no way to know for sure unless someone recognizes it.

important enough to someone to be marked for easy visual identification. For some of us the speculation is more interesting than certainty.

Guns owned by people unknown outside their communities, but well-known within them can sometimes provide more interesting history than might be expected, and can actually have real historical significance. Such is the case with a consecutively numbered pair of nickel plated SAAs made in 1935.

Among much fanfare and ballyhoo, Smith & Wesson introduced the .357 Magnum cartridge in that year. While the nation and much of the rest of the world were in the depths of one of the worst economic depressions in history, the new round still generated widespread interest. Colt was quick to chamber the SAA for the powerful extended .38 Special and made 525 of them in that caliber before production ended in 1941. Among the first to place an order was Chester C. Smith, of Verda, Kentucky.

Shipped to The Sutliff Co., of Louisville, the firm delivered a custom crafted pair of nickel plated revolvers with 4-5/8-inch barrels to Smith. Each bears the name of its original owner engraved on its backstrap and they are serial numbered consecutively; the only pre-war revolvers chambered for the .357 Magnum that bear that distinction. Among the special features that were added to the order were genuine mother-of-pearl stocks and triggers specified to release the sear with a weight of pull of 3.5 pounds.

While Chester C. Smith wore these revolvers in a floral-carved double Heiser rig as Grand Marshal of the Kentucky Mountain Laurel Festival for 15 consecutive years, they were not just for show. They were used on one occasion to stop a charging bear and were carried by him in his undercover law enforcement work for a federal agency.

Chester C. Smith's name may not command the recognition that a Frank Hamer, or Bill Tilghman will, but his sixguns are unique and have an interesting history, whether or not the world remembers.

Consecutively numbered pairs of Colt SAA revolvers are scarce and very desirable among collectors. They require a premium purchase price, because they must be specially selected and each must follow the other throughout the production process. Several trios have been made, however, in Colt's entire history, only one set of four consecutively numbered SAA revolvers has ever been made to fill a single order.

On March 24, 1981, four years after they were ordered, Colt shipped this remarkable quartet. As they neared completion the order was canceled, because the individual who had requested them

Fitted with genuine mother-of-pearl grips and tuned for a trigger pull of 3-1/2 pounds, these revolvers were custom crafted for their owner.

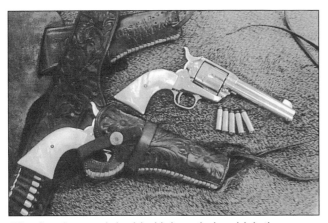

The floral carved double Heiser rig in which these revolvers were carried is almost as rare and desirable as the handguns.

had died. The estate had no interest in following through with the purchase. However, the guns were so near completion that cancellation of their production was out of the question. The distributor through which the order had been placed cast about for a new buyer and found one.

Chambered for the .45 Colt cartridge, these nickel plated revolvers have 7-1/2-inch barrels and all are engraved with D-coverage. Each is stocked in ivory and the engraving is so well executed that it is nearly impossible to tell one revolver from the other except by the serial numbers and the slight variances of the grain of the ivory.

These guns have never been holstered, let alone fired. They weren't ordered by someone well known to the public. Their only significance is in their consecutive numbers and similarity of construction and decoration. Those features alone make them among the most desirable of collectibles.

One of a set of four identical, consecutively numbered revolvers, each is desirable by itself. As a quartet, they are unique.

Wilbur Glahn was one of Colt's finest engravers between 1919 and 1950. Among the more interesting pieces attributed to him is a .45 caliber SAA with 4-5/8-inch barrel that was shipped in 1933 on a loan account to the prestigious Abercrombie & Fitch sporting goods store in New York City. It's listed in the factory records as having been provided with "B" coverage, which in modern terms means about half the revolver's surface was engraved. By current standards this revolver's embellishment would actually be regarded as close to "C" coverage; engraving of nearly 75 percent of the exposed surface.

The revolver rested in A&F's display cases for nearly two years, with no takers. In those lean depression days few had the wherewithal to be able to afford the luxury of a fancy handgun that cost more than twice the $36 price of an ordinary SAA Colt. It was returned to the factory for credit in January, 1935.

In April of that year, Colt representative Harry W. Lidstone borrowed the revolver from inventory to display it at an event in Dallas, Texas. In August it was taken to the National Matches at Camp Perry, Ohio, to be placed, once again, on exhibit. In November, it went back to Abercrombie & Fitch, who returned it two months later, on January 23. Five days after, the store requested that it be sent back. It had taken more than two and a half years for this beautiful handgun to find a home.

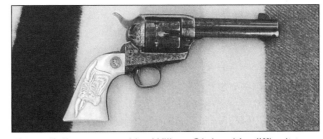

Beautifully engraved by Wilbur Glahn, it's difficult to imagine today that this revolver was hard to sell when it was new.

COLT'S 19TH CENTURY CAP & BALL REVOLVERS PRODUCTION TABLES

(R.L. Wilson's Figures)

The Patersons

No. 1 Baby Model, about 500 made 1837-1838

Nos. 2 and 3 Belt Models, about 850 made 1838-1840

No. 5 Holster or Texas Model, about 850 made 1838-1840

4th & 5th Model Ehlers, with loading levers, about 500 made 1838-1840

The Walkers

1847 Military - Companies A,B,C,D 1-220

Company E 1-120

1847 Civilian - 1001-1100

1847 Whitneyville-Hartford Transition Walker/Dragoon 1101-1340

The Dragoons

1848 The Fluck Pre-1st Model - 2216-2515

1st Model	1848 - 1341
	1849 - 4000
2nd Model	1850 - 8000
	1851 - 9500
3rd Model	1851 - 10700
	1852 - 12000
	1853 - 12500
	1854 - 13750
	1855 - 14000
	1856 - 15500
	1857 - 16250
	1858 - 16500

1859 - 18000
1860 - 18500

The Hartford-English Dragoon 1853 about 700 made (Serial numbers at start of each year)

Baby Dragoon

1847	1
1848	2000
1849	8000
1850	12000 - 14000

Model 1849 Pocket Revolver

1849	1
1850	12000
1851	16000
1852	25000
1853	55000
1854	85000
1855	100000
1856	110000
1857	130000
1858	140000
1859	150000
1860	160000
1861	184000
1862	197000
1863	223000
1864	250000
1865	270000
1866	280000
1867	290000
1868	300000
1869	310000
1870	320000

1871	325000
1872	330000
1873	331000 - 340000

1849 Pocket Revolver - London

1853	1
1854	1000
1855	5000
1856	9000 - 11000

1851 Navy Model

1850	1
1851	2500
1852	10000
1853	20000
1854	35000
1855	40000
1856	45000
1857	65000
1858	85000
1859	90000
1860	93000
1861	98000
1862	118000
1863	132000
1864	175000
1865	180000
1866	185000
1867	200000
1868	204000
1869	207000
1870	210000
1871	212000
1872	214000
1873	215000 - 215348

1851 Navy - London

Year	Serial
1853	1
1854	4000
1855	15000
1856	41000 - 42000

1855 Sidehammer .28 caliber

Year	Serial
1855	1
1856	5000
1857	15000
1858	18000
1859	20000
1860	22000
1861	26000

1855 Sidehammer .31 caliber

Year	Serial
1860	1
1861	1000
1862	4300
1863	6000
1864	8000
1865	9000
1866	10000

Year	Serial
1867	11000
1868	12000
1869	13000
1870	14000

1860 Army

Year	Serial
1860	1
1861	2000
1862	25000
1863	85000
1864	150000
1865	153000
1866	156000
1867	162000
1868	170000
1869	177000
1870	185000
1871	190000
1872	198000
1873	199000 - 200500

1861 Navy

Year	Serial
1861	1
1862	4600
1863	10000
1864	17000
1865	25000

Year	Serial
1866	28000
1867	30000
1868	31000
1869	33000
1870	34000
1871	35000
1872	36000
1873	37000 - 38843

1862 Pocket Police / 1862 Pocket Navy (concurrent production)

Year	Serial
1861	1
1862	8500
1863	15000
1864	26000
1865	29000
1866	32000
1867	35000
1868	37000
1869	40000
1870	42000
1871	44000
1872	45000
1873	46000 - 47000

COLT'S 20TH CENTURY RE-ISSUE CAP & BALL REVOLVERS

PRODUCTION TABLES

Model Number	Description	Year of Issue	Ser. No. Range	Total Made
C-1121	1851 Navy B/CH/Sl	1971	4201-24899	20699
C-1122	1851 Navy B/CH/Br	1971	Same as above	UNK
C-9001	1851 Lee Comm	1971	251REL-5000REL	4750
C-9002	1851 Grant Comm	1971	251USG-5000USG	4750
C-9003	1851 Navy Lee/Grant	1971	1GLP-250GLP	250
F-1100(1)	1851 Navy B/CH/Sl	1980	24900-29150	3951
F-1101(2)	1851 Navy B/CH/S/BL	1981	Same as above	300
F-1110	1851 Navy Stnls Stl	1982	29151S-29640S	489
F-1200	1860 Army B/CH/RebCyl	1978	201000-212262	7593
F-1200EBO	1860 Army BtrfldComm	1978	Same as above	500
F-1200MN(3)	1860 Army N/I	1984	Same as above	12
F-1200S(4)	1860 Army Antique Gold	1979	Same as above	100
F-1202	1860 Army Lmtd Ed	1980	Same as above	500
F-1203	1860 Army Fluted Cyl	1980	Same as above	2670
F-1210	1860 Army Stnls Stl	1982	211263S-212540S	1278
F-9005	1860 Army Cavalry Comm	1977	US1-US3025	3025
F-1200(5)	1860 Army Sampler N/I	1988	Same as F-1200	10
F-1200(5)	1860 Army Sampler B/I	1988	Same as F-1200	10
F-1300	1861 Navy B/CH/Sl	1980	40000-43165	3166
F-1300S	1861 Navy Stnls Stl	1982	43166S-43170S	5
F-1400(6)	1862 Pocket Navy B/CH/S	1979	48000-58564	5764
F-1400MN(3)	1862 Pocket Navy N/I	1984	Same as above	27
F-1401	1862 Pocket Navy Lmtd Ed	1980	Same as above	500
F-1400(5)	1862 P.N. Sampler N/I	1988	Same as above	10
F-1400(5)	1862 P.N. Sampler B/I	1988	Same as above	10
F-1500(6)	1862 Pkt Police B/CH/Sl	1980	48000-58564	4801
F-1500MN(3)	1862 Pkt Police N/I	1984	Same as above	25
F-1501	1862 Pkt Police Lmtd Ed	1980	Same as above	500
F-1500(5)	1862 Pkt Pol Smplr N/I	1988	Same as above	17
F-1600	1847 Walker B/CH/Br	1980	1200-3772	2573
F-1600	1847 Walker B/CH/Br	1981	32256-32500	245
F-9006	1847 Heritage Comm	1980	1-1853	1853
C-1770	3rd Mod Dragoon B/CH/Br	1974	20901-25099	4199
C-1770MN(3)	3rd Mod Dragoon N/I	1984	Same as above	20
F-17401	3rd Mod Dragoon B/CH/Br	1980	25100-34509	2856
F-1740EGA	3rd Mod Dragoon Grbldi	1982	GCA1000-GCA1200	200
F-11393(7)	Garibaldi in the white	1982	Same as above	94
C-1770(5)	3rd Mod Drag Smplr N/I	1988	UNK	25
C-1770(5)	3rd Mod Drag Smplr B/I	1988	UNK	25
C-1770DG(3)	3rd Mod Drag Bicent	1976	0001DG-1776DG	1776

Model Number	Description	Year of Issue	Ser. No. Range	Total Made
C-1770	3rd Mod Drag Statehood	1977	State-DC-USA	52
F-1720(8)	2nd Mod Dragoon B/CH/Br	1980	25100-34509	2676
F-1700(8)	1st Mod Dragoon B/CH/Br	1980	Same as above	3878
F-1700	1st Mod Drag Yorktown	UNK	Same as above	100
F-1760	Baby Drag B/CH/Sl	1981	16000-17851	1852
F-1761	Baby Drag Lmtd Ed	1981	Same as above	500

Key To Footnotes:

(1) There appears to be an overlap of serial numbers between the C-series and the F-series Navy Models in the 24900-25025 range and between the C-series and F-series 3rd Model Dragoons in the 25100 range.

(2) The rollmark normally associated with the 1851 Navy cylinder was left off the F-1101 series. It is believed that an enhanced rollmark was to have been put on these as a commemorative to sailing ships, but the project was canceled and the guns were issued as is, with smooth cylinders.

(3) Production of these guns was contracted by Aeromarine.

(4) Actual numbers produced may be as few as 25, not the 100 that were supposed to have been made.

(5) The engraved "Sampler" revolvers were a special sesquicentennial offering, featuring the styles of Colt engravers during four periods of the company's history. These were ordered by Bangor.

(6) The 1862 Pocket Navy and 1862 Pocket Police models share the same serial number range.

(7) The Garibaldi Commemorative series seems to have been cut short in its run, explaining the 94 guns left in the white.

(8) The F-series 1st, 2nd and 3rd Model Dragoons share the same serial number range.

Abbreviation Key:

B/CH/Sl = Blue, case hardened colors, silver backstrap and trigger guard

B/CH/Br = Blue, case hardened colors, brass backstrap and trigger guard

BL = Blank cylinder without rollmarks

BtrfldComm = Butterfield Commemorative

RebCyl = Rebated cylinder

Lmtd Ed - Limited Edition

N/I = Nickel finish with ivory grips

B/I = Blue finish with ivory grips

Bicent = Bicentennial

APPENDIX III

1ST GENERATION COLT SINGLE ACTION ARMY REVOLVER

PRODUCTION TABLE
(John E. Parsons Figures)

Year	Note	Serial	Year	Note	Serial
1873	.44 Colt and .45 LC cartridges chambered	1	1905		261000
1874	.450 Boxer ctg. added	200	1906		273000
1875	.44 RF until 1880	1500	1907		288000
	(their own serial number range 1-1863)		1908		304000
1876	.476 Eley introduced	22000	1909		308000
	First Buntlines appear serial number range 28800-28830		1910		312000
			1911		316000
1877		33000	1912	Bisley Model discontinued	321000
1878	.44-40 introduced	41000	1913	.44 Russian and .44	325000
1879		49000		S&W Special introduced	
1880		53000	1914		328000
1881		62000	1915	Long-flute cylinders used - serial range	329500
1882	Sheriff's Model introduced	73000		330001-331480	
1883	.22 RF introduced	85000	1916		332000
1884	.32-20 and .38-40 introduced	102000	1917		335000
1885	.41 LC introduced	114000	1918		337000
1886	.38 LC introduced	117000	1919		337200
1887	.32 Colt and .32 S&W introduced	119000	1920		338000
			1921		341000
1888	Flat-top Tgt. Model introduced - #126530	125000	1922		343000
1889	.32 RF, .32-44 S&W, .38 S&W and		1923		344500
	.44 Russianctgs. introduced	128000	1924	.45 ACP introduced	346400
1890	.44 Smoothbore .380 and .450 Eley and	130000	1925		347300
	.44 S&W introduced		1926		348200
1891	.38-44 introduced	136000	1927		349800
1892	Transverse cylinder	144000	1928		351300
	pin latch introduced		1929		352400
1893		149000	1930	.38 Special introduced	353800
1894	First Bisleys shipped to England - serial	154000	1931		354100
	numbers concurrent with standard SAA		1932		354500
1895		159000	1933		354800
1896		163000	1934		355000
1897		168000	1935	.357 Magnum introduced	355200
1898		175000	1936		355300
1899		182000	1937		355400
1900	SAAs first certified safe for use with	192000	1938		356100
	smokeless powder ammo		1939		356600
1901		203000	1940	Some SAAs were assembled from	357000 - 357859
1902		220000		parts during the war and just after	
1903		238000			
1904		250000			

COLT SINGLE ACTION ARMY CALIBER BREAKDOWN
(John E. Parsons figures)

Caliber	SAA	Flat-top Target	Bisley	Flat-top Bisley
.22 RF	107	93	0	0
.32 RF	1	0	0	0
.32 Colt	192	24	160	44
.32 S&W	32	30	18	17
.32-44	2	9	14	17
.32-20	29,812	30	13,291	131
.38 Colt to 1914	1,011	122	412	96
After 1922	1,365	0	0	0
.38 S&W	9	39	10	5
.38 Colt Special	82	7	0	0
.38 S&W Special	25	0	2	0
.38-44	2	11	6	47
.357 Mag.	525	0	0	0
.380 Eley	1	3	0	0
.38-40	38,240	19	12,163	98
.41 LC	16,402	91	3,159	24
.44 Smoothbore	15	0	1	0
.44 RF	1,863	0	0	0
.44 German	59	0	0	0
.44 Russian	154	51	90	62
.44 S&W	24	51	29	64
.44 S&W Special	506	1	0	0
.44-40	64,489	21	6,803	78
.45 LC	150,683	100	8,005	97
.45 Smoothbore	4	0	2	0
.45 ACP	44	0	0	0
.450 Boxer	729	89	0	0
.450 Eley	2,697	84	5	0
.455 Eley	1,150	37	180	196
.476 Eley	161	2	0	0
Totals	310,386	914	44,350	976

2ND AND 3RD GENERATION COLT SINGLE ACTION ARMY PRODUCTION TABLE
(R.L. Wilson's figures)

	SAA	New Frontier
1956	1SA	
1957	8800SA	
1958	18500SA	
1959	23400SA	
1960	28500SA	
1961	33600SA	3000NF
1962	35650SA	3006NF
1963	37300SA	4325NF
1964	38500SA	4700NF
1965	40000SA	5000NF
1966	41500SA	5500NF
1967	43800SA	5700NF
1968	46399SA	5800NF
1969	49000SA	5900NF
1970	52600SA	6000NF
1971	59400SA	7000NF
1972	61700SA	None
1973	64400SA	None
1974	69400SA - 73319SA	7088NF
1975	None made	7288NF
1976	80000SA 3rd Generation begins	None
1977	82001SA	None
1978	6000SA - 99999SA SA suffix ends mid-year	7501NF
1978	SA01000 SA prefix begins mid-year	
1979	SA13000	04426NF
1980	SA14809	06268NF
1981	SA30255	11373NF
1982	SA46920	16583NF
1983	SA58628	16829NF
1984	SA66496	

APPENDIX IV
TABLE OF VERIFIED SHERIFF'S MODELS

Serial Number	Barrel Length	Caliber	Finish	Year Mfgd	Comments
72638	2-1/2	.44-40	unknown	1881	
74821	7-1/2	.45	unknown	1882	
77370	4	.45	blue	1882	
77390	2-1/2	.45	blue	1882	
77399	2-1/2	.45	blue	1882	
77454	3-1/2	.45	blue	1882	
77456	3-1/2	.45	blue	1882	
77514	3-1/2	.45	blue	1882	
77527	4	.45	blue	1882	
77605	4	.45	blue	1882	
77612	3-1/2	.45	blue	1882	
77615	4	.45	blue	1882	
77616	4	.45	blue	1882	
77620	3-1/2	.45	blue	1882	
77623	4	.45	blue	1882	
77625	4	.45	blue	1882	
77626	3-1/2	.45	blue	1882	
77627	2-1/2	.45	blue	1882	
77629	3-1/2	.45	blue	1882	
77631	3-1/2	.45	blue	1882	
77634	4	.45	blue	1882	
77638	4	.45	blue	1882	
77639	3-1/2	.45	blue	1882	
77641	4	.45	blue	1882	
77644	2-1/2	.45	blue	1882	
77645	3-1/2	.45	blue	1882	
78158	4	.44-40	blue	1882	
80118	4	unknown	nickel	1882	Notes 1,2
84018	4	unknown	blue	1882	Note 1
84244	4	.44-40	nickel	1882	
91247	4	unknown	nickel	1883	
91253	4	unknown	nickel	1883	
91923	4	unknown	nickel	1883	
91960	4	.45	nickel	1883	
92057	4	unknown	nickel	1883	
92085	4	unknown		1883	Note 2
92088	4	unknown	nickel	1883	
92105	4	unknown		1883	Note 2
92116	4	unknown	nickel	1883	
92244	4	unknown	nickel	1883	
99504	2-1/2	.44-40	nickel	1883	Note 5
99556	2-1/2	.45	unknown	1883	
102257	2-1/2	.45	blue	1884	
102761	2-1/2	.45	blue	1884	
103270	4	.45	blue	1884	

Serial Number	Barrel Length	Caliber	Finish	Year Mfgd	Comments
105734	4	unknown	blue	1884	
105757	3-1/2	.44	nickel	1884	Note 1
105770	4	unknown	blue	1884	
105778	4	unknown	blue	1884	
105781	4	.45	blue	1884	
105805	4	unknown	nickel	1884	
105867	4	.45	blue	1884	
106996	4	unknown	blue	1884	
107781	3-1/2	unknown	blue	1884	
107784	4	unknown	nickel	1884	
107793	4	unknown	nickel	1884	
108330	3-1/2	.45	nickel	1884	Note 1
108372	4	.44-40	blue	1884	
108379	3-1/2	unknown	blue	1884	
108382	4	.44-40	nickel	1884	
108383	3-1/2	unknown	blue	1884	
108388	3-1/2	.45	blue	1884	
108389	4	unknown	nickel	1884	
108392	4	.44-40	blue	1884	
108394	3-1/2	unknown	blue	1884	
108400	4	.45	nickel	1884	Note 13
108401	4	.45	nickel	1884	Note 13
108753	4	.45	blue	1884	
109982	3-1/2	.45	blue	1884	
112311	3-1/2	unknown	nickel	1884	
115126	2-1/2	.44-40	nickel	1885	Note 1
121200	4	.44-40	unknown	1887	
122325	unknown	.45	blue	1887	
122355	3-1/2	.45	blue	1887	
122362	3-1/2	.45	blue	1887	
122376	3-1/2	unknown	blue	1887	
122380	3-1/2	.45	nickel	1887	
122386	3-1/2	.44-40	unknown	1887	
122393	4	.38-40	blue	1887	
122396	3-1/2	.44-40	blue	1887	
123304	3-1/2	.44-40	nickel	1887	
122306	3-1/2	.44-40	unknown	1887	
123207	3-1/2	.45	nickel	1887	
123309	3-1/2	.45	blue	1887	Note 12
123311	4	.45	blue	1887	
123314	3-1/2	.45	nickel	1887	
123318	3-1/2	.45	nickel	1887	
123321	3	.45	nickel	1887	Note 3
123372	4	.44-40	nickel	1887	Note 3
127740	3-1/2	.44-40	nickel	1888	Note 1
129132	5	.38LC	blue	1889	Note 4
130752	4	.32-20	blue	1890	
131409	7-1/2	.450 Eley	blue	1890	Note 6
132084	4	unknown	unknown	1890	Note 2
135666	4	.45	blue	1890	
141819	3-1/2	unknown	unknown	1891	
142314	3-1/2	.44-40	nickel	1891	
145289	4	.44-40	blue	1892	
145300	3	.45	blue	1892	
145305	3-1/2	.45	unknown	1892	
145312	4-5/8	.45	nickel	1892	

Serial Number	Barrel Length	Caliber	Finish	Year Mfgd	Comments
145319	4	.44-40	blue	1892	
145325	4	.41LC	blue	1892	
145346	5-1/2	unknown	nickel	1892	Note 1
145348	4	unknown	nickel	1892	Note 1
145895	4	.45	nickel	1893	Note 1
145044	4	.45	unknown	1894	
154046	3	.45	unknown	1894	
154062	3	.45	unknown	1894	Note 11
159323	4	.44-40	blue	1895	
159327	4	.45	unknown	1895	
162342	3-1/2	.32-20	blue	1895	
162343	4	.45	blue	1895	
162356	unknown	unknown	unknown	1895	
162357	4	.45	nickel	1895	
166943	3-1/2	.45	blue	1896	
166964	4	.38-40	blue	1896	
167102	3	.45	blue	1896	Notes 3,5
167537	7-1/2	.38-40	blue	1896	Note 6
168468	3-1/2	.41LC	blue	1897	
172723	4	.45	blue	1897	
172740	3-1/2	.44-40	nickel	1897	Note 1
183448	4	.45	blue	1899	Note 5
185258	4	.45	blue	1899	Note 8
185888	3	.45	unknown	1899	
186153	3-1/2	.32-20	blue	1899	Note 8
186154	4	.38-40	blue	1899	Note 8
192852	4	.45	blue	1900	
192884	4	.45	blue	1900	
196024	4	.38-40	blue	1900	
196027	3-1/2	unknown	unknown	1900	
200623	3-1/2	.44-40	blue	1900	Note 8
200625	3-1/2	.44-40	blue	1900	Note 8
200661	4	.44-40	nickel	1900	Note 8
222399	4	unknown	nickel	1902	
253691	3-1/2	.45	blue	1904	
259273	4	.45	blue	1904	Notes 3,8
259336	4	.45	blue	1904	Note 8
267322	4-5/8	.38-40	unknown	1905	
270585	4	unknown	blue	1905	
279736	3-3/4	.38-40	blue	1906	Note 8
282223	4-5/8	.45	blue	1906	Note 7
288374	4-5/8	.45	blue	1906	Note 7
305409	4	.45	blue	1908	
305410	4	.45	blue	1908	
305412	4	.45	blue	1908	
305413	4-5/8	unknown	blue	1908	
305416	4-5/8	.45	blue	1908	
319042	5-1/2	.41LC	blue	1911	Note 8
322123	3	.45	blue	1912	Notes 8,9
328915	4	.45	blue	1914	Note 10
329925	4	.45	silver	1915	Note 1
347834	4-5/8	.45	blue	1925	

Note 1: Factory engraved. Note 2: Shipped in the white. Note 3: No factory record. Note 4: Full (civilian) blue. Note 5: Known to be a fake. Note 6: Flat-top frame. Note 7: Bull-barrel. Note 8: Bisley. Note 9: A factory rework. Note 10: Long-flute cylinder. Note 11: A fake with the same serial number exists. Note 12: Made in 1887 - shipped 27 years later in 1914. Note 13: Both have been re-nickeled. Ivory grips on #108401 are replacements.

SINGLE-ACTION RESOURCES

COLLECTOR INFORMATION

Office of the Historian
Colt's Mfg. Co., Inc.
P.O. Box 1868
Hartford, CT 06144

Colt Collectors Assn.
25000 Highland Way
Los Gatos, CA 95030

National Rifle Assn.
11250 Waples Mill Rd.
Fairfax, VA 22030

Ruger Collectors Assn.
P.O. Box 240
Greens Farms, CT 06436

Office of the Historian
Smith & Wesson, Inc.
2100 Roosevelt Ave.
Springfield, MA 01104

Smith & Wesson Collectors
Assn.
P.O. Box 444
Afton, NY 13730

(E)NGRAVING, (S)CRIMSHAW AND (R)ESTORATION

John Barraclaugh (E)
Los Angeles area
(310) 324-2574

Ralph B. Bone (E)
718 N. Atlanta
Owasso, OK 74055

Rick Bowles (S)
556 Pheasant Run
Virginia Beach, VA 23452

Michael Dubber (E)
P.O. Box 4365
Estes Park, CO 80517

Robert Evans (E)
332 Vine St.
Oregon City, OR 97045

Firearms Engraver's Guild
Rex Pederson, Secretary
511 N. Rath Ave.
Ludington, MI 49431

William Gamradt (E)
111 W. Front St.
Missoula, MT 59802

Tim & Christy George (E)
5698 Dearborn Rd.
Evington, VA 24550

Jerome C. Glimm (E)
19 South Maryland
Conrad, MT 59425

Barry Lee Hands (E)
26192 East Shore Rte.
Bigfork, MT 59911

Benno Heune (E)
1205 Wileen Court
Modesto, CA 95350

Ken Hurst (E)
P.O. Box 2154
Kitty Hawk, NC 27949

Pete Mazur (R)
Grass Valley, CA

Paul Persinger (R)
10441 Mackinaw St.
El Paso, TX 79924
(915)821-7541

Scott K. Pilkington, Jr. (E)
P.O. Box 97
Monteagle, TN 37356

Eugene T. Plante (E)
P.O. Box 10534
White Bear, MN 55110

Gidgette Dove-Price (S)
P.O. Box 1783
Blacksburg, VA 24062

Martin Rabeno (E)
92 Spook Hole Rd.
Ellenville, NY 12428

Roger Sampson (E)
430 N. Grove
Mora, MN 55051

Ben Shostle (E)
1121 Burlington
Muncie, IN 47302

Ron Smith (E)
5869 Straley
Ft. Worth, TX 76114

Doug Turnbull (R)
P.O. Box 471
Bloomfield, NY 14469

Scrimshaw by Twyla (S)
J Bar T Ranch
16504 Lawrence 2100
Mt. Vernon, MO 65712

Rachel Wells (E)
110 N. Summit St.
Prescott, AZ 86301

AMMUNITION, COMPONENTS AND RELOADING EQUIPMENT

AA Ltd.
315 N. Bridge St.
Henryetta, TX 76365
Ph: (940) 538-4108

Bull-X
520 N. Main
Farmer City, IL 61842
Ph: (309) 928-2560
Fax: (309) 928-2130

Black Hills Ammunition
P.O. Box 3090
Rapid City, SD 57709-3090
Ph: (605) 348-5150
Fax: (605) 348-9827

Cor-Bon Ammunition
1311 Industry Rd.
Sturgis, SD 57785
Ph: (605) 347-4544
Fax: (605) 347-5055

Federal Cartridge Co.
900 Ehlen Drive
Anoka, MN 55303
Ph: (602) 323-3835
Fax: (602) 323-3738

Hornady
P.O. Box 1848
Grand Island, NE 68802
Ph: (308) 382-1390
Fax: (308) 382-5761

Lyman Products Corp.
475 Smith St.
Middlefield, CT 06455
Ph: (860) 632-2020
Fax: (860) 632-1699

Old Western Scrounger, Inc.
12924 Hwy A-12
Montague, CA 96064
Ph: (916) 459-5445
Fax: (916) 459-3944

PMC Ammunition
12801 US Hwy. 95 South
Boulder City, NV 89005
Ph: (702) 294-0025
Fax: (702) 294-0121

RCBS
605 Oro Dam Blvd.
Oroville, CA 95965
Ph: (916) 533-4191
Fax: (916) 533-1647

Remington Arms Co., Inc.
870 Remington Drive
Madison, NC 27025-0700
Ph: (910) 548-8546
Fax: (910) 548-7814

Starline Brass
1300 W. Henry St.
Sedalia, MO 65301
Ph: (660) 827-6640
Fax: (660) 827-6650

3-D Ammunition & Bullets
112 Plum St.
Doniphan, NE 68832
Ph: (402) 845-2285
Fax: (402) 845-6546

Ultramax
1221 Elk Vale Rd.
Rapid City, SD 57701
Ph: (605) 342-4141
Fax: (605) 342-8727

Winchester Ammunition
427 N. Shamrock
East Alton, IL 62024
Ph: (618) 258-2000
Fax: (618) 258-3609

GRIPS

Ajax Custom Grips, Inc.
9130 Viscount Row
Dallas, TX 75247
Ph: (214) 630-8893
Fax: (214) 630-4942

Altamont
901 N. Church St.
Thomasboro, IL 61878
Ph: (217) 643-3125
Fax: (217) 643-7973

Blue Magnum Grips
2605 East Willamette Ave.
Colorado Springs, CO 89090

Eagle Grips
460 Randy Rd.
Carol Stream, IL 60188
Ph: (630) 260-0400
Fax: (630) 260-0480

Herrett's Stocks, Inc.
P.O. Box 741
Twin Falls, ID 83303
Ph: (208) 733-1498

Hogue Inc.
P.O. Box 1138
Paso Robles, CA 93447
Ph: (805) 239-1440
Fax: (805) 239-2553

N.C. Ordnance
P.O. Box 3254
Wilson, NC 27895
(919) 237-2440

HOLSTERS

Backwoods Custom
Leather
3022 Tyre Neck Rd.
Portsmouth, VA 23703
Ph: (757) 483-4872

Bianchi International
100 Calle Cortez
Temecula, CA 92590
Ph: (909) 676-5621
Fax: (909) 676-6777

David Bullard
4418 Sherwood Dr.
Mesquite, TX 75150
Ph: (972) 270-8119

Classic Old West Styles
1060 Doniphan Park Circle C
El Paso, TX 79936
Ph: (915) 587-0684
Fax: (915) 587-0616

El Paso Saddlery
P.O. Box 27194
El Paso, TX 79926
Ph: (915) 544-2233
Fax: (915) 544-2535

Galco International, Ltd.
2019 West Quail Ave.
Phoenix, AZ 85027
Ph: (602) 258-8295
Fax: (602) 582-6854

GunMate Products
P.O. Box 1720
Oregon City, OR 97045
Ph: (503) 655-2837
Fax: (503) 655-4310

Kirkpatrick Leather Co.
P.O. Box 677
Laredo, TX 78042
Ph: (956) 723-6893
Fax: (956) 725-0672

Old West Reproductions
446 Florence South Loop
Florence, MT 59833
Ph: (406) 273-2615

Red River
P.O. Box 241
Tujunga, CA 91043
Ph: (818) 821-3167

River City Gunleather
P.O. Box 3883
Omaha, NE 68103
Ph: (402) 342-8267

Trailrider Products
P.O. Box 2284
Littleton, CO 80161
Ph: (303) 791-6068

Wild Bill's Originals
P.O. Box 13037
Burton, WA 98013
Ph: (206) 463-5738

MANUFACTURERS AND DISTRIBUTORS

Cimmarron F.A. Co.
105 Winding Oak Rd.
Fredricksburg, TX 78624
Ph: (830) 997-9090
Fax: (830) 997-0802

Colt Firearms Mfg. Co.
P.O. Box 1868
Hartford, CT 06144
Ph: (860) 236-6311
Fax: (860) 244-1442

Colt Blackpowder Arms Co.
110 8th St.
Brooklyn, NY 11215

Ph: (718) 499-4678
Fax: (718) 768-8056

European American
Armory
P.O. Box 1299
Sharpes, FL 32959
Ph: (407) 639-4842
Fax: (407) 639-7006

EMF Co., Inc.
1900 E. Warner Ave.
Suite One D
Santa Ana, CA 92705
Ph: (714) 261-6611
Fax: (714) 756-0133

Navy Arms Co.
689 Bergen Blvd.
Ridgefield, NJ 07657
Ph: (201) 945-2500
Fax: (201) 945-6859

Taylor's & Co., Inc.
304 Lenoir Drive.
Winchester, VA 22603
Ph: (540) 722-2017
Fax: (540) 722-2018

Uberti USA, Inc.
P.O. Box 509
Lakeville, CT 06039
Ph: (860) 435-8068/2846
Fax: (860) 435-8146

U.S. Fire Arms Mfg. Co.
55 Van Dyke Ave.
Hartford, CT 06106
Ph: (860) 724-1152
Fax: (860) 724-6809

PARTS & SERVICES

Belt Mountain Enterprises,
Inc.
P.O. Box 3202
Bozeman, MT 59772
Fax: (406) 388-1396

Brownells
200 South Front St.
Montezuma, Iowa 50171-1000
Ph: (515) 623-5401
Fax: (515) 623-3896

Dixie Gun Works
P.O. Box 130
Union City, TN 38261
Ph: (901) 885-0561
Fax: (901) 885-0440

Gun Parts Corp.
226 Williams Lane
West Hurley, NY 12491
Ph: (914) 679-2417
Fax: (914) 679-5849

Liberty Antique Gunworks
19 Key St.
Eastport, ME 04631
Ph: (207) 853-4116

Linebaugh Custom Sixguns
Rt2
Maryville, MO 64468
Ph: (660) 562-3031

Munden Enterprises
1691 Sampson
Butte, MT 59701
Ph: (406) 494-2833

Peacemaker Specialist
P.O. Box 157
Whitmore, CA 96096
Ph: (916)472-3438

Phariss Professional Services
P.O. 495
Big Timber, MT 59011
Ph: (406) 932-5191

Qualitè Pistol Repair
5580 Havana #6
Denver, CO 80239
(888) 762-3030

R.C.S., Inc.
522 Main St.
Elsmere, KY 41018
Ph: (606) 727-8008

R&D Gun Shop
5728 E. Co. Rd. X
Beloit, WI 53511
Ph: (608) 676-5628
Fax: (608) 676-2269

The Regulator
2295 Woodsfield Land
Marietta, GA 30062
Ph: (770) 973-3051
Fax: (770) 509-9919

GOVERNING BODIES FOR COMPETITION

National Rifle Assn.
11250 Waples Mills Rd.
Fairfax, VA 22030

Single Action Shooting
Society
1938 N. Batavia St., Suite M
Orange, CA 92865

World Fast Draw Assn.
P.O. Box 2039
Fernley, NV 89408

SUGGESTED READING

The books listed here are recommended for many different reasons. Each provides an important contribution. Some deal with the subject from the standpoint of the collector and historian, others consider practical use and mechanical aspects of the revolver. Artistry and accouterments are examined in some others. A few may have been dropped from the roles of their original publishers and been taken up by new ones. Many are no longer in print at all and some command collector prices in their own right. But, in this age of the internet the reader should have little difficulty locating those that are of interest with only the title and author's name with which to work.

Big Bore Sixguns, by John Taffin, Krause Publications, Iola, WI, 1997

The Book of Colt Firearms, by R.L. Wilson, Blue Book Publications, Inc., Minneapolis, MN, 1993

Colt - An American Legend, by R.L. Wilson, Abbeville Press, New York, 1985

Colt Engraving, by R.L. Wilson, Beinfeld Publishing Company, North Hollywood, CA, 1982

Colt Firearms From 1836, by James Serven, Stackpole Books, Harrisburg, PA, 1954-1981

Colt Peacemaker Dictionary & Encyclopedia Illustrated, by Keith Cochran, Colt Collector Press, Rapid City, SD, 1976

Colt's SAA Postwar Models, by George Garton, Beinfeld Publishing Company, North Hollywood, CA, 1979

Colt Scouts, Peacemakers and New Frontiers in .22 Caliber, by Don Wilkerson, printed by Walsworth Publishing Company, Marceline, MO, 1993

Colt's Single Action Army Revolver Pre-War Post-War Model, by Don Wilkerson, Boughton Printing, Inc., Minneapolis, MN, 1991

Fast & Fancy Revolver Shooting, by Ed McGivern, Follett Publishing Company, Chicago, IL, 1938-1962

A History of the Colt Revolver and the Other Arms Made by Colt's Patent Fire Arms Manufacturing Company from 1836 to 1940, by Charles T. Haven & Frank A. Belden, Bonanza Books, New York, 1940

History of Smith & Wesson, by Roy G. Jinks, Beinfeld Publishing Company, North Hollywood, CA, 1972-1992

Home Gunsmithing the Colt Single Action Frontier Revolver, by Loren W. Smith, Gun Room Publishing Company, Kenmore, NY, 1955

Know Your Ruger Single Action Revolvers 1953-63, by John C. Dougan, Blacksmith Corporation, Southport, CT, 1981

Loading the Peacemaker - Colt's Model P, by Dave Scovill, Wolfe Publishing Company, Prescott, AZ, 1995

Packing Iron - Gunleather of the Frontier West, by Richard C. Rattenbury, Zon International Publishing Company, Millwood, NY, 1993

Paterson Colt Pistol Variations, by Philip R. Phillips, R.L. Wilson, Published for Woolaroc Museum by Jackson Arms, Dallas, TX, 1979

The Peacemaker and Its Rivals, by John E. Parsons, William Morrow and Company, New York, 1949

The Post-War Colt Single Action Revolver, by Don Wilkerson, Taylor Publishing Company, Dallas, TX, 1978

The Post-War Colt Single Action Revolver 1955-1976, by Don Wilkerson, Taylor Publishing Company, Dallas, TX, 1980

The Post-War Colt Single Action Revolver 1976-1986, by Don Wilkerson, Taylor Publishing Company, Dallas, TX, 1986

Ruger Auto Pistols & Single Action Revolvers, by Hugo A. Lueders, Blacksmith Corporation Publishers, Chino Valley, CA, 1993

Shooting Colt Single Actions In All Styles, Calibers & Generations, by Mike Venturino, MLV Enterprises, Livingston, MT, 1995

Shooting Sixguns of the Old West, by Mike Venturino, MLV Enterprises, Livingston, MT, 1996

Sixguns by Keith, by Elmer Keith, The Stackpole Company, Harrisburg, PA, 1955-1961

Smith & Wesson Revolvers - The Pioneer Single Action Models, by John E. Parsons, William Morrow & Company, New York, 1957

The Standard Catalog of Smith & Wesson, by Jim Supica and Richard Nahas, Krause Publications, Iola, WI, 1996

The Story of Merwin & Hulbert & Co. Firearms, by Art Phelps, Graphic Publishers, Santa Ana, CA, 1992

A Study of Colt Conversions and Other Percussion Revolvers, by R. Bruce McDowell, Krause Publications, Iola, WI, 1997

United States Martial Pistols and Revolvers, by Arcadi Gluckman Col, US Army, Ret., The Stackpole Company, Harrisburg, PA, 1960

U.S. Cartridges and Their Handguns 1895-1975, by Charles R. Suydam, Beinfeld Publishing Company, Inc., North Hollywood, CA, 1979

FINAL WORD

No symbol better expresses the rugged individualism characteristic of Americans and the history of their young nation than the cowboy. The cowboy is, in turn, best symbolized by Colt's Single Action Army revolver. It has come to represent the causes of freedom and justice in the hands of the righteous, just as truly as the Stars and Stripes - *"Old Glory"* - waving proudly in the breeze. If this revolver could speak its words would likely be those of the Texas Rangers motto: *"No man in the wrong can stand up against a man in the right, who keeps on coming."*